A PRETTY S
TO CATCH ,
(THE ALICE IN WONDERLAND YEARS)

CHRISTIAN PARIS

First published in Great Britain in 2011

Copyright Christian Paris 2011 ©

This book is sold subject to the condition that it shall not, by way of trade or otherwise, be lent, resold, hired out or otherwise circulated without the publisher's prior written consent in any form of binding or cover other than that in which it is published and without a similar condition including this condition being imposed on the subsequent purchaser.

Magic Alice
www.parisitegraphics.co.uk

This book is dedicated to Carol for believing I could do it, to Clive without whom none of this would have happened, to Joe for taking the photos and being there for me and to all the lovely Alice people for keeping it going for so long.

CONTENTS

1.	THE EXPLODING VICAR	1
2.	HOOKED ON ROCK'N'ROLL	4
3.	DAY-GLO MURDER SUSPECTS	20
4.	THE WEIRD WILD AND WONDERFUL WORLD OF ALICE IN WONDERLAND	33
5.	I KEEP THINKING IT'S TUESDAY	51
6.	GOING UNDERGROUND AT CHISTLEHURST CAVES	71
7.	TRIP TO FAIRYLAND	88
8.	DID HE JUST SAY WHAT I THINK HE SAID?	97
9.	LOVE, PEACE AND BANANAS	111
10.	PLANET ALICE	127
11.	SARDINES IN WONDERLAND	139
12.	SPIRIT IN THE SKY	157
13.	THE ROCK'N'ROLL FRIDGE	172
14.	BIG IN JAPAN	188
15.	YOU'RE NOT BIG AND YOU'RE NOT CLEVER	206
16.	SNAIL FARMING	219
17.	THE CURSE OF THE GREEN DRAGON	231
18.	DROP KICK ME JESUS THROUGH THE GOALPOSTS OF LIFE	243
19.	THE WEIRDO TERRAPIN GIRL	251
20.	OOPS I'VE JUST SOLD MY SHOP	267
21.	PLANET ALICE GOES TO HOLLYWOOD	282
22.	HORSES	302
23.	THE FAT LADY SINGS	314

CHAPTER ONE

THE EXPLODING VICAR

In which, at a press of a button, a vicar literally explodes in front of 2000 people.

Legends come and legends go, but none so quickly as the Exploding Vicar. One minute he was there standing on stage at The Town And Country Club in London's Kentish Town and a split second later he was gone. At the push of a button his head literally exploded showering vicar-head-shrapnel over a gathering of London's finest freaks of nature. I will attempt to explain my act of ecclesiastical cruelty later, but first let us take a trip to the weird, wild and wonderful world of Alice In Wonderland...

In the summer of 1983 I had an idea. The plan was quite simple, to open a nightclub in London's west end that would play cool music that no where else was playing, a place where bands, influenced by that same music, would play and a place where 18 to 30 year olds could hang out. It didn't occur to me then just how successful it could become and how it would become the platform for many other associated projects. And so it was that a couple of months later Alice In Wonderland opened its doors. Mainly based around 1960's psychedelia it soon became the most successful one-nighter in London and led onto records, a film, film festivals, the now legendary Magical Mystery Trips, shops in London and Los Angeles and a number one pop group.

This is the story of Alice In Wonderland, admittedly not as impressive as Lewis Carroll's original, but a good story nonetheless. It's about the events we put on, the bands that played there and the people who experienced the whole thing and made Alice In Wonderland THE place to go in London in the mid eighties. It lasted nearly ten years and during that time many adventures were had, friendships were formed, enemies were made, relationships started and relationships ended, people were born and people died, some people found success and some sadly didn't. But it was those people who were the nucleus of the whole Alice scene that kept it going for so long, not just in London, but also up and down the UK as well as in Europe, America and Japan.

Random Alice people on the dance floor

CHAPTER TWO

HOOKED ON ROCK'N'ROLL

In which I detail my early years, my desire to be a pop star and my subsequent introduction to the music business.

When I first started writing this book I decided that it wasn't going to be about me, and I would just concentrate on the club, the special events, the shops, the bands and the people. But now I've changed my mind. In order to see how I came to be inspired to do the whole Alice thing perhaps my background may have some relevance.

I was born on 8th December 1958, Jim Morrison's birthday and what would later become John Lennon's deathday, so a suitably rock'n'roll day to make my debut. It was also the anniversary of the day America joined forces with England to declare war on Japan, which wasn't very rock'n'roll at all but there we are. I was born in Hemel Hempstead, Hertfordshire, about 25 miles northwest of London. My mother, an ex-communicated Catholic banged out six children in seven and a half years and I was the third.

I was causing trouble from the very first moment I entered the world, I almost died at birth as my umbilical cord was wrapped around my neck and I very nearly strangled myself. I was born at home and the midwife panicked and called the emergency doctor who sorted it all out and saved my life. My mother was convinced I was going to be a girl and had decided to call me Sophie Louise, she didn't have a boys name up her sleeve so intended to name me after the doctor, however his name was Colin and thankfully she thought better of it and came up with the name Christian so that was it. Christian it was.

Although my parents were originally from Leeds in Yorkshire they moved down to London when my father, an engineer, was offered a job at the BBC television centre. My mother's wish to have several hundred children meant that they couldn't afford to stay in the capital so they had to move a bit further out, they moved from Clapham, via Enfield to Hemel Hempstead.

My early childhood was fine albeit a little overcrowded; as if having six children wasn't enough, at one point my parents fostered another couple of kids as well. There were children everywhere and because there were only a few years between all of us it must have been an absolute nightmare for my parents. Financially it was a major strain on my dad, who although he had a very good job, six (or eight if you include the foster kids) children were a serious drain on resources, so much so that he had to do two other jobs as well, fixing radios in a shop in West Hampstead in the evenings after he finished at the BBC and working as a cinema projectionist at the weekends.

It must have been hell on earth for my mum in the early sixties bringing up all these brats without the current day conveniences we all take for granted, no dishwasher, no washing machine, no central heating. But somehow or other they coped. We did have a succession of au pair girls who helped out from time to time, glamorous they were not, usually German, usually called Beatta or Dowerty and always smelling of rhubarb and ginger jam, don't ask me why but they always did. Although I haven't seen or smelt it since (the jam that is, not the Germans) I reckon if I did it would immediately remind me of our au pairs.

We did have a Swedish au pair once, called Gizella, she was blonde and looked like Princess Diana, but despite being drop-dead-gorgeous she was a nasty piece of work who kept telling tales to my mum about me.

"Christian ran across the road without looking, Christian did this," Christian did that. I ended up hating her and the Rhubarb and Ginger girls, despite looking like Russian shot-putters and having little downy moustaches all of a sudden seemed the better option.

The most brilliant thing about my dad working at the BBC was that we got to be in the audience of various TV shows. At the age of about four I was on a TV show hosted by Rolf Harris called *Swinging Time*. Rolf used to call us The Miniature Beatles, because we all looked the same, wore the same clothes and had mop top haircuts. Even at the age of four that used to piss me off because I preferred The Rolling Stones and I wanted Rolf to call us The Miniature Stones instead. Among others we saw Billy J. Kramer And The Dakotas, Herman's Hermits, Gerry And The Pacemakers, Lulu and Cilla Black, not exactly rock'n'roll but it was a start. Meanwhile I went back to watching *Andy Pandy, Bill And Ben* and *Muffin The Mule* on TV.

In December 1963 as a special treat for my fifth birthday my dad took a few of us kids to see The Swinging Blue Jeans at some TV show or other. They were riding high in the charts with 'Hippy Hippy Shake' and they played their single to the small audience. I don't remember too much about it but apparently it was at the old Shepherds Bush studios. After the show we headed off to the lift to get to the ground floor only to find it was out of order, my dad, knowing the place like the back of his hand took us down a corridor to a service lift. We got in and as my dad was struggling to shut the doors The Swinging Blue Jeans arrived and squeezed in. As the lift bumped its way to the basement we were met by dozens of screaming teenyboppers who shook the cage-like lift doors shouting: "FOR GOODNESS SAKE, DO THE HIPPY HIPPY SHAKE!"

I was terrified but somehow quite excited by it all, stuck in the lift with my dad, a couple of siblings and The Swinging Blue Jeans. The band hid behind my dad who opened the doors and fought off the madding crowd and let the band run off to safety. I don't think I had quite grasped what it was all about then.

In the spring of 1964 we were in the audience of *Swinging Time* again, Cilla Black was there performing 'Anyone Who Had A Heart' and my sister Deborah and I were on a mission to get her to sign a copy of her single. We had even selotaped a piece of white paper on the label for her to write on. Deborah went up to a small red headed girl and asked if she would sign this record. The girl said "Of course, nobody's asked me for my autograph before." My sister then replied, "Can you write: To Deborah from Cilla?" I tugged Deborah's sleeve and said: "That's not Cilla, that's Lulu!" It was Lulu, just fifteen years old and promoting her new single 'Shout'.

Ten years or so later I bumped into Lulu again, this time at the *Top Of The Pops* studios when she was performing her latest hit, a cover of David Bowie's 'Man Who Sold The World.' I reminded her that my sister and I were the first people to ask for her autograph. "I remember," she said, "You thought I was Cilla Black."

In 1965 at the tender age of six I saw my first credible rock'n'roll band play live. Actually they were probably miming but at six years old, how could I have possibly known? It was on another TV show screened by the BBC and I was there. The programme was *Crackerjack* and the band was The Easybeats. They had just had a hit record with 'Friday On My Mind' an excellent single, which ironically in future years, was played virtually every week at Alice's in the early days. That day literally changed my life forever. I was hooked on rock'n'roll and there was no turning back.

I had a teenage aunt who gave me all of her old records once she had played them to death. In those days singles were disposable items, you'd buy the record, throw away the sleeve and put it in your record rack, which was a bit like a toast rack, a free standing plastic coated wire construction with little coloured stoppers that stopped the G-plan furniture and the Formica surfaces from being scratched. Everyone had one but everyone had at least one 'stopper' missing which meant that it wobbled. My rack was no exception and every time I visited someone else's house and checked out their record collection I coveted their 'stopper'.

My record collection was growing and I hadn't spent a shilling thanks to Marie, but one thing was for sure, I was going to be a Pop Star, just like Mick Jagger, it wasn't even up for debate. Fact. Christian, aged six was going to be a pop star. First of all I had to have a stage outfit, so I put on my bell-bottom (pre-flares) hipsters, which my mum had made, and a white vest. I had brown parcel tape stuck on my hair to make it look longer and a 'microphone' constructed out of an empty loo roll, a tennis ball, a sock and a long wire. I postured and preened just like Jagger (or so I thought) miming to 'Get Off My Cloud'. This was the future, I thought, move over Jagger I'm on my way, "Hey (Hey) You (You) Get Off Of My Cloud!" I mouthed whilst throwing my head back and running my hand through my parcel tape hair-do.

As the song started to fade out I turned my back on my imaginary audience to face the band, Keith, Brian, Bill and Charlie, but to my horror lurking in the doorway was my brother Julian grinning from ear to ear having witnessed my performance. Ouch.

In 1967 I bought my first album, it was by The Tremeloes released just after they had a hit with 'Silence Is Golden'.

Because this was my first album I proudly wrote the number '1' in the top right hand corner of the sleeve, I also wrote my name and address on the back, just in case it got lost. What? But worse than that, whilst the front cover had brightly coloured psychedelic swirls on it, the back was in black and white. As an eight year old I decided to brighten it up by colouring in the black and white Tremeloes logo with my crayon set. In future years, as a serious record collector, I would cringe every time I saw it. Although I couldn't possibly have guessed at that time, their version of 'Cool Jerk' would be played at Alice's often, although I would always make sure that no-one saw the sleeve.

Growing up in the early seventies for me was all about music and girls. That and the minor irritation that was school which I just had to do. Alice Cooper, T.Rex, David Bowie, Velvet Underground, Mott The Hoople, Queen, Sparks, Roxy Music, Cockney Rebel, The Stooges and The New York Dolls were what I lived for, my record collection was by now growing to phenomenal proportions. I also started collecting early rock'n'roll and blues records as well as classics from the sixties. I fell in love with The Shangri La's, The Ronetttes and any other sixties girl group. I had everything.

It was obligatory in my family to play a musical instrument, it wasn't up for discussion, we just had to do it. My father played wicked boogie-woogie piano and my mother sometimes played triangle with the local philharmonic orchestra, we were, however, allowed to choose the instrument, within reason. I was still convinced at this stage that I was going to be a pop star and having worked out that I couldn't really sing, and didn't want to follow in my mothers footsteps and play the triangle, I decided to play the saxophone.

My parents bought me my first sax and I had lessons at the Watford School of Music, I even had a one-off lesson with the legendary saxophonist Johnny Dankworth, set up by my mother and Johnny's wife, the jazz singer Cleo Laine.

As well as playing with the school concert band I also formed various schoolboy rock groups, Last Quarter and then Silver Thunder. We played a few gigs at school discos, youth clubs and even played at a bus driver's Christmas party. We weren't that bad for thirteen year olds. One night we were playing at the Hemel Art Club and just before I went on stage I sprayed my hair silver. I had decided earlier in the day that this would be my new stage look; trouble was the only silver paint I could find was a metallic silver aerosol that I had used to spray my pushbike.

It looked great but was a nightmare to get out the following day. Half a gallon of white spirit later and I still couldn't get rid of it. I then chopped bits of my hair off, as there was no way I could go to school like that on Monday. Feathered haircuts were all the rage at the time but my hair-do looked like Rod Stewart's, had he gone through a hedge backwards.

The silver hair became my 'stage image' from there on, however, for the following gig I used proper hair colour, which washed out. These days I don't have to bother, nature and old age do all that for me.

One day at school I had an appointment with the careers advice people who asked me what I wanted to do when I grew up. I thought about it and should have said, "I will never grow up." That would have been a correct answer. What I actually said was "I dunno, a doctor or a train driver or something." That would have been a wrong answer.

Imagine if I had said "Well what I want to do when I grow up is to run my own nightclub where I play my favourite music, watch my favourite bands, get pissed and chat up the girls, I will also run my own cool shop that sells the things that I want it to sell and I want to co-manage a number one pop group, oh and I want to make shed loads of money as well." They would have laughed me out of the interview. But actually that was exactly what would happen.

My dad's position at the BBC meant that now that I was older I could go and watch the rehearsals for *Top Of The Pops.* That was my special treat, every school holiday on a Wednesday afternoon my dad would get me into the studio and I'd watch the top bands rehearse for the show which would be filmed with the audience later that evening. I would also be allowed to meet them in their dressing rooms and get their autographs. For a thirteen year old it was fantastic times.

One day we arrived at the studios and I saw Noddy Holder of Slade standing by the stage with some guy in a hat. They were both wearing sunglasses. My brother Joe and I went up to 'Noddy' with me nervously clutching my autograph book. 'Noddy' looked at us and said "Alright boys?" in a thick Midlands accent. I looked at his little piggy eyes through his sunglasses and realised that it wasn't Noddy Holder at all and we both scuttled off. The man with the little piggy eyes was in fact Ian Hunter of the excellent Mott The Hoople who were there performing their new single, 'All The Young Dudes'. And the guy in the hat? That was David Bowie, who wrote the song. Oh well.

I got to meet dozens of the top pop bands at the time, including The Bay City Rollers. The Rollers were phenomenally successful, singer Les Mckeown had yet to kill the little old lady by running her over in his sports car, their manager Tam Paton had yet to be arrested for child sex crimes and their public image was still perceived to be whiter than white. I knocked on the door of their dressing room at the *Top Of The Pops* studios and they invited me in. Les was swigging from a bottle of wine, Alan was smoking a spliff, Woody was snogging some groupie, Eric was snorting coke and Derek was probably up to no good as well. So much for the squeaky clean Rollers eh?

One day in 1974 Mick Ronson the former guitarist of David Bowie's band, The Spiders From Mars, was due to play at my local music venue, the Hemel Hempstead Pavilion. He was promoting his new single, 'Love Me Tender' and his album, *Slaughter On Tenth Avenue*. The show had sold out and I hadn't got a ticket so I thought I would go down in the afternoon and hang around the stage door and I might at least get to meet him and get his autograph.

I had been there for about half an hour when two trucks arrived and a couple of stereotype longhaired, tattooed denim-clad roadies jumped out. "Are you the local humper?" one of them asked. Not knowing what they were talking about, I replied: "Err yeah." "Well how the fuck do we get in?" he said. Luckily I knew the answer; having played at the Pavilion with the school concert band I knew that there was a hidden intercom buzzer to the manager's office by the front door. "Leave it to me." I said and ran round the corner and pressed the button. "I'm with the band." I lied. Having blagged my way in I made my way back to the stage door. Suddenly a terrible thought entered my head, what if 'the local humper' was some music biz term for a gay groupie?

Luckily it wasn't, I opened the back door and let the roadies in, helping them unload the flight cases from the trucks and wheel them into the lift.

So that was it, I was now working in the music business, they called me a humper, I called myself a roadie, I called them roadies, they called themselves sound technicians, so actually no one was really a roadie. I got to meet Ronno and was given dozens of promotion packs consisting of a press release, a glossy photo and a flexi disc. I got Ronno to sign them and I sold them at school the following day. That was the beginning of my music business entrepreneurialism, it would do for now, I thought, I'm too young to be a pop star yet anyway. I hung around for the rest of the day and stayed for the gig in the evening. Fantastic. So that was it every Sunday for the next couple of years, I would hang out at the Pavilion, help the road crew, watch the sound check, meet the band and get in free to the gig.

In 1974 there was a bit of a rock'n'roll revival thing going on. Showaddywaddy, Gary Glitter, Alvin Stardust, The Rubettes and Suzy Quatro were all there doing their glam rock take on fifties rock'n'roll with flares. As were Mud who played at the Hemel Pavilion and, of course, I was there. Mud were great, okay so they won't go down in the history of the rock scheme of things as say, Led Zeppelin, Jimi Hendrix or The Rolling Stones, but they recorded some great records and, unlike many other bands at the time, had a great sense of humour.

After a string of excellent hit singles including, 'Dynamite', 'Tiger Feet', 'The Cat Crept In', 'Rocket', and 'Lonely This Christmas' they went on tour and Hemel was on the list. When the crew arrived, my first job was to take the bands' stage costumes up to their dressing room.

The outfits had just come back from the dry cleaners and were still covered in the plastic wrapping; drape jackets, brothel creepers, all the gear that was hip at the time. Alone in the dressing room I couldn't resist the temptation of taking a closer look. On TV they looked fine, but in reality they were the worst collection of cheap crap clothing I had ever come across. And this was coming from the boy who at that time bought his clothes from a market stall. (Three button two-tone tonic high waisters with 30-inch flares!) With no one around I secretly held Les Gray's pale blue jacket with the Las Vegas Elvis style collars against my body. I looked in the mirror and, curling my lip in a comedy Elvis fashion, thought to myself: This band needs a decent tailor.

After the sound check there was the usual hanging about period until the band came on at, say, nine o'clock. The road crew and I got down to some serious drinking. Well I was about fifteen years old so any drinking was serious. The crew had made a bit of a name for themselves on *Top Of The Pops* joining the band on stage and jiving to 'Tiger Feet' and decided they would do it again that night. Hanging about in the empty hall they practised and got me to join in. I hate dancing and I'm absolutely crap at it. Dancing like me dad? Dancing like me granddad more like. However when the show began and 'Tiger Feet' was the next song on the set list I was nowhere to be seen. I couldn't face the embarrassment so disappeared to the bar to get another pint of lager and lime.

Whilst hanging out at the Pavilion I worked at a Thin Lizzy gig and, after the sound check, Phil Lynott cracked open a bottle of tequila and taught me how to do slammers with salt and lemon. Licking your hand, sprinkling on some salt, licking the salt, swigging the tequila and then sucking on the lemon.

I did notice that no one wiped the neck of the bottle before they took a swig; that would not have been rock'n'roll, so I did the same, Phil's germs and everything.

Thin Lizzy never played at Alice In Wonderland, I wish they had, but the relevance of this story is that, ten years on, tequila slammers became part of the Monday night ritual for the DJ's at Alice's, we started off the evening with a couple of shots to get us in the mood, because the way we saw it was that if we weren't going for it how could we expect our audience to go for it?

When The Bay City Rollers played at the Pavilion at the height of Rollermania the screaming teenage audience, mainly girls, pulled the front entrance doors off their hinges. It was mayhem, two thousand teenyboppers surged towards the front of the stage and when the band came on they went absolutely ballistic. Girls were being crushed at the front of the stage and were fainting in their dozens. I was standing in the wings and the security guards, seriously struggling to cope, shouted at me to help them. I had to pull these semi-comatose youngsters to the safety of the orchestra pit, only to find that once they were by the stage they'd suddenly come to and run towards Les or whoever.

I was going out with a girl at the time who was a serious Rollers fan, and knowing that I was working that night she asked me if I could get her one of their drumsticks. After the show, as we were packing up, sure enough I found a broken stick next to the drum kit. She was absolutely delighted with her trophy but her friend, who also wanted one, was dead jealous. She offered to pay me if I could find one for her as well. I went backstage and found another broken drumstick by the side of the drums; I got £2 for it, which was not bad money in 1975.

Next thing I was besieged by dozens of other girls waving their £1 notes at me pleading for me to find them a stick as well. I hunted around the area at the back of the stage but to no avail. Derek was not known for his skin-pummelling hard-hitting stick-breaking drumming so that was it. However, under the raised stage area there were dozens of broken sticks from drummers of previous gigs lying among the dust and cobwebs. I scooped them into my arms and went out to the front where I did a roaring trade flogging these sticks. Del Boy would have been proud of me. I wrestled with my conscience for all of about ten seconds, whilst I didn't intend to deliberately rip the girls off, I didn't want to disappoint them by not coming up with the goods. Well they might have been The Rollers drumsticks; I didn't know that they definitely weren't.

I was also given a fist full of photos from the band, which I got them to sign, and I sold those as well. With the money for helping on the merchandise stall, the money for assisting the security guards and now the cash from the drumsticks and the autographed photos this was a very profitable gig for me. In fact I earned more in one day than I would normally earn in a month doing four jobs! I love this music business lark I thought to myself, I could seriously get used to it.

I didn't just work at the Pavilion, I had three other jobs, cleaning at a pub before school, cleaning factory offices after school, and on a Saturday I worked at a furniture shop. These jobs supported my teenage lifestyle, my vastly expanding record collection, gigs and with it clothes, cigarettes and alcohol. By early 1976 the current music scene was crap, glam rock was finished and most of the great bands of the early seventies had either split up or had had their day. Something had to happen to change all of that, what was needed was a completely new revolution in music, something to kick rock music seriously up its backside. That would be punk then.

What shall I do when I grow up?

Deborah, Joe, Me and Julian in 1960

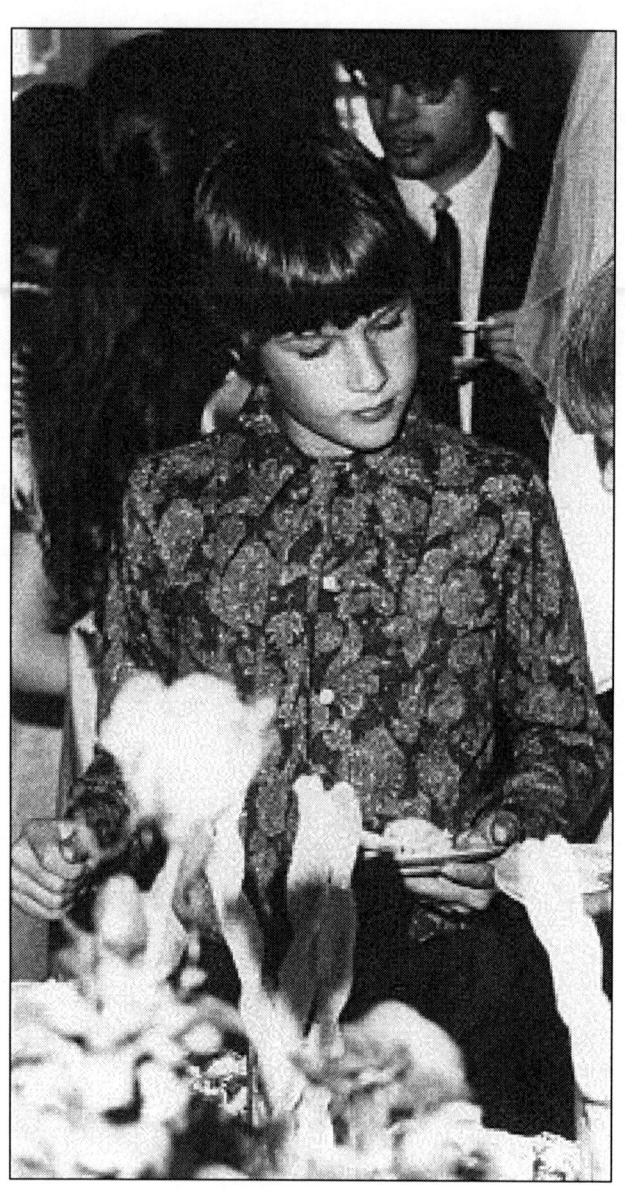

Psychedelic me in 1967

Me aged 14 pot-holing and NOT auditioning for The Village People

Moody me aged 16

CHAPTER THREE

DAY-GLO MURDER SUSPECTS

Punk comes along, I join The Bears, meet the Sex Pistols and get questioned during a murder investigation. I start work as a funeral director, get stalked by Morrissey and unwittingly meet my future business partner.

It was inevitable that I would get into punk rock. Born out of the ashes of influence from The Stooges, The Velvets and The New York Dolls, all of whom I loved to death, it wasn't long before I found out about the UK punk scene and went to check it out. I had already heard about what was happening in America with The Ramones and had got their first album on US import before it was released in the UK. I was at a Doctors Of Madness gig in St. Albans, this girl I met handed me a leaflet for a band called The Sex Pistols advertising a gig at the 100 Club, it was July 1976 and I trotted off to the small club in Oxford Street to witness a gig that would change my life forever. The next day I grabbed a pair of scissors and chopped off my early seventies locks and died my hair black. Earrings and tattoos followed together with the essential leather jacket and ripped drainpipe jeans.

I then trudged to every punk gig I could possibly get to, The Damned, The Clash, and any new band that seemed to appear from nowhere on an almost daily basis. I had by now left school and was at Watford Art School studying graphic deign. It was there that I met George Gill who was the guitarist of a band called Wire. At that time Wire were a five piece and George asked me if I would bring my sax and rehearse with them. I did and for a short while, became a member of Wire.

I played a couple of gigs with them until early 1977 when George was thrown out and I kind of left with him. It wasn't discussed whether I would stay or not, it was just assumed that I would leave with George.

In December 1976 the legendary punk venue, The Roxy Club opened in London's Covent Garden and I was there on the opening night to see Generation X. I got chatting with their singer, Billy Idol, and he asked me if I was in a band. I told him I was in Wire. "What, as in bog wire?" he asked. His comment has puzzled me for the past thirty five years. What the fuck is bog wire? The Roxy Club was fantastic, the atmosphere in the early days was like nothing I had ever experienced and I lived from one Roxy gig to another, everyone that was there knew they were experiencing something special. In years to come The Roxy would be, in part, an influence and inspiration for my own club, Alice In Wonderland, I wanted to re-create the sense of belonging and the excitement that I had witnessed and although I didn't realise it at the time; that was exactly what would happen.

In the summer of 1977 I left Watford art school and went down to Cornwall to work the summer at a caravan park while I decided what I was going to do next. By accident I saw a poster advertising a gig in Penzance for a band called SPOTS, I worked it out, Sex Pistols On Tour Secretly. The Pistols had been banned by virtually every venue in the UK so were doing a secret tour under this assumed name. The day of the gig I won £25 on a one-armed bandit machine, which was a lot of money then, more than a weeks wages. A few of us went down to Penzance that day and after messing about on the fairground we settled into the business of some serious drinking at a nearby pub.

I was sitting at the bar and got into an argument with some local who was going on about how much he hated tourists, or emmits as he called us, taking over Cornwall. I tried to reason with him but he was having none of it.

Someone came up behind me and said, "Don't worry about him, he ain't worth it, come and sit with us." It was Sid Vicious, bass player of The Sex Pistols. I followed him to his table where Johnny Rotten, the other band members and various hangers-on were sitting. They shifted over and I sat down with them chatting about punk and stuff for the next hour or so. Johnny Rotten was in a good mood and was really friendly, I reminded him that we had met in the toilets of The Roxy a few months previously where he had told me off for sticking safety pins in my ears. "They'll go septic you know." He said to me. That night at The Roxy I didn't give a shit, numbed by alcohol I couldn't feel a thing. "So how were you the next morning?" asked the Rottenmeister. "Septic as hell" I replied. Johnny Rotten cackled victoriously.

Sid was on top form and was incredibly polite, he said he would put me and my mates on the guest list and we could all meet up after the show. The gig was amazing but we never did meet up afterwards, we had to somehow walk and hitch back to the Park which took us about four hours. But what a night. Sid, or rather John Beverley as he was called then, went to school in Cleveden, North Somerset, which is not far from where I now live. In fact I have a property in Cleveden, maybe I should apply to get its name changed to 'Beverley Hills' in honour of the punk legend. Somehow North Somerset Council may have something to say about that.

They always used to say that everyone could remember where they were when they first heard that J.F. Kennedy had been killed. Well I can't, I was too young. However, I do remember where I was when I first heard that Elvis had died. I was still at the caravan park and on my way back to my caravan the DJ stopped his van as he was driving past and said; "Have you heard the news?" He then turned up his radio and the announcer informed their listeners that Elvis Presley, the King of rock'n'roll was dead.

As a punk I wasn't supposed to like Elvis, he was part of the old establishment, however, I loved Elvis, I still do, so whilst I pretended to be blasé about it on the outside, inside I was secretly hurting. At least I still had Marc Bolan, for a month anyway.

After finishing my summer stint in Cornwall I went back to Hertfordshire to work out what I was going to do with the rest of my life. Whilst I did quite well at Art School, I couldn't see me with a career in graphics. I had this bizarre idea that I wanted to be a funeral director. Originally I thought it would be a bit of a laugh, *Billy Liar* style, but once I started I did actually take it very seriously. I studied hard and passed my diploma and even qualified as an embalmer. It was a job and until such time as I became a pop star (so I thought) it would do just fine.

The day I went to my interview to be a funeral director was the day Marc Bolan died. He was killed in a car crash when his mini, driven by his girlfriend, hit a tree and that was it. What a bummer. Years later I was in a mini being driven by my girlfriend at that time, we were trying to find Richmond Park but had got lost, we were driving down an unfamiliar road when I suddenly felt this weird chill going down my spine, the hairs on the back of my neck stuck out and as we turned a corner there in front of us was the tree. I had never been there before and had no idea I was in Bolan tree territory. That was weird.

I was actually based in the office originally but I do remember my first funeral, it was hilarious you couldn't write a better script for a situation comedy. Due to staff shortages I had to fill in as a bearer at a funeral at West Herts Crematorium, after managing to lift the coffin onto my shoulder I realised that I was about four inches taller than the other bloke at the back so I had to bend my knees and walk in a comedy manner hanging onto the coffin as if my life depended on it. To make matters worse the coffin was only short and I kept treading on the heels of the bloke in front, I was completely out of step and the coffin was wobbling about all over the place.

Halfway down the aisle a plastic bell top that hid one of the screws on the coffin lid fell off and bounced down the crematorium in front of us. Boing! Boing! Boing! That was it, I just started giggling uncontrollably, I couldn't help myself and I couldn't stop. After placing the coffin on the bier, and putting up with the gesticulations from the crematorium workers below, I had to lead the bearers quietly out of the service. I had never been to the place before so hadn't a clue where the side exit was.

I headed towards a door and opened it, I looked to my left to see the other guys walking towards another exit and then realised I had opened the door to the cleaner's cupboard. Without thinking I walked into the dark cupboard and shut the door. As the vicar started the service I thought, shit, I can't stay in here for half an hour, so I gingerly opened the door and after tripping over a mop and bucket I crept out towards the proper exit door. The vicar stopped the service as I made my way out still giggling to myself like a demented child.

The next funeral was even funnier, this time it was a burial, and after lowering the casket into the grave we had to take the floral tributes off of the roof of the hearse and place them by the side of the grave.

As the mourners stood over the open grave I unclipped the elasticated bungee and let go. It flew through the air and landed on top of the coffin. A dozen heads peered into the grave wondering what had happened. Was this a sign from above? Meanwhile, I got those giggles again, and once more I couldn't stop myself, and with tears of laughter streaming down my face I inexplicably let go of another bungee.

Once again it shot through the air, this time whacking the balding heir of the deceased on the back of his head. I was led away by a more mature colleague who sat me down behind a gravestone and told me to pull myself together. "Funerals are no laughing matter," he said. You could have fooled me, I thought, as I wiped the tears from my eyes.

Whilst I was in Cornwall my friend George had joined another Watford art school punk band called The Bears, I was also going to join once I returned. After getting the job as an undertaker I was in Hemel Hempstead's bank court opening a bank account. I bumped into Mick North, the lead singer of The Bears and we chatted for a while. I remember the meeting vividly, he was eating a jam doughnut, what would be his last supper.

He was highly amused at my new choice of career and asked when I was going to hook up with The Bears. "Soon." I said. He then jumped on the back of a motorbike driven by another punk called Pete Perspex who played with a band called The Paper Doilies. On their way back to Watford they crashed into a bridge and were both killed. I was the last person to see them both alive.

Mick North died far too soon, The Bears were just getting a bit of a name for themselves, getting a good local following and he was the main influence. His scruffy bespectacled looks and hilarious lyrics were what made The Bears different from the other more serious punk bands.

"Wots up mate where d'ya get your bananas? Down by the pickle jar, first shelf in the larder! Where's me hammer and where's me pliers? Out there in the shed dear, NO THEY'RE NOT YOU LIARS!"

Soon after Mick died he was replaced by Johnny Entrails and I too joined The Bears on sax. We played various gigs in London and Watford including The Roxy Club on a number of occasions. Once we were supported by Crass, although I have absolutely no recollection. We recorded a track for the *Farewell To The Roxy* album; a song called 'Fun Fun Fun' which was chosen by the producers because at first they thought it was called 'Fuck Fuck Fuck'. I was recently interviewed for a book about The Roxy Club and reading through it the memories of the club and the gigs I attended or played at came flooding back. Amazing times.

Being a punk was risky business and for some reason teddy boys and general meatheads took exception to this new breed of kids who just wanted to have fun. Once the tabloids had stirred it up a sense of hatred from virtually everyone was directed towards us. In the early days whilst living in Hemel Hempstead I normally had to run home from the train station after going to The Roxy or wherever as I was chased by the local lads cruising for a bruising. Luckily I could run quite fast and they never caught me.

The Bears were featured in a documentary about punk hosted by goofy Janet Street-Porter and shown on London Weekend Television. Soon after I was walking home from the pub with George and his girlfriend, Petra, when a bunch of Watford wallies spotted us. "Look! It's the punks from the telly, let's get 'em!" shouted one and we were duly attacked by the idiots and given a bit of a pasting.

There were six of them and only three of us, George and I were pissed and Petra was a girl. Still, it was reported in the press which gave us a bit more much-needed publicity although I'm not sure the cuts and bruises were worth a few lines in *Sounds*.

We went into the studio towards the end of 1977 to record a single and an album. The single, a double A-side, 'On Me / Wots Up Mate?' was released the following year and got some great reviews. It even got single of the week in *Sounds* beating John Travolta and Olivia Newton-John's 'You're The One That I Want', their single was a massive hit, ours sold a few hundred copies. However, it was played often on John Peel's radio show. "Dig that harmonica, man." John commentated referring to my two minute long sax solo.

During my stint with The Bears I had moved in to share a house in Watford with George and Petra, none of us had any money and what we did have was spent down the pub. We had to take it in turns to cook and one night, George's turn, with nothing in the cupboard but a bag of lentils he rustled up the supper from hell. I can't stand lentils but had to eat something to soak up the alcohol so staring at the grey dish I attempted to force a spoonful down. Petra looked at me and we both looked at George and said in unison: "George, this is rubbish." George then decided to spruce it up by adding the only other ingredient he had in the cupboard, a bottle of fluorescent green food dye. The meal now looked positively radioactive.

We were interrupted by a knock on the door and I opened it to find two policemen standing there. They showed their ID's and marched into the sitting room. They announced that a local corner shop owner had been stabbed to death and two people matching mine and George's descriptions had been seen running away from the scene of the crime. (The only match, it transpired, was that they were both wearing leather jackets, like us.)

The policemen stared at the three bowls of day-glo

fluorescent green lentils as George exclaimed: "Murder? What do you think we are? Weirdos?"

Luckily for us we both had cast iron alibis as we could prove that at the time of the murder The Bears were playing at the Art Club in Hemel Hempstead. They took another glance at our fluorescent feast and left the house shaking their heads. I guess they thought that even real murderers wouldn't eat something as disgusting as that.

The Bears split up soon after releasing the single and apart from going to Ireland to record another great single 'Descisions,' (sic) and play a few more gigs, we faded into punk history. The Bears album wasn't released for another ten years when, by complete coincidence, Phil Smee, an occasional Alice DJ put it out on one of his labels as part of a *Roots Of Punk* thing, but its actually quite good. We played live in the studio but among the bum notes and feedback there are some great songs. Apart from a few dalliances with various other music projects, that was it for my pop star ambitions, for a few years anyway.

By the end of 1981 I realised that I had had enough of funeral directing, and as the mop and bucket and flying bungee incidents proved I just wasn't serious enough to carry on, I was twenty two going on seventy two, something had to change. I wanted to be more creative, which was what I was always supposed to be about and I still had these cravings for pop stardom so decided to have a proper crack at it. I gave up my job and formed a tacky glam rock band called The Lollipop Sisters.

I had by this time moved to London, via Pinner to Muswell Hill and then Hampstead.

We played a few gigs around London; Dingwalls, The Batcave, The Kensington Ad Lib club and even The

Brixton Academy. (Well it was actually at a club in the foyer of The Brixton Academy.)

One night at the Marquee club we were approached by a bloke called Terry Doran who wanted to be our manager. Terry was part of the original Beatles set-up in Liverpool, had hung out at the cavern, worked as their roadie, worked for Apple and ended up being George Harrison's estate manager. He had a lot of contacts and set up a photo session with the photographer, former model, former Mrs. George Harrison and at that time, the current Mrs. Eric Clapton, Layla herself, Patti Boyd. We went to Eric Clapton's house and had the photo session in his garden.

Through our temporary bass player we attracted the attention of a bloke called Steve from Manchester. He was an avid New York Dolls fan and hearing that we were the next worse thing kept writing me letters asking me to send photos of the band. I ignored his constant requests and after about six attempts he gave up. That Steven from Manchester turned out to be Morrissey, soon to be huge with The Smiths. I never kept the letters, I wish I had, they would make amusing reading now. But I never got The Smiths. How someone obsessed with the remarkable New York Dolls could turn out such drivel is beyond me. They're supposed to be good but I still don't get it.

Terry next set up a recording session to record our first demo and had a word with his old mate Ringo Starr who agreed to let us use the recording studio at his house in Ascot. It was a strange place with acres of gardens containing massive fibreglass dinosaurs and had a lake with a rowing boat.

We recorded four tracks, which were quite good really, although even then I was beginning to realise that actually we stood bugger all chance of making it, something wasn't quite right.

Whilst we were recording the demos I came face to face with Ringo's petulant eleven year old daughter, Lee, she didn't say anything but just stared at us before being whisked away by her nanny. I could never have predicted then that many years later the sullen girl in the kitchen, Lee Starkey, would be my future business partner.

Not long after recording the demo at Starr studios The Lollipop Sisters split up. I wasn't really that bothered, I knew it wasn't going to happen for us so that was it, Christian wasn't going to be a pop star after all, it just took me a while to realise it. I'll just have to do something else now.

When I gave up my promising career as a funeral director, my parents weren't too pleased. My dad said to me: "You've got about as much chance of making it in the music business as I have of winning the pools, and I don't do the bloody pools". He was spot on with regards to The Lollipop Sisters, but I was going to prove him wrong in the end.

Me aged 17
"Do you feel lucky, punk?"

Me on stage with The Bears 1977

The Bears 1977 George, Cally, Me and Ron

CHAPTER FOUR

THE WEIRD, WILD AND WONDERFUL WORLD OF ALICE IN WONDERLAND

In which I come up with the idea of starting the Alice In Wonderland nightclub, hook up with the Doctor and his band, Doctor And The Medics, and go on a boat trip with the fabulous Flower Children.

The London nightclub scene in early 1983 was mainly dance and disco and unless you went to a rock venue like Dingwalls, The Marquee or The Clarendon that was all you had. New romantic was finished, goth had temporarily crawled under a stone, and The Batcave, previously the best alternative club, had had its day. There was an opening for someone to start something new and exciting. I wasn't the only person who was bored with nowhere to go, surely? At that time in the absence of much good current music I was listening to music from previous decades, 1960's psychedelia and 1970's glam. The Doors, The Stooges, The Velvet Underground, T.Rex, Alice Cooper and The New York Dolls sounded just as good then as they did in the ten or fifteen years previously.

I started digging around second hand record shops for classic 60's garage stuff by bands like The Seeds, The Chocolate Watchband, 13th Floor Elevators etc. If they looked the part, had a quirky name and a wacky title I would buy it, regardless.

Some of the eighties bands were also taking their influences from the sixties scene, Siouxie And The

Banshees released 'Dear Prudence' and The Cult, The Cure, Teardrop Explodes, Bauhaus and The Damned started to move towards a slightly more psychedelic sound. The answer was written on the wall. It was all there just waiting to happen but nowhere at that time for it to happen in. Someone had to start a nightclub playing new psychedelia and it might as well be me.

I didn't want the club to be a pure revival of 1960's psychedelia, although that was the obvious backbone to it all. It had to be a mixture to include current music that fitted in that genre as well. 70's punk and glam, surf, goth, with a bit of blues, country and heavy metal thrown in. What I wanted to achieve more than anything though was a fun atmosphere, new romantic was far too serious and goth was just down right depressing.

Having decided on the format I had to have a name. Originally the club was going to be called Pandora's Box. I am so glad I carried on thinking, that would never have worked. Alice In Wonderland was a perfect name for this club, a bastardised title taken from the classic children's novel by Lewis Carroll, *Alice's Adventures In Wonderland,* with its psychedelic overtones and quirky characters it seemed to epitomise the feeling I hoped to create. With a theme and now a name sorted I had to find a venue. I picked up a copy of *Time Out* from my local newsagents and started phoning the clubs listed, starting with 'A' and working my way down the list.

It was the middle of the afternoon and not surprisingly no one was answering their phones. I got to 'G' and phoned Gossips a 400 capacity club on the corner of Dean Street and Meard Street in Soho, situated next to a brothel called The Golden Girl Club and below the infamous Gargoyle Club the venue would be perfect.

By a strange quirk of fate, Mick Collins, the manager and

future owner of the club happened to be there that afternoon taking charge of a beer delivery and answered the phone. I told him about my idea and he suggested we discussed it further. We met up and struck a deal, the Monday night would soon be free and I could be open in early October. It was as easy as that. Little did Mick or I know then that his decision to give Alice In Wonderland a chance would make him, Vince (the owner at that time) and me an awful lot of money over the next ten years.

There were two things bothering me. Firstly, Monday nights were the quietest nights of the week, first day back at work after blowing all your cash at the weekend and it's a long way until pay day. Secondly, and more importantly, I hadn't really got a DJ The plan was that I would play the records. I had DJ'ed before and it's not that easy. Getting people up on the dance floor is challenging, keeping them there is hard work.

And then there's P.D.S. (Pissed DJ Syndrome) where, after copious amounts of beer you put on what you thought was the extended album version of a song but was actually the shortened single version. You then go to the loo and half way through the six pinter you suddenly hear the music stop. Nightmare. You run back to the decks and the dance floor is deserted, you panic, and the record you put on, which you thought was a really up-beat song was actually a dreary ballad.

I was having sleepless nights worrying about this, I had designed the leaflets, written the press release, organised a light show and we were ready to go, but without a DJ this enterprise was apparently doomed to fail before we had even started. I spoke to my elder bother, Joe, about this. Joe, as you will discover was the unsung hero of Alice In Wonderland. Joe was always there, and when I was in danger of going off in the wrong direction he could always be relied on to bring me back down to earth.

Joe had a realistic approach to everything, and he had seen me DJ before. After listening to my concerns he reminded me of the fact that not everyone finds 'Chirpy Chirpy Cheep Cheep' funny at two o'clock in the morning. Hmmm.

A couple of weeks before the opening night, Alex, my girlfriend at the time, went to see a band called Doctor And The Medics. She came back raving about their singer, a bizarre six foot five myopic beanpole in flared trousers and a cape rolling around the floor singing a version of the Sweet's 'Blockbuster'. Unbeknown to me Clive Jackson, AKA the Doctor, had been a DJ a couple of years previously at a club called The Clinic, ironically also at Gossips. A meeting was arranged at a wine bar in Covent Garden.

That was the beginning of what would become a business partnership that would last almost ten years and a friendship that lasts to this day. Clive told me on that first meeting that he didn't think it would work but was willing to give it a try. He said that if he had to crawl around on his hands and knees with a cucumber between his teeth and a banana up his backside he would do it. Thankfully it never came to that. Well not the cucumber bit anyway. So that was it, all posts covered and we really were now ready for it. For the first time since I had started the Alice ball in motion I was beginning to think that it actually really might work.

Although everything was in place and we were all quite confident that we could put on a good night we were yet to convince Joe Public.

The deal I did with Gossips was this: I would hire the club for the night for a set fee, Gossips would take the bar money and I would get the door takings and pay for the receptionist, the DJ's, the band and the P.A. The publicity and the advertising was also down to me, I managed to scrape together £4 and printed some leaflets advertising the opening night. £4 didn't buy a lot of leaflets. I needed thousands, I had a few hundred.

After handing them out in Camden and Kensington markets and outside various gigs I was running out rapidly. I then had this cunning plan of how I could hit my specific audience with the least amount of cost and work. Quite simply I went to the most popular specialist record shops and stuck my flyer directly above the psychedelic section. I then went to HMV and Virgin and slid the flyers inside Doors and Stooges albums. We had a few mentions in *Time Out, City Limits* and the music press, we had our friends and family and the rest was down to word of mouth.

The opening night had arrived and I set off from my flat in West Hampstead on the tube to Soho. Laden down with records, oil wheel projectors and leaflets and posters (for the second night) I arrived at Gossips to prepare. Clive arrived at about the same time and set about hanging long loops of toilet paper from the ceiling. He explained the method in his madness, as the first punters arrived they wouldn't know that the club was empty as they couldn't see for the Andrex. Whilst I was dubious at first, the toilet paper would become part of the Alice set-up for the next ten years.

We hung up white backdrops for the oil wheel projectors and Clive set up his film projector with the only cine film he possessed, a clip of some sixties surfers doing what they do, surfing.

Problem with this, as we soon discovered, the film was only two minutes long and took about fifteen minutes to thread into the machine. Needless to say it only actually got shown once. Blink and you missed it.

James Bloomer, Clive's manager at that time, was also there sticking strategically placed objects around the club, a surprise for later he explained. James was a bit of a nutter but it was he who introduced me to Clive so I gave him the benefit of the doubt.

At ten o'clock we started the music and opened the doors. Clive put on a long record and we went to the bar and had a couple of tequila slammers to get us in the mood. People started drifting in, mainly friends, family and fellow band members at first and then various strangers who actually paid to get in. Phew. There was no band on the opening night and Clive and I took it in turns to play the records. The broad mix of people was exactly as I had hoped and planned for, psyches, punks, goths, surfers, glam rockers, hippies, bikers and just ordinary people who were there to experience Alice In Wonderland and have a good time. Clive was on top form, cackling his soon to be legendary psycho-babble through his echo box and playing great music, getting people up on the dance floor whether they wanted to or not. It was a fantastic evening and everything was going according to plan.

A young punk was innocently walking out of the girls toilet when BANG! there was an explosion. The poor girl nearly jumped out of her black leather mini skirt. Everyone on the dance floor stopped dancing when BANG! Another explosion went off, this time right by the DJ booth. What the fuck was happening? I thought, and then I saw James Bloomer grinning like Alice's Cheshire cat, his thumb hovering over the red button on some hand held device. That was his surprise, he had planted pyrotechnics around the club and now he was setting them off!

The whole plot was a Health and Safety nightmare but luckily no one was injured. This was not the last time we pushed the boundaries of safety for the sake of entertainment, I'm afraid, but it was hilarious and helped to make the evening one not to be forgotten.

The opening night drew to a close and the music had to stop at three thirty so we packed up to go home. The evening had gone better than I could have hoped for and I actually began to realise that I might be onto something here. The club was by no means busy, but there were enough paying people through the door to satisfy the club owners. After the printing costs (£4) we all earned £10 each, not bad for the first night.

More importantly the reaction and feedback from those first night revellers was encouraging enough that we had to carry on. So a second night there would be. After leaving Soho a group of us went back to my flat and carried on partying until the sun came up. This became a bit of a norm after Alice's, not always at mine but we would usually find somewhere to carry on.

I am under no illusion whatsoever that without the Doctor Alice In Wonderland would not have become the great success that it was. Clive was the magic that made Alice's so different from any other club in London at that time. London night clubbers had learnt the art of pretending to suck on a boiled sweet until Alice In Wonderland showed them how to spit it out and smile. In between the records Clive would talk in manic fashion through his echo box, it could be about the resident fish in the corner of the club, suggesting the clubbers go up to them and say hello, or it could be his story about Shakin' Stevens being in the club in disguise and for the first person who correctly identifies him they could have free drinks all night.

Of course Shaky wasn't there but the Doctor's tale did what it was supposed to do, lighten the atmosphere and set the tone for the rest of the night.

One night at Alice's, the day after Steve Marriott of The

Small Faces died, Clive played 'Itchycoo Park' in his memory. He then said his spiel about what a great hero he was and how he would be sadly missed, and dedicated the following record, Arthur Brown's 'Fire' to the Small Faces front man. Steve Marriott of course died in a fire at his house in the country. Clive then returned to the mic and apologised after people had complained that his chosen record was in poor taste. He then played The Move's 'Fire Brigade'.

Clive has to be one of the funniest people I have ever met, a born entertainer but not necessarily a born sex god idol. By his own admission he has to wear his hair long as he has a head like a peanut. I have seen him instruct a crowd full of strangers to lie down on their backs and wiggle their arms and legs in the air like a confused beetle. Hundreds of people did exactly that and the odd few people who thought they were too cool to participate ended up looking ridiculous standing alone in a sea of 'beetles' that they too would get down on the floor. Only Clive could do that and get away with it. I'm convinced. With that sort of charisma Clive should be a number one pop star, but that would never happen, surely?

In case you hadn't guessed, Clive isn't really a Doctor; he is however a Reverend, I kid you not. Clive is these days a fully ordained member of the *Holy Church Of Elvis Presley* (or something similar) and is qualified to officiate at marriage ceremonies. (Only in America or thirteen miles off the coast of Britain though.) But in 1983 he was a former scout leader, an ex-civil servant and the singer of the band Doctor And The Medics.

Doctor And The Medics were the first band to play at Alice In Wonderland. Performing on the second night they became the resident band in the early days and usually played about every three weeks. Their first Alice gig was, ironically, the least attended Alice night in it's entire ten years, but The Medics were superb and had a small but loyal following who turned up that evening and became Alice regulars from there on. A psychedelic glam punk band fitted the bill at Alice In Wonderland and Doctor And The Medics were always superb entertainment.

Playing a mixture of their own songs, 'The Goats Are Trying To Kill Me', 'Love Peace And Bananas', 'The Molecatcher's Boot' etc. and covers of 'Blockbuster', 'These Boots Are Made For Walking', 'Motorhead', 'Gloria' and 'Silver Machine' they pulled off every gig they did. As well as Clive, of course, Steve, Richard and Vom hung out at Alice's whether they were playing that night or not. But just as The Medics helped Alice's get established, Alice returned the favour and, whether we liked it or not, Alice In Wonderland and The Medics were, for a while, joined at the hip.

The Annadin Brothers were the female vocalists and dancers with The Medics. Led by Wendi, soon to be Clive's girlfriend, wife and then mother of their four children, they were essential to The Medics sound and stage show. With matching outfits, wigs and make-up their unique image and dance routines were often copied but no one could do it quite like Wendi. Originally partnered by Sue and Jane and then a few years later by Colette, Wendi could be found at Alice's every Monday night in the early days, as could the other girls.

It took a while for Alice's to get totally established, some weeks were desperately quiet and some weeks were busy enough to give us hope. We knew we had a good thing going; we just needed to convince a few hundred more.

After a few months we had built up a steady group of regulars who spread the word and turned up week after week parting with their hard earned cash, student grant, handouts from wealthy parents, dole money or in some cases maybe even pocket money. Whilst they all had a great time regardless of how many people turned up, we had to satisfy the management of Gossips that the turnover at the bar was sufficient to allow us to continue. Thankfully the Alice crowd liked to drink and the Alice staff alone probably spent enough behind the bar to keep it going. The band playing sometimes made a difference to the number of people who turned up, as did other events going on that night and of course, the weather. Back combed hair-dos, Mohicans and flat tops didn't do well in the rain. So if it was wet or windy they would stay at home.

One night, when a band ironically called Bad Karma Beckons played, the weather was foul and the night was a disaster. The band were rubbish despite the great name and hardly anyone turned up, the temporary caretaker manager of Gossips at the time, a bloke called Don, told us that unless things picked up, the next week would be our last. Clive and I pulled out all the stops and rang everyone we knew asking them to turn up the next week; we leafleted Camden, Kensington and Soho and hoped for the best. Word was out that the next Monday could be the last of Alice In Wonderland. Doctor And The Medics played and the night was quite busy. Phew, we had a stay of execution. Other bands that played in 1983 were Persian Flowers, Billy London, Jeremy's Secret and Ring Of Roses.

I knew Jim Vane before he formed Ring Of Roses and before I started Alice's. He was their charismatic lead singer, not unlike an early David Bowie or Jim Morrison. I booked them to play on the fourth night of Alice's, Hallowe'en 1983.

They were a sort of goth psychedelic glam band so suited the evening perfectly. We decorated the club for the occasion with a massive pumpkin by the door and giant scary masks were hung on the wall. We had *Hammer*

House Of Horror videos playing and a slide show featuring Boris Karloff. Ring Of Roses were excellent and had quite a following which meant that Hallowe'en became the busiest night of Alice's so far.

That was it, I thought we had made it, however, I was brought crashing down to earth the following week, Guy Fawkes Night when, with no band playing, my pathetic indoor firework display did not exactly go down in history as the very best in entertainment. I lit the fuses and watched as hardly anything happened apart from a small puff of smoke and some pathetic fizzling, Clive was doing a running commentary through his echo box, taking the piss out of me relentlessly. Admittedly it was quite funny, but only because it was so bad, good job hardly anyone was there to witness it.

Ring Of Roses signed a £100,000 record deal with RCA the following year and things started going down hill from there on. Although they were amazing live they couldn't pull it off in the studio, after spending a year recording their first single, 'According To The Weatherman,' and it still not sounding right, RCA ran out of patience and dropped them.

They never had any material released officially but there are some great tapes out there. In later months, once Alice's really got going, those Ring Of Roses followers became Alice regulars, and many of them ended up working for me in one way or another.

The lead singer of Siouxsie And The Banshees, Siouxsie Sioux was one of the first minor celebrities to walk through the doors of Alice's.

It was absolutely dead that night, the club was almost deserted, it was early and Siouxsie looked around the place wondering where all the others were. I think she half expected a whole group of people to burst through the toilet paper like they do at surprise parties. That was not going to happen. She left before the band played at twelve and, to my knowledge, didn't come again. We used to play her latest single, a cover version of The Beatles 'Dear Prudence', virtually every week in the early days so we were quite glad to see her.

It prompted speculation that she was going to do a secret gig at the club and I have to admit I did nothing to quell those rumours. When asked if it was true I replied: "I think she's thinking about it." Well she might have been for all I knew. Anyway, some people came back over the following few weeks just in case it was true. It wasn't.

The first group of regulars who supported the club from day one were mainly known to us; friends, family, band members and their partners and friends. Youth, from the bands Killing Joke and Brilliant used to come down with Mark Manning, soon to become a rock star himself. Genesis P. Orridge from Throbbing Gristle and Psychic TV was an early punter together with Dave Vanian, Roman Jugg and Captain Sensible of The Damned. But then there were those who seemed to appear from nowhere, no-one knew who they were or where they came from.

One night two such strangers arrived on the scene, nicknamed the Flower Children Emma and Louise were two young teenagers who ran away from their comfortable family lives in Shrewsbury to a squat in Brixton, south London only to find that the streets weren't paved with gold. There was, however, Alice In Wonderland.

They turned up a month or so after we started and way before the club was truly established, with enough money to pay to get in, buy a pint and get the night bus home, they came back week after week. They dressed in authentic sixties psychedelic clothes and danced all night, when the press started to turn up and photograph the audience they were always the first in line. After a few weeks I let them in free on the guest list, they were great for the club and the club was great for them, I usually had to give them their bus fare home as they had spent it on another beer or lost it on the dance floor.

One night after Alice's a bunch of us went back to someone's flat in Battersea to carry on partying. At about five in the morning the Flower Children came with me as I went walkabout and we ended up climbing over a fence and going into Battersea Park. We came across a rowing boat on the grass by a lake but unfortunately there were no oars. Not to be deterred I found a plank of wood and we all climbed into the boat and paddled out across the lake. I was doing the rowing and Emma and Louise were sitting opposite me, it was just beginning to get light and as I gazed across the park a kangaroo came bounding out through the early morning mist.

"Oh my God I've just seen a fucking kangaroo!" I said. Emma and Louise looked over their shoulders but the kangaroo had jumped behind a bush, "Yeah right." they said in unison, turning back to face me. Suddenly Skippy jumped back into view, this time with a youngster faithfully following her. "There are two of the buggers!" I said, totally gob smacked at what I was witnessing. The Flower Children turned round again to see, just after Skippy and Jerry disappeared behind the bush once again. "There's nothing there, Christian," said Lou, "You're seeing things." "I'm not joking," I replied, "I really did see them!"

Next thing about half a dozen of the blighters came bounding out through the mist, "Look!" I said, "The whole place is full of bloody kangaroos!" Emma and Louise refused to turn round and the group of marsupials stood by the lake and stared at us. "They really are there, look,

look!" I said. Louise sighed and turned around "Shit!" she screamed as she saw them, startled by the noise the kangaroos hopped off into the distance. I later found out that they weren't kangaroos but wallabies, which are smaller, and they lived in the park, but when you're not expecting them....

The wallabies were probably just as freaked out at coming across us in a boat at five in the morning as we were of seeing them. "Mum, mum, there are three weirdos in a boat on the lake!" "Yeah right," said Skippy, "You must be seeing things."

The Alice In Wonderland regulars helped to make up the personality and identity of the club and over the years tens of thousands of people passed through the doors, dozens of whom stick in my mind as being instrumental in it's success. I couldn't possibly mention all of them but some stand out as being relevant in some way that I couldn't write this book without telling their story. Old friends of Joe's from our home town of Hemel Hempstead, Elvis, Jesus and Iain, (a car mechanic,) supported the club right from the early days, driving the 30 mile trip from Hemel and staying 'til the end.

The three of them, bored with their mundane lives in Hemel, suddenly found a new place to go and turned up week after week, regardless of the journey. Not only that, but they all had full time jobs, and less than two hours after returning home they had to get up and go to work.

That was dedication. It changed their lives, Iain went out and bought a leather jacket, Elvis already had one, of course, and Jesus dug out a more be-fitting sheepskin coat. They were also regulars at the other events and added to the eclectic mix of punters that made Alice's so different from anywhere else at that time.

Clive: Love Peace and Bananas

Me on stage in the early days at Alice In Wonderland (No it's not Jimmy Saville)

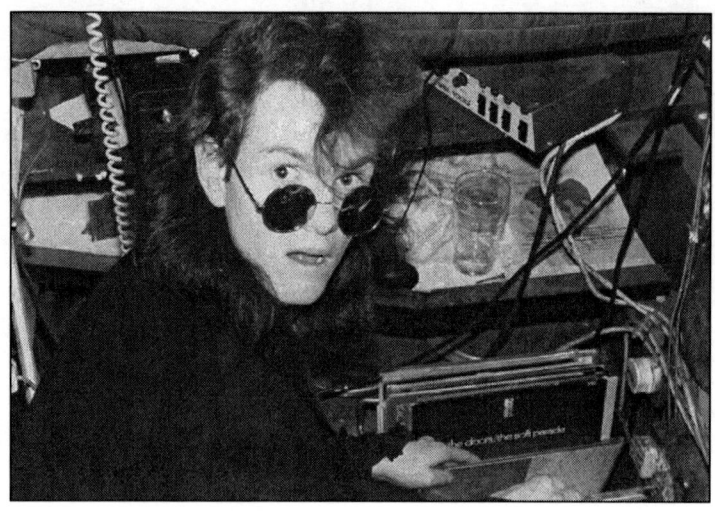

Doctor Clive in the DJ box

Emma Flower Child
(Yep, the bloke in the background is flat on his back)

Louise Flower Child

CHAPTER FIVE

I KEEP THINKING IT'S TUESDAY

Alice In Wonderland begins to be the place to be, The Damned play their first gig there, we make our first record, and a film. The first all night psychedelic film festival takes place, the Custard Beasts arrive on the scene and the toilet paper is explained.

Doctor And The Medics had, at this time, a very small but loyal following. They always went down well with the crowd but didn't always end up getting paid. One night after I witnessed another great Medics performance and yet another night of no money, Clive asked me if I would help them out. That was the beginning of what would be many years of working with Doctor And The Medics.

Towards the end of 1983 I bumped into an old familiar face at Alice In Wonderland. At the back of Gossips there were a series of alcoves that were designed to look like caves, and one night I came across Dave Vanian of the classic punk band, The Damned, lurking in the darkness, (no he wasn't hanging upside down.) I had met him many years previously during the early punk days. He lived in Hemel Hempstead at the time, as did I, and we would sometimes end up on the same milk train at five in the morning after a night at The Roxy Club. He was with Roman Jugg, the then guitarist of The Damned and we got talking. They had just formed a spin off band, Naz Nomad And The Nightmares, and were about to release an album of cover versions of sixties pyschedelic classics.

This meeting was the beginning of what would result in many joint ventures between Alice's, The Medics and The Damned.

We became good friends, with Roman Jugg especially and spent many evenings at one or other of our flats partying. We set up a gig for Naz Nomad to play at Alice's, the first attempt had to be cancelled as drummer Rat Scabies had something else on but we re-organised it for a few weeks later for January 30th 1984. The joke was that Naz Nomad And The Nightmares were an obscure original psychedelic band from Sweden and had reformed. Fact of the matter was that the singer was from Hemel Hempstead and the guitarist was a Welsh Yugoslavian. Everyone knew they were The Damned really.

When we arrived at the club to set it up at nine as usual, we were surprised to see people queuing outside already. When the doors opened at ten the place was packed in no time, we had to turn away a hundred or so people and hadn't, up 'til then, experienced anything like it. Naz Nomad were amazing, dressed in sixties clothes and wearing wigs they belted out such classics as 'Can't Stand Your Love, Goodbye', 'I Had Too Much To Dream Last Night', 'Cold Turkey' etc.

They went down a storm and the crowd were uncontrollable, we had not anticipated such a turnout and were not prepared for it. Joe and I were forced into doing security, the crowd had spilled onto the stage and the band were virtually forced up to the backdrop with nowhere to go. We tried to hold back the audience but two against loads was never going to work. So if you were wondering if we took any photos that night, the answer is no, we were otherwise engaged.

Naz Nomad released their album, *Give Daddy The Knife Cindy* and roped in a whole bunch of Alice In Wonderland regulars to be photographed for the sleeve. The day of the photo session a major bomb went off in Harrods departments store and London was in chaos.

Dave Vanian, Roman, the Flower Children and a bunch of others struggled to get across London and we all ended up at my flat where we carried on partying until the following morning.

After the amazingly successful Naz Nomad gig, Alice's was now past the point of no return. We earned shed loads of brownie points from Gossips and they were happy for us to carry on. Although it was pretty much back to normal over the next few weeks, there was a definite buzz about the place, gradually more and more people started to frequent the club but as the paying people increased, so did the guest list. Doctor And The Medics were also growing in popularity. The Damned booked them as a support act for a few shows and the exposure did them good. Damned fans started turning up at Medics gigs and Alice's as well.

Doctor And The Medics were invited to support The Damned at a festival at Nostell Priory, up north somewhere and fair play to The Damned they let us share their tour bus. So off we set, The Damned, The Medics and their respective entourages for what would turn out to be a totally mental weekend. Rat Scabies, The Damned's drummer, went off on one. It started before we had even left London when he demanded the coach stopped so he could have a wee. As two policemen approached, Rat shouted "In Pain!" three times. He then explained to the cops that it was an ancient English by-law that if you needed to piss in a public place you could, providing you shouted "In Pain!" three times. He got away with it.

The following night after the show we all went and got slaughtered. For some reason Vom, The Medics drummer fell out with his Damned counterpart and they had a fight, the following morning it carried on and Rat ordered a bottle of Champagne at breakfast and broke the bottle over a chair.

Why would you do that? As we headed south to London we stopped at a service station when it all kicked off again. That night I was glad to get home.

The Volcanoes started hanging out at Alice's from the very formative days. Their lead singer, Jan Volcano, was the cousin of The Damned's Roman Jugg so, nepotism and all that, The Volcanoes became the next resident band. Nepotism aside, they were a great band and joined the Alice crowd on anything going. Brought up in Wales by Yugoslavian parents, Jan sang in a different way than most singers, I can't really explain it, their first single, a version of 'Strangers In The Night' is excellent, as are their other records.

Apart from being a great singer, Jan was also responsible for a classic comedy moment that could only have come from him. In the summer of 1984, Clive, Roman and Jan went to the final Summer Solstice festival at Stonehenge. In the early hours of the morning Clive and Roman found Jan, worse for wear after a handful of magic mushrooms and a Pink Panther tab, crouched down staring through the wire fence to a field beyond. "What are you doing, Jan?" asked Roman, puzzled. "I'm watching the little people." replied Jan, seriously. Clive and Roman followed his gaze to the empty field and Clive said: "There are no little people there, Jan." Jan continued to stare at the field for a few moments before he turned around with an angry look on his face and said: "They're not there now, you've frightened them away!"

Sadly The Volcanoes split up a few years later and that was the end of that. I was reminded that I played saxophone on a few recordings and played with them at Alice's alongside my brother Julian and his mate Nick. We were called The Volcanic Brass and I think it was quite good, I must dig out those recordings.

The Surfin' Lungs were four guys from Bracknell, Berkshire, nowhere near the coast, and just like The Beach Boys two decades earlier, they had never been surfing in their lives. The only time they got on a board was for publicity shots, but they wore Hawain shirts and played great music so that was alright. If you crossed The Beach Boys with The Ramones, you'd get The Surfin' Lungs, and, like The Volcanoes, they too became a resident band and also joined us on our outside events.

One of the Alice In Wonderland door girls, the gorgeous Sandra, was responsible for almost re-naming the band once. Sandra was so laid back she was virtually horizontal but whilst she may have been right at the top of the list in the beauty stakes she was half way down the clever list. One night she was asked by a punter who the band were that night, unable to read my psychedelic graphics she replied; "Errr, The Urfin' Slungs." Quality.

The Surfin' Lungs (and not The Urfin' Slungs) often came to Alice's as punters, even though they lived miles away, and became good and respected friends of the Alice crew. I came across some clips on YouTube recently that are brilliant, they released some great records and are still playing today.

Although Captain Sensible had left The Damned, for now at least, he still hung around and was a regular face at Alice's at the beginning. One night he turned up with a camera and took loads of weird photos, taking pictures of people through a beer glass, pushing people in front of the oil wheel projector and then lying on the floor and snapping shots of the toilet paper. He really was off his head, but then what was new? He made a few impromptu appearances, jumping on stage to join The Medics on more than one occasion.

Completely out of the blue he had a freak hit single with a

cover version of 'Happy Talk', a song from the musical, *South Pacific.* He frequently mentioned Alice In Wonderland in press interviews which helped to raise our profile further and make sure that we were probably the most talked about and written about club in London's 1984. Tragically Captain's baby daughter died and he stopped coming to Alice's, quite understandably deciding to stay at home and support his girlfriend.

In the early part of 1984, Clive, Roman and I had a five o'clock in the morning idea. After a night at Alice's and our usual post gig party somewhere we decided we would record The Medics playing live at Alice In Wonderland and release it as a single. We wanted to keep it fairly low key as we were hoping to sign a 'proper' record deal in the not too distant future. And so it was, the single was recorded, a four track EP with 'The Goats Are Trying To Kill Me', 'She Grows Flowers By Candlelight', 'Ride The Beetle' and 'Blockbuster'. Before writing this paragraph I found a copy of the single and listened to it for the first time in over twenty years and it really is very good. Clive does his psychobabble bit between each track and the disc ends with a cover of 'Motorhead,' which irritatingly fades out after thirty seconds.

Produced by Roman and organised by me, the record cost just £500 to make and manufacture and a total of just 1000 were pressed. In true bootleg fashion the label and the sleeve were plain white with no pictures or script at all. We had a rubber stamp made which simply said *Doctor And The Medics Live At Alice In Wonderland* and painstakingly stamped each copy manually. We even held a rubber stamp party to launch the single, although as Clive commented when he saw the first copy, "No I don't, I live in Blackheath."

The single was only sold at Alice's and at gigs and is now apparently quite collectable. When it was first 'released' it retailed for just £1 but if you can find a copy now prepare to pay a lot more.

Listening to the single today I noticed that the crowd in the background shouting Medics! Medics! sounded more like a crowd at Wembley Arena rather than 400 or so punters at an underground club in Soho. This leads me to a confession. Some of those that bought a copy probably realised that they were duped and some had absolutely no idea.

The single wasn't recorded live at Alice's at all but in a four-track studio somewhere with Clive singing the vocal track whilst crouched in the toilet. The crowd noise did indeed come from the Wembley Arena, from a U2 live concert. We drowned out the audience chanting U2! U2! With Medics! Medics! Hilarious. If anyone feels cheated by our little prank then I apologise, but you would have to admit that it was quite funny and the record is great.

In the late spring of 1984 we had another of those ideas. We had the club, we had the band, we had the single, what about a film? These ideas were usually formed in the early hours and were becoming quite a regular thing, with many more still to come, some of them seemed like a good idea at the time but in the cold light of day we thought better of it. Other ideas, discussed after however many bottles of wine were completely forgotten the following day. Some, however, did reach fruition. *I Keep Thinking It's Tuesday (Two Pieces Of Cloth Carefully Stitched Together)* was the title dreamed up by Clive.

Just as we had done with the record I'm afraid we cheated a bit. It wasn't actually a film as such but a video that was transferred onto film. Sorry.

We hired a crew to video people at the club dancing, Alice regulars messing about in a park somewhere, someone being body painted (can't think who,) and some footage recorded at Clive's bed-sit. Clive did a storybook and we enlisted the help of my dad, using his technical skills and access to the editing suites at the BBC. Clive and I trotted off to the BBC studios where my dad was waiting for us outside to get us past security. A couple of young girls were hanging about as it was *Top Of The Pops* day and asked Clive and I for our autographs. "You want Don's autograph", Clive said, referring to my dad, "He's much more famous than us." Prophetic words from the Doctor, perhaps things will change one day....

My dad took us into his editing studio and we got to work chopping it about, adding the credits, and inserting a previously recorded video of early Medics doing 'The Goats Are Trying To Kill Me.' He then transferred it onto 16mm black and white film. It wasn't too bad considering we had never done anything like that before and actually gives a good inside view as to what the Alice scene was about in 1984. However, I don't remember it being reviewed on *Film '84* and if it was ever up for any Oscars I must have been out when they tried to phone me. Funny that.

Another of our ideas at the time was to form a Medics spin off band. It consisted of the majority of the then current Medics line-up, Clive, Steve, Richard, Wendi and Sue together with a previous Medics drummer. Roman was on keyboards and me on sax. We called ourselves; Masher Mik And The Mastic Asphalt Spreaders and did cover versions only, 'Gloria,' 'These Boots Are Made For Walking,' 'Motorhead,' 'Wild Thing,' 'Jack The Ripper' and '96 Tears' were some of the songs we played. We did a few gigs at the club and went down as well as The Medics always did.

Most people didn't actually realise that we weren't really The Medics, just a bunch of friends having some fun.

By the spring of '84 Alice's was becoming quite a happening place and word of mouth meant that each week was busier than the last. We were getting quite a few mentions in the press, *Time Out* and *City Limits* always gave us good reviews and a few journalists from *Sounds,* the now defunct music paper, became Alice regulars and mentioned us in their columns whenever they could. Jane Simons was always a familiar face as was Neil Perry and Tibet. Tibet was responsible for our first full-page article, it appeared in *Sounds* in early April entitled *Down The Rabbit Hole.* Not a particularly original title and in future years we had the lot, *Through The Looking Glass* (dozens of times), *White Rabbit, Ask Alice, Off With Their Heads* etc.

Tibet raved about Alice's because he genuinely loved it and it certainly did the trick. The following Monday we arrived at the club at nine as usual to set up, and as the taxi pulled up outside I saw a queue of brightly dressed Alice people winding round the corner, just as it was at the Naz Nomad gig. That was it, we had got there, there was going to be no stopping us now, not for many years at least.

Rock journalist, Kris Needs, was an Alice regular from the early days and was a well-known face in the music business. In April 1984 he was helping to promote two bands from New York, Certain General, who were a powerful angry psychedelic garage band and their friends, Band Of Outsiders. Kris organised a few gigs for them in the UK and asked if they could play at Alice's.

We put them on the same bill and they were both excellent, the club was packed that night, as usual, and the show received a rave review in the music press, probably written by Kris himself.

Kris was a loveable reprobate, but not the most together

of people and although the Alice show was a great success the other dates on the mini tour didn't go quite so well, mainly because Kris hadn't actually got round to advertising them. I went to see them at The Railway in West Hampstead, me and about six other people.

Not only had Kris not organised any flyers or posters he had also forgotten that he was DJing and hadn't brought any records with him. As I lived just around the corner, I nipped home and fetched some records and I DJ'ed that night. Helping to avert a crisis went a long way with both the bands and Kris and we became quite good friends from there on. Both bands played at Alice's on a couple more occasions and released a brilliant album together with Certain General on one side and Band Of Outsiders on the other.

A group of Doctor And The Medics fans, collectively called the Custard Beasts, came down to Alice's in the early days and were regulars at some of the outside events as well. They were a bunch of psychobillies with flat top hair-dos led by a lad called Bogey. When they turned up they would head for the dance floor and enthusiastically push each other around as they strutted about in a circle.

They were having fun but in a crowded club they started to piss off the other punters who were getting fed up with having their feet trodden on or their drink spilt over them. When The Medics played once, the half a dozen or so Custard Beasts took up so much room at the front of the stage with their mushing that none of the other few hundred people could see the band. Enough was enough.

Whilst I didn't feel it was necessarily my place to tell someone not to dance like that, I had to consider the majority as opposed to the handful of Custard Beasts.

I took Bogey aside and told him that if he was going to

continue coming to the club he would have to alter his dancing habits. "You can't do that." He said, incredulously. "Yes I can." I replied. I then told Chris and Clive not to play psychobilly any more and that seemed to do the trick. Now everyone could have a good time.

Such was Alice In Wonderland's success, in May '84 we thought we could expand, so when the Wednesday night became available at Gossips we decided to do an Alice spin off night called The Magic Roundabout. The idea was that, seeing as how Alice's was becoming too crowded people could come to the Wednesday night as well as or instead of. Of course it didn't work like that, Alice's was Alice's and no one would accept a substitute. So after three weeks, which were quieter than any Alice night ever, we closed it down. Alice's was busier than ever but it was a lesson learned.

The Mystery Girls were more glam than psychedelic, but they had a record to promote and they did a set on the *Old Grey Whistle Test,* a popular late night live in the studio rock TV show, presented by 'whispering' Bob Harris. I booked them to play at Alice's and they were great. They had a sax player who was about seven foot tall, he only just fitted on the stage and you couldn't see his head which disappeared among the strips of toilet paper hanging from the ceiling.

Officially the first Alice event outside Gossips was at The Fulham Greyhound, Doctor And The Medics headlined with The Volcanoes and The Surfin' Lungs supporting. We had the Alice In Wonderland DJ's and it appears the night was fairly busy.

This was in June 1984; trouble is I can't really write about it because I have no recollection of the night whatsoever. I know it happened because the advert for the gig is in one of my scrapbooks and the financial record is in one of my account books. But other than that I really can't remember it, which is odd as I can recall most of the other future events.

Clive came up with a unique idea one night. Why don't we combine film and music and put on a film festival showing classic cult sixties films with a band playing live? What a great idea, to my knowledge it probably hadn't really been done before and if it had it was a long time ago. So I set about organising *The Alice In Wonderland All Night Psychedelic Film Festival*.

It was to take place on Saturday 7th July 1984, Clive's 23rd Birthday, and would consist of a selection of favourite films and, of course, Doctor And The Medics live on stage. The Scala Cinema in London's King Cross is often used these days for gigs and parties but in the eighties it was strictly films only, I thought it was worth asking them if they would let me hire their cinema and to my surprise they agreed.

The films chosen for the first festival were *Barbarella, I Keep Thinking It's Tuesday* (our own classic), *The Trip, Head* and *Grateful Dead Live In Concert*. The last choice was not ours, but The Scala themselves said that it always pulled in a few people, so to keep them happy I agreed. Actually, it worked quite well, it was shown at about six in the morning when most people were asleep, the only people who watched it were the 'Deadheads' who, after the event, joined the growing mass of Alice followers.

I designed the flyer and it was handed out at the club and sent out to the mailing list, we had a few mentions in the press announcing the show and I sold about fifty tickets in advance.

The cinema held five hundred people so from then on it

was in the lap of the Gods. Setting the venue up for the gig was quite challenging, the cinema used to be a monkey house decades earlier so in the front of the screen there was a deep monkey pit hardly visible from the seats. So we hired staging to build it up, setting it up ourselves, we had to carry dozens of scaffold tubes and planks up two flights of stairs and bolt the whole structure together, it took half a day. Never mind, I reminded everyone it would be easier taking it down the stairs the next day.

We set up the P.A. the light shows and in the café, the Alice In Wonderland disco. After the band sound checked it was back to the flat to get cleaned up and then back to The Scala for the show. I was beginning to wonder what on earth I had let myself in for, I had been working flat out setting up since seven that morning, it was now ten at night, the show started at 11.30 and went on until 8.30 the next morning. Trouble is, I had only sold fifty tickets and I was starting to get a bit concerned.

An hour before the doors opened Vom, The Medics drummer burst into the dressing room, The Scala's office, and said: "Have you seen the queue outside? They'll never all get in!" We looked out of the window and sure enough there were hundreds of people queuing half way round Kings Cross. Amazing. Vom was right; they couldn't all get in, not a chance. And so, after letting in the first five hundred, we had to lock the doors and turn away a few hundred more. We could not believe it.

The night went extraordinarily well. The Medics rose to the occasion and were superb, joined on stage by Dave Vanian in his Naz Nomad garb they really went for it. The atmosphere was electric and the crowd were dancing in the aisles, it couldn't have possibly gone better.

There was a bit of an altercation in the dressing room between a pissed Captain Sensible and an equally pissed Rat Scabies, they started throwing drink around until Dave Vanian reminded them that I was responsible for the place and could lose my damage deposit. Fair play, they stopped immediately.

And then there was the shoe incident. Locking the doors once we had squeezed more than enough people inside proved to be a very unpopular decision, especially for one guy who really got upset. "You've got to let me in" he wailed, "I'm a friend of Charlie Harper's!" Charlie Harper was the singer with the punk band UK Subs and a regular at Alice In Wonderland. "So what" I replied and forced the door shut. The so-called friend of Charlie's managed to kick it open and in doing so his shoe fell off inside just before I was able to lock the door. So I confiscated it, which, unsurprisingly, pissed him off even more. If I had unlocked the door dozens of people would have forced their way in, there was no security just me. Anyway it served him right; we didn't do violence at Alice's. I have visions of that bloke walking the streets of London to this day, with just one shoe, a worn out sock and a seriously blistered right foot.

That first film festival was a milestone for Alice's. Our first major event outside the club had far exceeded our expectations and gave us the confidence that perhaps we could do it again. It was damned hard work but the feedback from those that were there made it all worthwhile. Our new friend, Tibet, gave the show a full-page rave review in *Sounds* and letters demanding another one flooded into the office. We'll just have to wait and see.

Flesh For Lulu were regulars at Alice's in the early days and blagged their way in on the guest list on the pretence of wanting to play there.

I had known their guitarist, Rocco, for years, way before Alice's. In fact we used to play in a band together, (I can't remember the name.) until he left to join east end smackheads Wasted Youth. Flesh For Lulu were getting a bit of a name for themselves and although the band members were up for it and booked a date to play, their management wrongly thought that Flesh For Lulu were too big for Alice's and cancelled the gig.

The strips of toilet paper hanging from the club's ceiling was one of our trade marks. The weekly ritual of splitting the Andrex into single ply, tearing them into strips and selotaping them to the ceiling was something that happened every Monday night in its entire ten-year history. The toilet paper created a perfect backdrop for our light and laser shows and, as was its intention, freaked people out when they arrived for the first time, especially as they couldn't see that they were the first arrivals.

Over the course of Alice's life I estimate we used about a million sheets of paper, not exactly environmentally friendly admittedly but when it was pulled to the floor it soaked up the beer which stopped people from falling over, breaking their legs and being a strain on the National Health Service. So as I'm sure you'll agree, we were doing our bit. However one person who was less than impressed was Pat, the cleaner. He was the poor sod that had to clean up the next morning and was, quite justifiably, pissed off by the additional mess caused for the sake of entertainment. He wrote me a letter, which I kept. It reads:

'Christian. A man's word is his bond!! What about this toilet paper and selotape on the ceiling every Tuesday morning? Bad show = and certainly not cricket. Has stumps been drawn for the winter? The "mad" Doctor could give a hand, or paw??

When Big John Wayne - Audie Murphy = (was he a paddy we ask) and Steve McQueen stormed Iwo Jima = they didn't chicken out half way up the hill. Oh - no = right to the top = Hoist old glory = and capture 10,000 Japs. And only three of them. This is not Iwo Jima. Pat. P.S. Take care - see you one Monday night'

What? This letter goes to prove that, at Alice In Wonderland, even the cleaner was completely bonkers.

Flyer for the first Scala film festival
(Spot the spelling mistake)

Naz Nomad and Annadin Brother Jane on stage at the Scala

Masher Mik And The Mastic Asphalt Spreaders on stage at Alice's

A still from the film 'I Keep Thinking It's Tuesday (Two Pieces Of Cloth Carefully Stitched Together')

The Volcanoes

CHAPTER SIX

GOING UNDERGROUND AT CHISTLEHURST CAVES

We meet the Smeg Monster and The Jesus And Mary Chain play their first London gig at Alice's. The legendary Magical Mystery Trips kick off, Nico sobs her heart out, Lemmy marks his territory and Hanoi Rocks end in tragedy.

I could not write a book about Alice In Wonderland without mentioning a high profile character who came and went as he pleased and was, in the early days, a regular at the club. Gossips was not exactly a swish state of the art venue and if it had been it would not have suited Alice's. But what was that smell often prevalent in the toilets and from time to time the dressing room and the DJ box? Ladies and Gentlemen let me introduce you to, the Smeg Monster. Smeg, as he became affectionally known, was short for smelly gas.

He was a legend in his time, often talked about, mentioned in interviews and he even featured in a comic drawn by my brother Julian. Clive would tell everyone over the microphone, "The Smeg Monster is in the building. Repeat. The Smeg Monster is in the building. Do Not Panic!" Before fading out with his manic echoed cackling. The Smeg Monster disappeared one day never to return, and I can't say I was particularly disappointed.

I later found out what caused the smell. Sewer rats are prolific in certain parts of London, living off half eaten kebabs and Kentucky Fried Chickens discarded by careless night time revellers, they could grow to be as big as cats.

They hung out in dark, noisy underground places, like the London tube network and the basement club that was Alice In Wonderland. They would somehow get behind the wood panelling and became such a nuisance that they had to be poisoned. After eating the poison they would crawl off and find the most inaccessible place to die. Problem was until such time as they started to decompose there was no way of knowing where they were. Eventually the problem was sorted and the Smeg Monster was out of our lives forever.

For the first few months at Alice's, Clive and I were the only DJ's. I tended to do the early spot and then we'd share a deck each before the band came on at midnight. Clive would then DJ for most of the rest of the night. Once Alice's had established itself we enlisted the services of Big James, a chubby chap from the east end of London, he didn't quite look the part but he was a record dealer and had an amazing collection of rare sixties psyche.

He used to arrive on a Monday night with a paisley shirt in a plastic bag that he then got changed into. (The paisley shirt that is, not the plastic bag.) "I couldn't walk around the east end wearing this." He'd say. Hilarious, compared to Clive and I he really shouldn't have worried. When we took Jim with us to the Alice show in New York he'd walk ten paces behind Clive and I (obviously sans paisley shirt) because he didn't want to get beaten up. But hey, he played some wicked stuff.

In 1977 whilst playing in The Bears, we were signed to Waldo's Records run by a bloke called Phil Smee. Some seven or eight years later Phil turned up at Alice's with a boxful of rare classics and asked if he could DJ for half an hour. He had no idea I had anything to do with Alice's. It's a small world. And then came Chris Duffell. Chris was an Alice regular from the very early days, and begged me every week to let him DJ.

Trouble was Chris was always pissed and I didn't want to take the risk, he offered to work for free and once even offered to pay me to give him a chance. Eventually his persistence paid off and I told him I'd let him have a go the following week providing he stayed sober.

The next week he had his moment and he was great, he played an excellent selection of music, different from Clive, Jim or I. Further more, he drank orange juice all night. Bless. So that was it Chris started DJing at Alice's and did so for the next eight years or so. The staying sober bit went out the window after the first week but that was okay.

Kris Needs, who I had helped with Certain General and Band Of Outsiders turned up one night with a carrier bag full of records and asked if he could DJ. Kris was once the editor of *Zigzag* magazine and was well known in the nightclub and music business. He loved Alice's and often came down with other influential people who helped towards raising our profile. Long hair, scruffy, leather jacket and a total pisshead, Kris Needs fitted the bill perfectly and got the job. He joined the crew for about a year until disappearing back to America.

Kris was also responsible for one of the most unforgettable 'back stage at Alice's' quotes. One night whilst flicking through Clive's record box, he pulled out an album by the American punk band, The Plasmatics. He pointed his stubby fore finger at the lead singer, Wendy O. Williams on the front cover and said, with a sly grin on his face, "I porked that."

Now Kris was a well-respected journalist, however, his use of the English language on this occasion was exceptional. We never forgot it and to this day whenever I come across that record in my own record collection, I think to myself, Kris porked that.

These days he's still DJ'ing and sometimes come across his name on the bill of some fairly high profile events, touring with The Prodigy and Primal Scream among others.

He has also written a succession of rock'n'roll books, biographies on Keith Richards, Joe Strummer, Primal Scream, and more recently The New York Dolls. He has also written his own autobiography, it's on my list of books I must read.

Other DJ's were Wizz (who did the light show) and his girlfriend, Kit, otherwise known as Suzy Creamcheese. Wizz was a cool bloke but Kit let me down really badly. That's another story. Towards the end, a bloke called Gideon played the records, and fair play, when I couldn't afford to pay him on the night he would still turn up the following week when I'd pay him double.

In the early days of Alice's there was a brothel in the building next door called The Golden Girl Club. The 'girls,' most of whom were actually transsexuals, would occasionally filter into Alice In Wonderland to add even more to the strangeness. We didn't encourage them to hang out there but they were quite harmless really. Every now and again a businessman in a suit would come into our club thinking we had something to do with the place next door and demand his money back. Apparently it was a well-known trick (it has a name but I can't remember it,) to take money from some naïve punter and disappear round the corner and not return.

Most of them would realise they had been had and disappear off to the nearest peep show; others would kick up a fuss and call the police. The police would pretend to take their complaint seriously and would ask them for their name and address.

They would always give false details, so the police would suggest they telephoned their wives for confirmation. They soon scuttled off. After a while The Golden Girl club closed down and was replaced by a more respectable Thai restaurant.

After the success of the first film festival, we received dozens of letters from all over the country from our new Alice fans demanding more. The format was in place that worked so well, so it wasn't that difficult to set up another. So on the 29th September 1984 the second festival took place. Films shown that night were: *Pop Down, Blow Up, I Keep Thinking It's Tuesday, Psyche Out, Stones In The Park* and *Wonderwall*. Doctor And The Medics were live on stage and were excellent once again. They loved these shows and continued to just get better. We had the Alice disco, light and mini laser shows, the event sold out and it couldn't have gone better.

Doctor And The Medics were growing in popularity and I felt I had taken them as far as I could. It was time to bring in someone with more knowledge, experience and contacts in the music business than myself. Andrew King was the former co-manager (along with Pete Jenner), of Pink Floyd and was at that time managing the legendary Ian Dury And The Blockheads and the not so legendary Mari Wilson And The Wilsations.

Andrew King had a variable C.V. a friend of the original Floyd at university he was in there at the beginning. Pink Floyd released the fabulous early albums and the classics, 'See Emily Play', 'Arnold Layne', 'The Scarecrow' etc.

When the other band members decided to split from the lead singer, Syd Barrett, because of his drug problems, Andrew decided to side with Syd and became his manager severing all connections with the rest of Floyd.

Syd Barrett went completely off the rails, and despite releasing two excellent albums disappeared into hermit like obscurity until his death in 2006. What a bummer. Pink Floyd of course went on to being absolutely massive.

Andrew King's secretary in the late sixties was a girl called June Child, wife of the soon to be pop superstar Marc Bolan. Marc introduced Andrew to a friend of his looking for a manager, an up and coming singer songwriter called David Jones. David auditioned for Andrew who declined the opportunity of managing him describing him as 'a talentless poof.' David Jones changed his name to David Bowie and the rest is history. Oops.

A couple of decades later and Andrew, still working in the music business, witnessed an audition by a three piece all girl group. He listened to them, he watched them and shook his head saying they couldn't sing, they couldn't dance and they had as much stage presence as a can of lager. These three girls were Bananarama, who became the most successful all girl-group ever at that time.

With that sort of chequered history he was the perfect man for the Medics. Andrew King has of course had many successful acts and I've only mentioned the ones that got away because it's amusing. However, by his own admission, he was not in touch with the current scene and that was where I came in. We struck a deal that with Andrew, his partner, Jenny Cotton, and myself, we would manage The Medics between us. And so that was it for the next six years.

On the 17th September 1984, a band from the states called Green On Red were booked to play. I got a phone call from Alan McGee of Creation Records asking me if I would let this new band that he had just signed play as the support act.

The band from East Kilbride were The Jesus And Mary Chain, it was to be their first London gig. They came on stage at about 11pm and were absolutely slaughtered, they were far too drunk to play their instruments properly and just thrashed around the small stage tucked away in the corner of the club, falling into the P.A. speakers and knocking mic stands over. They were so appalling that, after a few numbers, Clive and I pulled the plug on them and threw them off stage.

The band were none too pleased at being stopped in full drunken flight but that gig resulted in them getting their first bit of publicity, I was quoted (or rather misquoted) in the music press as to the reason why I threw them off stage, apparently we only wanted "nice" bands to play at Alice In Wonderland. That wasn't the case at all, The Jesus And Mary Chain were just passing through whereas our P.A. guys were there every week and their equipment was getting trashed, I owed it to them to stop that from happening.

Some people thought they were brilliant that night, others thought they were awful, either way they got the publicity they wanted and they went on to be very successful, had a few hit singles and released some great albums. I paid them £40 that night; I should have charged them that for damages. When I researched for this book I discovered that they had been previously booked to play at Alice's in June that year, supporting a band called Jasmine Minks, but I have no recollection of them playing at all so I can only assume that they cancelled.

Alan McGee, the owner of Creation Records, was so taken with Alice's that he decided to start his own club so that he could showcase his latest signings. He called his club The Trip and opened one Wednesday night. Problem was he chose Gossips as his venue and I was having none of it.

I spoke to the management and told them there was room for only one psychedelic club so they closed him down after just one week. As well as the success of The Jesus And Mary Chain, Alan McGee went on to manage and sign to his label, among others, The Charlatans and a fairly well known band these days called Oasis. Oh dear.

Alice In Wonderland's Magical Mystery Trips may now be legendary to those that went on them or heard about them, but the concept wasn't planned, it just happened.

After the success of the film festivals we wanted to expand on the idea of alternative and different ways of putting on shows featuring our house band, Doctor And The Medics. Clive told me about Chistlehurst Caves in South London, 23 miles of underground caverns, how excellent would it be to put on a show there? Apparently both Jimi Hendrix and The Rolling Stones played there in the sixties but a girl died at the Stones gig after wandering down a tunnel and falling into a deep pit and so they stopped allowing gigs there.

I managed to track down the bloke who was looking after it and he agreed to let me hire the caves but only for a private party as they didn't have a drinks, music or dancing license. Also the local residents must not be aware that the show was taking place. Hmm how was I going to get around that one?

What if, I thought, people bought a ticket to see Doctor And The Medics playing at a secret venue, met at a specified place and were transported to the show with no idea whatsoever where they were going? It was then that the legend that was to become the Magical Mystery Trip was born.

Like I said, it wasn't so much an idea, more of a solution. So, with the venue sorted I started planning the show.

Coaches weren't that expensive and as I had decided, in true Alice tradition, that the event would be non profit making I worked out the running costs and divided them by the maximum number of tickets I could sell. That set the price, £3.50 and that included transport there and back. I could have easily doubled or even trebled the price and it would have still sold out, but that was not the way we worked. I booked eight coaches to pick up from Speakers Corner, in London's Hyde Park, and for the Romford and Stamford contingent (the loyal Medics Essex fans) a coach at each of those places.

The flyer was designed and mailed out and press releases were sent to all the relevant papers and magazines. I booked Another Green World, Paul Chousmer, ex-Ring Of Roses keyboard player, to play by the entrance of the caves, organised a video machine (playing *Magic Roundabout* episodes and the original *Batman* movie) and arranged for decks and a P.A. for the Alice In Wonderland disco. Shiva Photonics were booked to do the light show and we were pretty much ready to go.

One potential problem I hadn't quite overcome was how I was going to get 525 excited party people from the coaches to the caves through a built up residential area without the locals being aware that the show was taking place.

The solution was pretty obvious. I would get two stewards, dressed in furry bear outfits, to creep silently to the caves leading the crowd in single file through the streets of Chistlehurst. Every time someone would speak or make a noise they would be told to Shhhh! by the furry bears. Amazingly it worked.

The second problem was the electricity supply, unsurprisingly caves aren't usually kitted out with major power points everywhere; in fact Chistlehurst had just two

13 amp plug sockets, and from that they had to supply the P.A., the amps, the light shows, the disco, the video machine and Another Green World. As the people arrived, totally bemused by the furry bears telling them to keep quiet, the party began. The Medics were excellent of course and the atmosphere electric. Everyone that was there that night witnessed a show that they would never ever forget.

Halfway through the evening, not surprisingly, the power tripped, the music stopped, and the caves were plunged into total darkness. 525 Mystery Trippers trapped underground with no fire escapes, just 23 miles of tunnels that lead nowhere other than more caves. That was scary. I half expected the ghost of the girl from the Stones concert to make an appearance. She didn't. The fuse box was sorted, the lights came back on, and the show continued without any more problems. Phew what a night.

The least likely person on the trip that night was my youngest brother Sam. Sam followed in my footsteps to become a funeral director and took over where I left off. Whereas my other brothers Joe and Julian were regulars at Alice's and the outside events, it wasn't Sam's thing at all. So as an engagement present I gave him two free tickets to the Chistlehurst Trip and left him and his fiancé trapped underground with London's finest weirdos until it was time for the coach to take them all home. What a kind and thoughtful brother I am.

The caves trip received rave reviews in the music press and it began to dawn on me that, although not entirely planned, this was more unique than I had originally realised. When I went to my office a few days later I was amazed to find dozens of letters from people who were there that night and loved it so much they had to let us know.

One of the first things I learned on how to run a successful nightclub was how to run the guest list. The guest list was the fine line between someone adding to the turnover and someone adding to the footfall. It was only a matter of time before Lemmy of Motörhead and Hawkwind would show his face at Alice's and he became a familiar regular until the end. I don't remember Lemmy ever playing at Alice's, but I could be proved wrong, he usually came down late, normally on his own but sometimes with Wurzel, Motörhead's guitarist at that time. He tried to chat up every girlfriend I ever took to Alice's and on an anniversary night even tried to chat up my mother!

Lemmy hasn't changed a bit and is much the same now as he was in the sixties, seventies, eighties, nineties, noughties and tennies, he never paid to get in but it was good news for us. As far as others saw it, if Alice In Wonderland was good enough for Lemmy, it was good enough for them. One night at Alice's there was a bunch of us standing by the cigarette machine talking, Lemmy and Wurzel from Motörhead, Ian Astbury from The Cult and the Damned's roadie, Smiffy. For some bizarre reason Lemmy said to Ian Astbury, "There are three Ian's here, my real name is Ian, so is Wurzel's and you as well." And me, my name is Ian Smith." Said Smiffy. "I feel left out." I said, "Well," said Lemmy "You're half way there, Christ-Ian." It's funny the things you remember.

On Monday 8th October 1984 we celebrated our first birthday. Blimey, who'd have thought it? Surprise, surprise, The Medics were the live act that night, this time playing under the pseudonym of Jonathan The Tap Dancing Giraffe And The Irritated Rug.

We couldn't advertise that The Medics were playing as, by now, their popularity was such that we couldn't possibly accommodate their ever-growing following as well as Alice's own loyal fans. Gwyllym And The Raspberry

Flavoured Cat, Doc Tour And The Mudlarks, Bad Acid And The Spooks and The Axemen were other names that The Medics played under at Alice's. The night was packed out, of course, and most of the regulars as well as our growing fan club of minor celebrities made the effort and it was yet another excellent Alice night.

A few weeks after the birthday party, Nico came to Alice In Wonderland. Nico was once the beautiful singer performing with Lou Reed in The Velvet Underground. As a fourteen year old I was totally in love with her, I always thought she was French, but apparently she was German, however, she was gorgeous and she was in the sensational Velvet Underground. She was also part of the Andy Warhol Factory scene that I found so fascinating, I used to listen to 'Femme Fatale' and 'Chelsea Girls' over and over again and they would send a shiver down my spine. They still do today.

I was totally gob smacked when I saw her, Nico at Alice's? Never. Somehow we got talking, I can't remember whether she approached me or vice versa but she was pretty much off her face, exactly where she'd been for the past twenty years, but was friendly enough. I asked her if she would play at Alice's and she agreed so I gave her my home phone number and suggested she called me. The club closed at 3.30 and after packing up and getting home it was by then 4.30am and I went straight to sleep. An hour later I was woken up by the phone ringing. Who on earth could be calling me at this time? It was Nico; even more worse for wear than she had been earlier.

She was clearly upset and was slurring her words, she said she would love to play at the Club and we booked a date for 19th November, in the meantime, she sobbed, did I know anyone who could get hold of some gear, heroin. What! Firstly, I didn't get involved in drug dealing in any shape or form, never did do, and never would do.

The Good, the Bad, the Lemmy and Vom

A packed night at Alice's

CHAPTER SEVEN

TRIP TO FAIRYLAND

The second Magical Mystery Trip takes place, the Alice In Wonderland beer mountain takes shape and Primal Scream show their faces.

After the Chistlehurst Caves Mystery Trip I was constantly asked when the next one would be. The club regulars, our out-of-town followers, The Medics as well as Andrew King and Jenny Cotton all wanted more. Finding the right venue that had the necessary facilities, was large enough to house the anticipated crowd and was sufficiently different enough to carry on in the same vein as the caves was challenging to say the least. Someone told me about a disused factory in Battersea, south London, which used to belong to the record company, Decca. Decca was the early Rolling Stones label so that was sufficiently rock'n'roll enough for me.

I went to check it out, it was basically a shell of an old building with a concrete floor, broken windows and blocked toilets. But it had potential and, most importantly, electrics. The show was planned for 22nd December 1984 and so to give it a Christmas theme, it was called *The Alice In Wonderland Trip To Fairyland*. Transforming the building was seriously hard work, we hired a vast expanse of industrial carpet to cover the concrete and I went to Brick Lane market and bought every roll of white cotton I could find. The entire warehouse, walls, windows and ceilings were clad in the fabric giving it a tent like feel and would provide the perfect backdrop for our light and laser shows.

We built a stage for the band to play on and a scaffold tower in the centre for the lighting and sound equipment.

We had video machines playing non-stop *Magic Roundabout* episodes and tucked away in the corner was a secret fairy garden, to get there you had to go through a maze like tunnel which I had built out of white sheeting with a few corridors leading to dead ends and only one to the secret space. The garden itself was covered with artificial grass on the ground, giant toadstools and a pond. Another Green World played chill out music in the background and the tent like walls and ceiling were the backdrop for bizarre black and white films and light show projections. One thousand people gathered at Battersea Bridge and were led pied piper style by a bunch of musicians jamming. Dan Carpenter of Ring Of Roses and myself played sax and I think some others joined us, I just can't remember.

We walked over the bridge to the south side and after turning a few corners arrived at Fairyland, the disco had started and people just went for it the minute they arrived. The support band were The Cockroaches, who weren't a band at all but a couple of Medics roadies, the twins from Boys Wonder and The Medics bass player, Richard Searle. Because they were wearing wigs some people thought they were Naz Nomad And The Nightmares (The Damned's alter egos) but sorry to shatter your memories I can assure you they weren't.

Halfway through the evening it was discovered that the pond in the secret garden was leaking and the artificial grass was now sopping wet, but the twenty or thirty people chilling in there sitting cross legged on the floor didn't seem to notice or care. It had taken half an hour for them to find their way in, what was a wet bum in the scheme of things? Just wait until you go out into the cold December night.

The Medics, once again, were their exceptional selves, rising to the atmosphere fitting for a Mystery Trip; Clive ripped his trousers and played for most of the set with his man bits hanging out. Did he care? Of course not, and nor did anyone else, this was The Medics, this was Alice's, this was a Mystery Trip and pretty much anything goes.

The show went amazingly well and everyone had a thoroughly good time, however, it was after the event that it dawned on me that I was lucky to have got away without anyone getting hurt. When we were setting up the show, earlier in the day, it was pointed out to me that the place was bloody freezing and what had I done about heating?

Oh dear, it hadn't occurred to me (although broken windows and December should have been clues enough.) Andy Veg, who was helping out, suggested getting some industrial blow heaters and set off to see what he could find. He came back a few hours later with two gas fired rockets, one of which had no guard so was shooting out four foot long naked flames, just a few feet from acres of inflammable cotton backdrops.

If that wasn't bad enough, half way through the evening, a bloke called Chief who was one of the security people decided to tie up the fire exits after a couple of gate crashers had managed to get in. 95% of the Alice people were just cool kids who just wanted to have a great fun evening, but then there was always the odd idiot who had to try and ruin things.

This night's idiot decided to hot wire a mechanical digger, just outside the factory, and proceeded to try and demolish the building. Thanks mate, you've just lost me my damage deposit. Luckily there was no fire, thank God, and everyone left the place safely, leaving us to clear up the mess.

For those of you reading this book that were there that night, I would like to apologise for inadvertently putting your lives at risk, I didn't mean to. However, I would like to be able to say that I learned from my error of judgement and that I would never put humans in jeopardy again, but I'm afraid that was not the case as you will discover.

Whilst the thousand party people may have had the night of their life, and may have gone to sleep smiling, we were left to clear up the mess. Literally. As the sun rose the following morning, the punters had all gone home, the P.A. equipment, lightshows, staging etc. had all been taken away and myself, Clive and a few others were faced with clearing up after the party. We stared at the thousands of empty beer cans and the filthy carpet the size of a football pitch and the stark reality dawned on us. Part of the contract with the carpet hire people, was that we had to leave it in the same condition as it was delivered. Not a chance.

However, we made the effort and set about cleaning it up. We had a broken vacuum cleaner and a dustpan and brush, which were hardly adequate to clean an acre of carpet, half of which was sopping wet thanks to the artificial pond we set up. There goes that damage deposit as well. Needless to say it took us ages, and after dealing with the angry builder and his hot-wired digger we then saw the thousands of unsold beer cans.

When I hired the factory there was obviously no bar facilities so it was up to me to sort it out. Having previously been turned down for a drinks licence at a previous event I thought of a way of cutting through the red tape and side stepping regulations. Basically, anyone who wanted a drink would try and win one by buying a raffle ticket for £1. Amazingly, and I don't know how it happened, every ticket was a winner, and their prize? A can of beer.

When I bought the beer I estimated the number of beer cans needed based on my own nightly consumption, multiplied it by a thousand (the number of tickets sold) and halved it, because I thought, quite correctly, not everyone drinks as much as me.

Thousands of cans were sold and drunk, but thousands remained, stupidly I hadn't bought them on a sale or return basis so I was stuck with them, thousands of them. We packed The Medics tour van (the Medicmobile) with the unsold crates and brought them back to my flat in West Hampstead where they were piled up on the pavement outside.

I then had the unenviable task of carrying the crates up to my flat, trouble was, I lived on the third floor of a huge mansion block and after numerous journeys up and down the hundreds of steps. I was totally knackered. I hadn't slept for about thirty hours and there in the middle of my flat was this huge pile of beer crates. It became affectionally known as the Alice In Wonderland Beer Mountain.

Bit by bit I sold it off running bars at various shows until I was down to the last 500 cans, I then noticed to my horror that they were just about to reach their sell-by-date. I discovered that nail polish remover wipes off sell-by-dates printed on the bottom of beer cans, so I painstakingly removed every date from the last 500 cans and sold them on as a job lot. Whew, the mountain had gone, what a relief.

After the Fairyland show I reflected on events and taking into consideration the hassle factor and the fact that I didn't earn a penny from the night, I decided that I would never put myself through that again and that would be the last Mystery Trip.

The days that followed made me feel a whole lot better about the trips, the punters loved it and couldn't stop talking about it, the letters flooded into the office raving about the show and asking when the next one would be.

I have often thought, as I'm sure many others have, what a difference it would have made if, in the early eighties, we had had the technology that these days we take for granted. There were no mobile phones. There were no personal computers except the Sinclair ZX Spectrum and the Amstrad; I even bought a Spectrum with a view to creating a database for our ever-growing mailing list.

It was so ridiculously involved that I abandoned that idea and just used it to play games on. My 'data base' consisted of a series of very large address books and when we mailed our fans alerting them of future events and stuff, everything was hand written.

There was no Internet, of course, and I can only imagine what effect a website, YouTube or Facebook would have had on my enterprises. Still there wasn't and that was it. These days, however, I've been told about all sorts of sites that talk about Alice In Wonderland and it's associated projects, one particular site, Pooterland sent a shiver down my spine when I saw it.

These guys, who were obviously at virtually all of the Alice events set up this site about psychedelia in general and have dozens of pages about Alice In Wonderland, including reviews of most of the special shows. What I like about their reviews is that they are written by genuine Alice followers who lived it and loved it and were what Alice In Wonderland was meant to be about, they saw it with a different set of eyes and could write about the events in a way that I couldn't possibly.

Bobby Gillespie, the drummer of The Jesus And Mary Chain, also had his own band, Primal Scream, these days a huge and respected act, but in 1984 no one had heard of them. After The Mary Chains played at Alice's, Bobby became a regular at the club for a while. Unfortunately they never played there, it was talked about but it never happened. It may have been because of Clive and I throwing The Mary Chains off the stage when they played earlier in the year. Or maybe it had something to do with him and his girlfriend being accused of stealing Wendi and Sue Annadin's leather jackets from the dressing room. I also remember him slagging us off in an interview once. Even so, he put all that aside when he blagged his way in on the guest list. Welcome to the wonderfully two-faced world of rock'n'roll.

The year ended in fine fashion with Ring Of Roses playing on Christmas Eve and The Medics, under the guise of Bad Acid And The Spooks, playing on New Years Eve. Both nights were packed out and the punters, still buzzing from the Fairyland trip, went for it in true Alice style. 1984 had been an eventful year for Alice In Wonderland and some great bands had played, whilst I can't name them all, among those, other than the bands already mentioned, were Persian Flowers, The Missing, The Kissing Bandits, The Surfadelics and The Prisoners. We were all left wondering how the next year would pan out.

*Me and Emma Flower Child at the Fairyland Trip
(Check out the guy in the background)*

Alice people just going for it

Clive forgets his lyrics on stage at Alice's

Inside Alice In Wonderland

CHAPTER EIGHT

DID HE JUST SAY WHAT I THINK HE SAID?

A bloke decides to kill himself at our film festival, The Medics sign a record deal and Clive gets thrown through a car windscreen in Paris. We do a one-nighter in New York, and The Cult play a secret gig at Alice In Wonderland.

By the time it came to the next All Night Psychedelic Film Festival we were becoming old hands at the game. The system was in place and it was just about rolling it out for another. Because the previous two festivals had sold out and we had to turn away hundreds of punters we decided to do a double show, the club and the Mystery Trips had raised our profile considerably, The Medics popularity was increasing and we couldn't possibly cater for that in only one show.

The two shows would run concurrently with Doctor And The Medics playing live on the Friday 25th January 1985 and The Treatment were booked for the next night, the Saturday. The films were the same for both nights: *You're A Big Boy Now, Blue Sunshine, Performance, The Model, 1969 Mick Jagger Interview* and *Jimi Hendrix Live In Concert.* This time we added some films of original 1960's adverts and a never before seen promo film by an early Pink Floyd performing 'Arnold Layne', (courtesy of Andrew King.) The Friday night went like a dream so on the Saturday I decided in my wisdom to let my hair (and, it transpired later, also my guard) down and have some fun.

Every show I put on I had to keep myself reasonably together, after all I was in charge and I was responsible for everything, but after the Friday going so well for the

Saturday I got totally slaughtered. Well what could possibly go wrong? Not the best idea I've ever had that's for sure. The first couple of films were well received although the cult psychedelic classic, *Blue Sunshine,* unnerved a few people. It was a film about a group of people who had all taken LSD in the sixties and years later started having flashbacks that made them lose their hair and jump out of apartment block windows. Well it didn't always have to be about peace and love.

It was during Mick Jagger's *Performance* film that things took a rather dark turn. I was sitting next to my brother Julian watching the film when my other brother, Joe, tapped me on the shoulder and said, "I don't want to worry you Christian but some bloke has just killed himself and the place is crawling with police."

"I DON'T WANT TO WORRY YOU CHRISTIAN BUT SOME BLOKE HAS JUST KILLED HIMSELF AND THE PLACE IS CRAWLING WITH POLICE!!!" Yeah, why would that worry me?

I stood up immediately and just stared at the cinema screen rooted to the spot, my head was spinning. What did he say, what did he say? I thought to myself, trying to get my head around it. After a short while people behind me shouted at me to sit down as they couldn't see the film. I sat down and said to Julian, "Did he just say what I think he said?" "I think so." Replied Julian.

Oh shit, I thought, trying to make sense of it all, the place was well over capacity, I was running a drinks bar without a proper license (raffle tickets, beer mountain,) someone was dead, the place was full of police, I was completely off my face and I was in charge. I went into the lobby and Joe filled me in. Apparently, some guy had been found splattered on the pavement outside the cinema. Passers-by ignored him thinking he was just pissed but eventually the police arrived on the scene and worked out that he had jumped out of the toilet window on the fifth floor. They entered the cinema and kicked in the toilet door where they found a suicide note.

Joe was an absolute rock, I told him that I was in no fit state to talk to the police and I was putting him in charge. He talked to the police who surprisingly weren't that bothered but said that they wanted to speak to the crowd. So, much to the annoyance of 500 psyched out party people, the film was stopped and the lights came on. The chief policeman walked down the central aisle, stepping over fazed out Alice people, to the stage area amid a barrage of pig grunts from the audience.

Nobody took him seriously, especially as, earlier in the evening, The Treatment's bass player wore a policeman's helmet during their set so most people thought it was just another Alice wind-up. Fair play to the police though, they said that they didn't care what was going on but that a man had killed himself and if anyone knew who he was could they come forward. Nobody did, so the show continued, the police left the building and the poor unknown soul was scraped off the pavement and taken away.

The next day, still reeling from the events of the previous night, I rang the journalist, Jane Simons, who I knew had been in the audience and pleaded with her not to print the story. I could see the headlines *All Night Party Death Plunge* or something. She agreed, and the incident didn't even get to be yesterday's chip wrappers.

I then got a phone call from Adam of The Treatment who asked me if I had seen the previous weeks' *Time Out* magazine, I hadn't and he told me to go and buy a copy. The magazine was out a few days before The Scala show and there was a short piece about the forthcoming event with a photo of a person splattered on a pavement with blood coming out of their head. It was a still from the *Blue Sunshine* film. How weird was that? Either, it was a complete coincidence or the troubled dead man had deliberately chosen to end his life at that show. Whatever the reason, I wish it hadn't happened.

Doctor And The Medics had signed a record deal with IRS records, distributed through MCA, IRS was the label run by Miles Copeland, brother of Stewart, the drummer in The Police. The first Medics release was an EP called *Happy But Twisted*, which sold well and climbed up the Indie charts rapidly. At that time the main charts were normally pop and disco and it was hard for alternative rock bands to chart. So the Indie chart was set up for all of those bands on smaller independent labels that couldn't get a look in.

The band continued to play small gigs up and down the country, Dudley J.B's, The Croydon Underground, Dingwalls, The Zap Club in Brighton, and, God forbid, Scunthorpe Baths. They were gaining a bit of a following but the shows attracted nothing like the numbers that the Alice events achieved. I needed to organise another show.

Jon Brodel turned up at the very first Scala film festival with boxes full of lighting equipment and offered to do a light show. He said he didn't want paying, he just wanted to be part of it, from then on we couldn't get rid of him, (not that we ever tried.) Jon and his crew, collectively called Shiva Photonics went on to do all of the UK Alice events over the next few years or so. He had a fabulous collection of oil wheel projectors, slide projectors, lasers and all things psychedelic, he became an integral part of the Alice team and even when, as the events got bigger and we may have had four or five lightshow people, he was always top dog and had the main stage to himself.

However, sometimes his enthusiasm ran away with him and, when he told me of this fantastic idea he had had, I had to rain on his parade. Whilst I was planning one of the film festivals at The Scala Cinema he came up with this scheme where he would string a wire from the top row of seats to the screen and fix a rocket with rings attached to it and set it off. He was grinning from ear to ear as he told me his plan and said that when the firework hit the screen he would simultaneously shine explosive slides and films showing scenes of utter devastation onto the canvas. Hmmm. Sorry Jon, great idea and I'm sure it would be amazing, however, who would pay the £5000 for a new cinema screen?

At one of the festivals we showed the spaghetti western classic, *For A Few Dollars More.* Every time someone got shot, Jon would flash an image of a fried egg covered in tomato ketchup (or something similar) on the screen, trouble is he was usually a second or two late which was even more hilarious.

In the spring of 1985 The Medics were booked for a low budget gig in Paris. There were no hotels as part of the deal, just a space on the floor at the promoters' apartment. The night before the gig Clive joined their hosts on a trip to see the Eiffle Tower, Clive, being the tallest, sat in the passenger seat and off they set. Their car was involved in a bad accident colliding with another and Clive was thrown through the car windscreen.

Clive had blood pouring from his face and, rather than wait for an ambulance, the hosts drove the smashed up car to the hospital themselves as it would be quicker. Lying on the back seat with blood gushing out of his head, Clive slipped in and out of consciousness, as they passed the famous Parisian landmark, Pascal, the promoter, prodded Clive and said "Look Clive, zee Eiffle Tower!" Like he was bothered at this stage.

I didn't go to Paris but I received a phone call from Andrew King the following morning and he told me what happened. The first thing I did was go straight to my typewriter (well it was 1985) and started tapping out a press release, I typed out the graphic details, going through a list in my head of who I was going to send it to when I suddenly realised that I hadn't actually asked how Clive was, for all I knew he could be dying.

It would have made for a more impressive story but then it would have meant that I would have lost my close friend and business colleague. I phoned Andrew back who assured me that Clive was going to live and I breathed a huge sigh of relief, I didn't have to find a replacement DJ after all.

The girls that worked on reception played their part in helping Alice's run as smoothly as possible. They were the first 'Alice' face that the punters saw and it was important that they looked and acted the part. In the early days of Alice In Wonderland, Gossips was a members only club so everyone had to fill in a membership form. It wasn't a major problem at first but once Alice's started getting busy it was a nightmare. We had to have two girls on the door to deal with it all, I never knew that there were so many people called Donald Duck, Cruella DeVille, Margaret Thatcher and Mr. Purple Dragonfly, but according to the membership records there were.

Alice's got to the point that we had to have a door policy as to who we would let in and who we wouldn't. It wasn't that we were getting elitist it was just that twice as many people wanted to get in than we could possibly deal with or we were licensed to accommodate. If we let in the first 500 people who had queued since whenever, the place would be full of tourists and the regulars wouldn't get in.

Alex, my girlfriend at the time, was the girl on the door in the early days and she did a great job at stopping casuals, drunks and stag parties from spoiling good Alice fun. Wendi (Annadin Brother) worked at Alice's for a while and she wouldn't take any crap from anyone. Others that came and went were Sendrine, Sandra, Janine, Penny and Marcella.

There was another girl, whose name escapes me, who sat at reception wearing just her underwear. She was studying corsetry at college and wearing warm comfortable clothing for work was not on her agenda, a black leather corset, matching knickers, stockings, high heels and hair extensions and that was it. She always complained that it was cold (I can't think why) and used to bring a portable electric heater with her, which she plugged in under the desk. Still, if people came to the club just to gawp at the scantily clad door girl that was okay by me, providing of course they paid to get in.

Kris Needs came up with the idea to take the Alice In Wonderland club to do a show in New York. He introduced me to Ruth Polski, a promoter at The Danceteria, a large New York nightclub on three floors and she thought it was a great idea. Kris was working with a couple of New York bands, Certain General and Band Of Outsiders who had both played at Alice's a couple of times and suggested they would play live. The idea of an Anglo-American night appealed to the bosses at The Danceteria and we were booked for a gig in April 1985.

I arrived in New York ahead of Clive, who was coming in on the next flight and started to set up the club, painting backdrops and hanging up toilet paper. We had to pretend to the authorities that we were in New York to DJ at a private party as we didn't have green cards, so when Clive arrived with his boxes of records and his echo box he was on strict instructions to play the innocent.

It was no great surprise that the custom and immigration officials gave him the third degree at the airport and refused him entry to the USA, they reckon it was because he didn't have any money on him whatsoever (I was going to pay his taxi fare when he arrived at the hotel.) But I reckon it was the long hair and the flared trousers that they objected to. Luckily he was allowed to make a phone call and luckily I happened to be in my hotel room when he phoned. (No such luxury as a mobile phone.) Somehow or other I managed to sort it out and they let him in. Watch out America, the Doctor is in your country.

The show itself was a great success, Band Of Outsiders and Certain General were excellent and Clive was on top form, Big Jim also DJ'ed and we handed out sweets to the bemused Americans who hadn't experienced anything quite like it. We had achieved what we had set out to do, re-create the atmosphere of London's Alice and put on a show that would stick in people's minds forever.

When I started writing this book, this paragraph began: Guess what? Madonna was the coat check girl! I read in a magazine article that the legend that is Madonna used to work at The Danceteria taking in people's coats around the time of our show, and for the past twenty years believed that she may well have been working that night. I have told the story dozens of times in interviews believing it to be true, but in checking the accuracy of my stories I discovered that, yes she did work at The Danceteria, and yes, she was a coat check girl, but a few years earlier than the Alice show. Oh shit, there goes my story....

Ian Astbury, the lead singer of The Cult came to Alice's one night and loved it so much he turned up virtually every week for the next year or so. He would either arrive early and sit in one of the alcoves reading a book for a while, or he would turn up late with one or other of his band members and party. Ian didn't party hard and, unlike the majority of the Alice crowd, as I remember, didn't drink that much. But party animal or not we became good friends.

He also lived in West Hampstead and he would come round to my flat, or me his, and we would talk, listen to records and watch videos. One day at his flat he told me he had just recorded a new song that was inspired by, and written after a night at, Alice In Wonderland. He played me the tape and asked me what I thought of it.

The song was 'She Sells Sanctuary,' which was then released as a single and became a big hit. It is still recognised today as being an all time classic and I'm proud of the fact that the song would probably never have been written had it not been for Alice's. The album, *Love*, was also heavily influenced by Ian and the band's nights at Alice's and for the follow up single, 'Rain,' Ian asked the Annadin Brothers, Wendi and Sue, to dance in the video. Ian was well known for his image plagiarism and the black love heart painted on his cheek in the 'Rain' video was lifted directly from yours truly. But I didn't mind, I was kind of flattered.

The Cult were originally called Southern Death Cult, they shortened it to Death Cult and then finally The Cult. We always thought they should change their name again to C. Ian had had many image changes in his career, Red Indian, goth and now chic hippy psychedelic.

One night Ian asked me if The Cult could do a secret gig at Alice's to celebrate his and Billy Duffy's (the guitarist) birthdays. At that time they were playing to huge crowds and could demand huge fees. However they wanted to play at Alice's and they did, for the princely sum of just £150 with a £10 rider.

The gig was superb and will stick in my mind as one of the

most memorable shows ever in Alice's long life. They played some of the stuff from the *Love* album and cover versions of 'Hey Joe,' 'I Can't Explain' and 'Stepping Stone' and although only playing to a few hundred people (half of which couldn't see the stage) the gig was one of the band's favourites ever as well.

Ian Astbury and The Cult constantly mentioned Alice In Wonderland in press interviews, raving about how we were doing stuff quite unlike anything else going on at that time, this exposure helped to increase our profile even further. We were flattered.

Sonja Kristina was the gorgeous lead singer of the popular early seventies hippy band, Curved Air, who also featured Stewart Copeland of The Police, brother of Miles Copeland the boss of Doctor And The Medics record label, IRS. (Although that had nothing to do with anything.) Sonja Kristina was playing with a new band called Christie. (I don't think it was anything to do with Tie A Yellow Ribbon Round The Old Oak Tree' Christie although I couldn't be sure.)

Sonja played at Alice's and, it has to be said, was pretty mediocre, but what Sonja didn't know (until I reminded her) was that we had met ten years previously. As a sixteen year old in 1975 whilst working at the Hemel Hempstead Pavilion, Curved Air played, Sonja took a bit of a shine to me, she was a good few years older than me but that didn't seem to matter to her. She took me out for a cheeseburger at the Hemel Wimpy bar so she must have fancied me.

The Magic Mushroom Band approached me at some point in 1985 desperate to play at Alice In Wonderland. I loved the name, I loved the band and I loved their music. So, I booked them, not just to play at Alice's but at some of our other events as well.

Led by Garry Moonboot Masters and his gorgeous wife, the singer and dancer Kim, they were always great people to deal with.

What we have now that we didn't have then, of course, is YouTube. In the eighties I collected literally hundreds and hundreds of hours of video clips of my favourite bands and dragged them around with me every time I moved. Leaving them in barns and garages they all went mouldy and I had to sling them out. If I'd known YouTube was coming along I would have got rid of them long ago.

Many of the bands mentioned in this book have clips on YouTube, including The Magic Mushroom Band and they in particular are definitely worth seeking out. As I said: Great name, great band, great music, great dancer.

Garry of The Magic Mushroom Band

Kim of The Magic Mushroom Band

The Cult's Ian Astbury after the secret gig at Alice In Wonderland

Clive, myopic beanpole DJ'ing

The Treatment at The Scala

CHAPTER NINE

LOVE PEACE AND BANANAS

In which Doctor And The Medics rock out at the third Alice In Wonderland Magical Mystery Trip, the Alien Green Jelly Girl, an astronaut, the Underwear Girls, the Bisto Gravy Kids, the Nuns In Shades and the Crucified Teddy Bears all make an appearance. Doctor And The Medics play on the same bill as Hawkwind and Dame Vera Lynn.

After the Fairyland Mystery Trip I had vowed never to do it again, however, I changed my mind. Things were just going from great to greater at Alice In Wonderland and so I started to think that a summer event would be the next logical step for both Alice's and The Medics. Those that went on the first two trips wanted more and those that had heard about it wanted to experience the action for themselves.

One of the things that made the trips different from any other live music event was, of course, that no one had any idea whatsoever where they were going. Apart from myself the only other person who knew the locations was Joe, who drove me there. Not even Clive, the other bands or my staff knew where we were going. I would let the lighting, laser and sound guys know a week in advance so they could sort out logistics like power, water, access etc. The bands were told the night before the show, that way the secret was protected.

The next trip had to be bigger and better than the previous two so the venue had to match up to my expectations. I looked into a few venues, including a former lunatic asylum in Virginia Water, which had been the setting for Adam Ant's *Goody Two Shoes* video.

Unfortunately it wasn't quite right, the main hall wasn't big enough and the rest of the building consisted of dozens of small padded cells. I dread to think what would have gone on if we had had a trip there, the mystery trippers would probably still be there now.

The guys who had put up the staging at the film festivals and the Battersea trip told me about a disused Butlins Holiday Camp in Clacton, Essex. I contacted the owner and drove over with Joe to check it out. It was perfect, the main bar and stage area, called the Crazy Horse Saloon, was big enough for up to two thousand people and there were various other areas that we could use as well. Clacton was a bit far out, but Alice liked far out, rather than coaches this time I thought we could go by train. So I contacted British Rail and to my surprise they agreed to let me charter two private trains from Liverpool Street station in London, direct to Clacton. The walk from the station to the venue was a bit much, so I organised shuttle buses as well.

It was coming together quite nicely, needless to say The Medics were booked to headline the show planned for the eve of Clive's Birthday, Saturday 6th July 1985. Support bands were booked, Ring Of Roses, The Magic Mushroom Band, The Treatment, The Volcanoes, Voodoo Child, Perfect Disaster, The Surfin' Lungs and Bad Acid And The Spooks. Light shows, laser shows, discos and side events were organised, leaflets, tickets and t-shirts designed and printed, press releases went out and we were ready to go.

Once again the trip was planned as being non profit making and the tickets were priced at just £5, which even in 1985 was incredibly cheap, especially as it included the train fare there and back. The tickets had to be bought in advance and I was anticipating selling 1500, the number of seats available on the train and a 50% increase on the last trip. I was overwhelmed by the response, the applications for tickets came flooding into the office, and we sold the 1500 in a matter of weeks. It was a full time job just dealing with the mail, problem was the applications continued to arrive and we had oversold by almost 500. Oh shit.

By a complete bit of luck I received a phone call from my chap at British Rail who told me that due to rolling stock logistics I would have extra carriages on my train giving me another 500 seats, but I wouldn't have to pay extra for them. Problem solved, Cinderella you can go to the ball. It also meant that by selling another 500 tickets I had extra funds to plough into the show, which meant even more treats for the lucky 2000. Maybe now we could afford lasers. How brilliant would that be?

Setting up the show was great fun; everyone involved was in a great mood, excited about the event, which was already looking like it would be an event like no other. Shiva Photonics and a new recruit, laser man Jim Webb, set up their equipment in the Crazy Horse Saloon and it looked amazing. We may now take lasers for granted, but in 1985 they were in their infancy and were expensive. Pink Floyd could afford them, Alice's couldn't. Jim reduced his fees considerably because he too wanted to be part of this thing.

In the late afternoon 2000 Alice people congregated at Liverpool Street station, and although I wasn't there I've seen a photo and it was an amazing sight. There were psychedelics, hippies, punks, goths, glam rockers, bikers and hundreds of brightly coloured weirdos all wondering where they were going and what was going to happen. It was Ascot Day (or something) and, among the Alice crowd, there were dozens of top-hatted race-goers totally bemused and wondering what the hell was happening. The departure board read Platform 3 and 4: Alice In

Wonderland Magical Mystery Trip. Destination????? Good old British Rail, on this occasion they proved they could have a sense of humour and entered into the spirit of things. Not always the case as you will find out.

Just before midnight I went walkabout on a mission to find my brother Joe. Green and red laser beams shot through the air above my head as I gazed at the amazing lightshows projected onto the backdrops hung around the hall. The smell of incense, mixed with patchouli oil, sweat and alcohol, hung in the air.

I couldn't see him in the main hall so I escaped out into the cool summer night air and walked towards the outdoor swimming pool. There was some dude who had obviously had far too much to dream that night throwing up in the corner of the pool as another guy practised his backstroke 'swimming' backwards and forwards. Problem was there was no water in the pool; it had been empty for years, apart from a few inches of stagnant rainwater, which had collected in the deep end. However, that didn't seem to bother Mark Spitz or the other guy who dived into the rancid puddle to cool down.

No sign of Joe here, so I wandered back into the ballroom, a girl slithered towards me, totally naked, covered in green jelly and wrapped from her neck to her ankles in cling film. She smiled at me as if to say "Why not?" the jelly sliding about her slender body as she moved. She squelched out of sight and I shrugged my shoulders, oh well.

To the side of the main hall there was a large corridor, which had all sorts of strange things going on. There were jugglers, fire breathers, some bloke called Mix-Up wearing a mask citing psychedelic poetry and another bloke banging car hubcaps in time to the music. My other brother, Julian, was sitting cross-legged on the floor playing his bassoon, jamming with an early version of Spannerman. I asked him if he had seen Joe. Julian stopped playing for a moment and said he'd seen him go past about half an hour ago.

I walked to the end of the corridor where I bumped into the Bisto Gravy Kids. In fact I actually tripped over them and after picking myself up off of the floor I realised that they weren't the real Bisto Gravy Kids but impostors, life size cardboard cut-outs. Even so, what the fuck were they doing here?

After the Bisto Kids altercation I entered this bar area, fifty or sixty people were packed in dancing their heads off to '96 Tears' pumping out of the sound system. The whole room was bathed in a technicolour sea of psychedelic lights and then I spotted the Flower Children giving it loads on the dance floor. Either they didn't hear me or they were on a planet of their own, but they didn't answer my question: "Have you seen Joe?"

I left the disco area and moved onto another room where there were equally bizarre things happening, someone had turned up with his body painting kit and people were just stripping off and letting him carry out his art. There was a tunnel, which led to a secret room. That's where Joe would be hiding, I thought. The tunnel was lined with netting, which had teddy bears impaled on crucifixes with blood splattered on their fur. I followed the eerie sounds coming from the other end of the tunnel, negotiating past the teddy bears until I reached the secret room where Another Green World were playing chill out music and video machines were playing the *Banana Splits* shows.

I became engrossed in the Sour Grape Gang and the Dilly Sisters for a while before remembering I was on a mission. I left the secret room via the tunnel but by now the netting had fallen down and the only way out was on your hands and knees across the beer sodden carpet to the exit. The massacred teddy bears were a bit too close for comfort but after completing the assault course I eventually got out.

I made my way back into the main hall and came face to face with an astronaut. I'm not kidding you, a real life Neil Armstrong spaceman, walking towards me in slow motion, helmet and all. This was now really getting freaky. Standing next to me were two young girls with massive black back-combed hair-do's who obviously couldn't make up their minds what they were going to wear to the party so decided to wear nothing, just their underwear and not a lot more. It was a hot night but this was going some. Oddly enough no one hardly gave them a second look. The underwear girls made the green jelly girl look like a nun in comparison.

Oh yeah, there were a couple of those as well, not real nuns but two young lads dressed in full habits and wearing sunglasses. Nuns in shades? How cool was that? This wasn't a fancy dress party; this was a wear-what-the-fuck-you-want party.

I bumped into Ivor who was dressed as a vicar and he told me he had seen Joe by the main stage. I squeezed my way through the thronging mass and sure enough there was Joe struggling with the crash barriers at the front of the stage. "Where have you been?" I asked, "I've been looking everywhere for you, The Medics are on soon and I need your help." Joe glared at me and said, "What the fuck do you think I've been doing? This lot are going mental!" At that point the crowd surged forward and the barriers toppled over. Dozens of people ended up in a heap, arms and legs everywhere. I jumped in to help Joe untangle the bodies from the metal bars and we managed to push the barriers back into place and retain some sort of order. Amazingly no one was hurt.

Suddenly the lights dimmed and the DJ stopped playing records. A cloud of dry ice flooded the stage and Doctor And The Medics emerged. The Annadin Brothers weaved their way towards the microphones as the music started slowly, a mysterious figure wearing a cape appeared through the cloud. "There are hippies on the beach, there are hippies on the beach," snarled the Doctor "The night of the long hair! The night of the long hair!" Then, all hell broke loose, the lights flooded the stage the music exploded and the Doctor jumped into the air "LOVE PEACE AND BANANAS!" he screamed. "LOVE PEACE AND BANANAS!" The crowd went crazy, dancing like lunatics as if their lives depended on it. The crash barriers groaned under the weight of the masses, but somehow or other stayed upright.

As the song ended and the audience screamed and cheered, the Doctor shouted "LADIES AND GENTLEMEN WELCOME TO THE THIRD ALICE IN WONDERLAND MYSTERY TRIP!" I gazed out over the sea of hyped up punters, every one of them with a smile on their face, and thought to myself; FUCK, I DID THIS.

The night went perfectly, all of the bands played brilliantly and despite Clive injuring himself during Bad Acid And The Spooks set, nothing else went wrong. The show went on all night and the next morning, after some people had gone for a swim in the sea fully clothed, it was time to go home.

I never did get to find out what the Green Jelly Girl was all about. No one saw her arrive and no one saw her leave. I can't imagine what her parents thought when she told them the night before the show that she was making her outfit and then proceeded to pour gallons of hot water over bucketfuls of lime flavoured Chivers, and then raided the kitchen cupboard in search of cling film. There's no way she wore that costume on the train, the jelly would have oozed out all over the seats and I would have lost my damage deposit. So how when and where did she get dressed? Who was she and where did she come from?

Maybe she had actually been transported from another planet, sent to check out what went on at these weird and wonderful Magical Mystery Trips. But after being stalked by the astronaut decided to fuck off back home.

However, I did get to hear from the Underwear Girls. They wrote to 'Alice' after the show and told their story. They were two Geordie lasses who had travelled down from Newcastle wearing just their underwear under their coats. When they arrived at the show they ditched the coats, hiding them around the back of one of the disused chalets, unfortunately by the end of the night they had forgotten which one it was. Luckily they had the foresight to tuck their return train tickets and a twenty-pound note in their knickers. Where they kept their loose change doesn't bear thinking about.

Apparently they staggered out of the place the following morning looking like extras from a low budget seventies horror film. The walking dead sought out a local newsagent to buy a couple of bin liners to use as makeshift dresses. Mr. Patel's eyeballs nearly fell out of their sockets as he looked up from marking the Sunday papers to see the zombies standing there in front of him, all thigh length boots and suspenders.

Their previously neatly coiffured hair-do's now looked like they had been attacked by a combine harvester and their mascara and eye liner was now streaked across their faces. Mr. Patel must have wondered what on earth had happened that sleepy Sunday morning in that quiet seaside town. Or more to the point what the hell had happened the previous night.

After changing trains at Liverpool Street the girls travelled all the way back to Geordieland sitting opposite two totally freaked out elderly spinsters who didn't know where to look. That was their story and, as they said in the letter, it was an adventure that they could never ever forget.

One of the Mystery Trippers, someone calling himself 'The Orange Coloured Artichoke' summed it all up perfectly in a letter he wrote to *Sounds*:

'I had a dream... First of all there were the crucified teddy bears, then there were the Bisto Gravy Kids climbing up enormous mushrooms.... Two thousand hippies? I counted two million (in between the purple alien dancing with the spaceman.) And then there was the vicar, and what about the pixie flower child talking to the giant jellybean? Doctor And The Medics...yeah!! I lost my brain somewhere in between the magnificent Ring Of Roses and the brilliant Magic Mushroom Band... I swear I saw an oddball playing a bassoon (or was it an oboe?) and were those people really trying to fish for the moon in an empty swimming pool? Any second and I'm going to wake up, but first I must ask that wizard how he managed to fly over a passing fire engine playing 'Silver Machine' on its siren... Bad Acid And The Spooks are playing their last song and it's time to go home... I had a dream, and it all came true... the Alice In Wonderland Magical Mystery Trip... and some very strange things happened... Love, Peace and Strawberries - The Orange Coloured Artichoke, Planet Earth (but only just.)

Hmmm. Something tells me that guy was another one who had far too much to dream that night.

Whilst everyone would have liked a Mystery Trip every month or maybe even every week, it was never going to happen. The sheer scale of the organisation needed to carry out one of these events was massive and if they had been more frequent and there had been more of them, the ones that did happen wouldn't have been quite so special and memorable, if you see what I mean.

However, on a considerably smaller scale we did put on some Alice In Wonderland picnics. They were low-key happenings where people would just meet at a specified place, for instance, Isabella Plantations in Richmond Park, on a Sunday afternoon. Fifty or sixty people would turn up and just hang out, people would play musical instruments and the rest of the people in the park would wonder what on earth was going on.

At the end of the day the park warden would arrive to turf us out as he had to lock the gates. Richmond Park is hundreds of acres massive but he still managed to find us, even though we were hiding in the long grass. I reckon it was Parsley (of the band The Herbs, of course) who gave us away in his bizarre costume straight out of the sixties classic series, *The Prisoner,* complete with bright yellow and purple cape and a top hat he was spotted a mile away.

The picnics became the inspiration for at least two people to write songs about them, Jim Vane of Ring Of Roses wrote 'Garden Of Earthly Delights' and Spannerman recorded 'California Sunshine,' both written about the Isabella Plantations day trip.

That summer, The Fuzztones came over to England for a short series of dates. We had met them previously at the Alice New York show and it was only fitting that they should play at Alice In Wonderland in London. They had previously released some great records so there was a lot of interest in them when they came to the club. They didn't disappoint anyone, banging out a load of old psyche classics and it was an excellent gig.

In August 1985 Doctor And The Medics were booked to play a gig supporting awareness for an anti-heroin campaign at the Crystal Palace Concert Bowl. Also on the bill were Hawkwind, Spear Of Destiny, Alice regulars Balaam And The Angel, and, wait for it, the forces sweetheart Dame Vera Lynn!

The Crystal Palace bowl is an outside venue consisting of a field with a lake, the stage is on the other side of the lake. The last time I had been there was a decade previously when I witnessed Steve Harley of Cockney Rebel fame pull off one of the most embarrassing stunts in rock'n'roll history. Harley, with delusions of God-like-genius, intended to walk on water, just like his hero, Jesus, had apparently done many years previously.

He had organised for a platform to be submerged just below the surface of the lake and at a poignant part of a song, dressed from head to foot in white clothing (what no shroud?) he would walk across the water with his arms outstretched. Amazing. What Harley hadn't reckoned on, was that some members of the restless crowd dived into the water prior to Harley's performance and discovered the partly submerged jetty and after running up and down on it, lifted it up into the air for all to see.

Instead of abandoning his walking on water trick, Harley decided to go through with it even though everyone knew it was so obviously fake. As he walked bare footed towards the crowd he was met with a barrage of boos. Watching from the grassy bank on the other side of the lake (you wouldn't catch me diving in) I shook my head in utter disbelief, cringing with embarrassment for my former idol. Harley, a born again Christian, never ever lived that one down.

Back to 1985, and what a day it was. The Council authorities who had organised the event, decided in their wisdom that not only would it be drug-free (fair enough), but it would also be alcohol-free. Bad move. With no bar at the gig, everyone turned up with bottles and cans purchased from the local off-licences. Security personnel wouldn't let them in with their booze, so they drank it, all of it, outside. The net result was that everyone was totally slaughtered before the show had even begun.

Wherever there's water and pissed people, the twain shall meet, and this event was no exception, it was a typical dull English summer day but that didn't stop dozens of people jumping into the lake, just like they did ten years previously at the Steve Harley gig. Only this time, no one in any of the acts that played that afternoon (including Dame Vera Lynn) was pretentious enough to believe they could walk on water.

Because the event was organised by the Council, and because no one had got round to sorting out a drinks license, there was apparently no drinking allowed. Yeah right. Back stage there was a limitless free bar and everyone on that side of the lake got totally legless. The Medics were their usually superb selves and Hawkwind, joined by their former bass player, the legend and serious Alice regular, Lemmy, finished off the day in fine fashion.

Oh yeah and then there was Dame Vera Lynn, I really don't know what that was all about but sing she did in front of an audience consisting of people who didn't know who she was or what relevance her appearance made to a booze free (yeah right), drug free (really?) Anti-Heroin Campaign. As the show drew to a close, she invited all the bands and their entourages onto the stage for a rendition of 'White Cliffs Of Dover' or was it ('We'll Meet Again'?) for the final number.

We all piled on stage, including my brother Joe and I. Clive, however, never one to miss an opportunity pushed his way to the front and stood in poll position next to Vera Lynn whilst totally pissed. The photo appeared in all of the major newspapers and heralded the fact that the whole event was a total farce. Nevertheless, it was great publicity for Doctor And The Medics.

Clive at the Clacton Mystery Trip

An Alice In Wonderland picnic

An Alice girl dresses to get noticed

Sue and Wendi Annadin Brothering it

CHAPTER TEN

PLANET ALICE

The first Planet Alice shop is planned, Johnny Thunders gets barred from Alice's, Chrissie Hynde hangs out there, The Troggs beg for a gig, and we put on another New York show where Clive falls out with Joey Ramone.

A year and a half or so after starting the Alice organisation it became apparent that this was not a flash in the pan success story and showed no signs of slowing down. Alice's was packing in the punters week in week out, the film festivals and the mystery trips were must see events and The Medics popularity just kept growing. I had begun to sell various merchandise mail order. Tee shirts, records, cassettes etc. and I was using Andrew King's office in Greek Street, Soho as a mailing address. However I was using my home phone number for the business and my flat was used for storage. One Tuesday morning after another wild night at Alice's the phone rang. I had crashed out with a half drunk can of beer in my hand, without thinking I grabbed the phone and, still half asleep, shouted into the receiver "Shit I've just spilt beer all over me!" The person on the other end of the phone was my Bank Manager. Oops.

This was hardly professional behaviour of a serious entrepreneur. Later that day, still smarting from my early morning embarrassment, I looked around my flat and saw the boxes of Alice and Medics merchandise, the tee-shirts, the records and the last of the remaining unsold crates from the beer mountain. It was then that I came to the conclusion that I really did need my own office.

I spent the rest of the day, whilst nursing my hangover, planning my new office idea. I thought about where it was going to be and what it was going to look like, probably Soho and definitely purple and black. A few hours later and my imaginary office was now the size of a football pitch on the top floor of a glass skyscraper with leather sofas and high speed lifts. I even planned how tall and how blonde my secretary was going to be. As the hangover wore off I started to think a bit more sensibly. Who was I trying to kid, I couldn't justify having this swish office and a blonde secretary, what would she do all day once she'd opened the post and filed her nails?

Yesterday's hangover had disappeared and as it was by now early evening, it was time to start working on tomorrows. I cracked open a can of Stella and then suddenly a new thought came into my head. Oh no, here comes another idea. What if... I thought. What if... No, it would never work. What if... I opened an Alice In Wonderland shop?

It was obvious, the shop manager could also be my P.A. and the shop assistants could help me with the mail order business. They could also help me deal with the ever-increasing amount of fan mail that both Alice's and The Medics were getting.

The name came to me straight away. Planet Alice. It couldn't have been called anything else. I didn't put the two words together myself, one of our followers sent a letter to us and on the back of the envelope she wrote, 'Special Delivery From Planet Alice'. And so there we have it, that was what the shop was going to be called.

My idea for the shop was to sell clothes, tee shirts, records, posters and various other psychedelic paraphernalia. Among the club regulars there were dozens of people aspiring to create their own psychedelic products, Wendi of The Medics and Cathy, wife of Chris, the drummer of Ring Of Roses, were both primed to design and manufacture the clothes, and so the concept was now in motion.

Finding the right premises was almost as challenging as finding venues for the mystery trips, so Clive and I plumped for the easy option, Kensington Market. We set up a meeting with their manager who told us that there was a waiting list of about two years for units but there may be a way of jumping the queue. She was basically asking for a backhander. I didn't like that idea at all so I declined and started looking for alternative options. Ironically a year or two later I was approached by the new management team for Kensington Market who literally begged me to take on a unit there. No backhander would be necessary.

The plan was that Planet Alice would have the same sort of look, feeling and branding as Alice In Wonderland. It had to be special, and as Alice's was like no other club, Planet Alice would have to be like no other shop. No pressure then. So over the next few months the search was on for premises and plans were made for the stuff we were going to sell.

Our friend and DJ, Kris Needs, came to Alice's one night together with everyone's favourite Rock Chick in 1985, Chrissie Hynde of The Pretenders. She was absolutely slaughtered, as was Kris, but then he usually was. Kris introduced us and after saying hello, she looked me up and down, Kris quickly told her that I was spoken for and she turned her attentions towards an Alice regular and friend of mine called Izzy.

Izzy was a psychedelic glam rocker and although you would never guess was the son of a Tory MP, a direct descendent of Isambard Kingdom Brunel and was actually titled The Honourable Izzy... He proved to live up to his title because, despite the endeavours of Miss Hynde who had made up her mind that he was going back to hers that night, he refused, saying that he didn't want to leave the club then as the band hadn't played yet. Now let me get this right, he had the opportunity to go home with leather clad rock goddess Chrissie Hynde or stay at Alice's and watch The Herbs and he chose to stay at Alice's and watch The Herbs?

I have a very vivid memory of a totally pissed Chrissie Hynde staggering up the stairs trying to drag poor Izzy out of the club, she was pulling one way he was pulling the other. It was hilarious. In the end she went home alone.

As well as the picnics we also organised various small-scale coach parties to see Doctor And The Medics or Ring Of Roses. One such event that sticks in my mind is the day we took several coaches to see Ring Of Roses play at The Zap club in Brighton. A well-known character at Alice's, Big Steve, was there and gave a display that no one who witnessed it could possibly forget. Big Steve was not far off seven foot tall and he was on the coach, he had brought with him a holdall, which, he explained contained his props for some entertainment later.

The coaches arrived in Brighton late afternoon and we all went off to the funfair, after messing about on the dodgems and stuff we hit the pub and then went to The Zap club. As we were queuing outside, Big Steve revealed his equipment stuffed into his holdall. It consisted of a wooden stick with a bit of old carpet nailed to one end and a can of petrol. Oh dear, I sense another Health and Safety nightmare coming up, I wasn't wrong. It started reasonably sanely with Big Steve, in the open air, dousing the carpet with petrol and swigging a mouthful of fuel and spitting out fire. It was quite impressive; we all stood back and enjoyed the show.

However, later on as Ring Of Roses were playing, Big Steve discovered that an Alice regular, who he had a crush on, was having an affair with one of the members of the band. He kind of flipped, he stripped down to his underpants and in the middle of the club produced his fire breathing equipment and started spurting ignited petrol in all directions. He was dancing round the club like a lunatic, nearly seven foot tall, wearing just his underpants and breathing fire. It was scary to say the least and a sight that I definitely won't forget. Even the security guys were scared and it took a while before they were able to back him into a corner and get him to stop.

Doctor And The Medics follow up to *Happy But Twisted* was 'Miracle Of The Age,' an excellent single produced by Andy Partridge of XTC, it didn't make an impact on the main charts but was once again a hit in the Indies. I was asked to design the sleeve and came up with this mega mechanical revolving op-art design that was considered far too complicated and expensive by the record company so was toned down considerably. Spoil sports. Alice In Wonderland had reached its second anniversary, The Medics played under the name of Doc Tour And The Mud Larks and hilariously mimed to their new single during their set. The club was packed and a few well-known faces turned up. Lemmy and Wurzel from Motorhead, Stiv Bators from The Dead Boys, The Cocteau Twins, The Damned and The Cult all got in to the Birthday party, however, one hero of mine didn't.

I first met Johnny Thunders at the punk hang out, The Roxy in 1977. Thunders used to be the lead guitarist of the superb early seventies trash glam band, The New York Dolls. In 1977 he was the singer guitarist with The Heartbreakers and I went to see them at The Roxy's American Night. After the gig I bundled up to Johnny and asked him why The New York Dolls had split up, I was totally pissed and eighteen years old. He wasn't very polite to me and basically told me to fuck off. Still, I guess I might have asked for it. Johnny Thunders turned up at Alice In Wonderland's second birthday party and this time it was he who was pissed and our over enthusiastic door girl refused to let him in. When I heard about it later I was incredulous, my hero, Johnny Thunders, turns up at my club and he's told to basically fuck off. Revenge indeed, even if it wasn't planned.

He came back another night and this time we let him in, I didn't speak to him and he never played at Alice's. He did, however, play at Gossips on a Tuesday night. He was totally wasted and it took them an hour and a half to coax him onto the stage. He struggled to sing and play his guitar for about fifteen minutes before staggering off in an angry stupor.

Needless to say, it wasn't long before Thunders joined another member of The New York Dolls, Billy Murcia, in the over crowded graveyard, another victim of heroin. Something tells me there will be other Dolls to follow.

My elder brother Joe, as I mentioned previously, was a bigger part of Alice's than he was ever credited for. He was there from day one and loved the club to bits. A fellow nightclub promoter at that time, Phillip Salon, who worked at another venue, was mugged of his takings after leaving his club and it got me worried. There I was staggering out of Alice's at four in the morning every Monday night with a pocketful of cash, I was just asking for trouble. So I enlisted Joe as my minder, he would make sure I left the club safely and got home in one piece.

One night at Alice's I met up with The Medics tour manager and he handed over the cash from their latest tour, I also had a load of cash from the Mystery Trip ticket sales as well as merchandising money and the nights' takings from the club. Joe escorted me out of the club to his car, we had just driven round the corner when we were pulled up by the police. These weren't ordinary police; they were special branch or something. They told us to get out of the car and we were searched, they kept pulling bundles of cash out of different pockets of my leather jacket, The Medics cash, the Alice cash, tickets and merchandising cash, it just went on. The police were looking for drug dealers and they thought they had got their man.

The other policemen surrounded me and asked me where I had got the cash from. I tried to explain, this I got from that and this I got from that and so on. Luckily I had the paperwork to back up my story and they turned their attention to searching Joe's car. In the back they found a broken snooker cue and various toilet roll paraphernalia, empty rolls, half used rolls and various empty Andrex multipack bags. The police asked what the snooker cue, which they said was an offensive weapon, was doing in the back of his car to which Joe explained that he used it to push the back seat down. Still not satisfied, they questioned why we had all the toilet roll paraphernalia in the back of the car, I then explained that we hung toilet paper from the ceiling of my nightclub. The police looked at each other, shrugged their shoulders and let us go. I guess if they thought that we really were drug dealers we would have thought up a more conceivable story than that.

Elvis Presley never visited England so he couldn't have gone to Alice In Wonderland even if he had wanted to, besides, he died six years before Alice's started. However, one Presley who did come down to Alice's was Reg Presley, the lead singer and songwriter of the excellent sixties band, The Troggs. Reg came up to me and introduced himself, it was hard to take him seriously at first with his comedy Devonish accent and his obsession with crop circles, but this is the bloke who, among other great records wrote and sang the classic 'Wild Thing'.

He was really keen to play at the club and gave me a promotion pack consisting of a tape, a press release and an out-of-date photo. The photo was hilarious, it consisted of the four members of the then current line-up, but one of the members had changed and instead of arranging for a new photo, they had cut out the face of the new arrival and super-imposed it onto the shoulders of his predecessor. The problem was that apart from the fact that the new head had been cut out really badly and made the bloke look like he was wearing a crash helmet, it was a lot smaller than the rest of the photo and perched on this massive pair of shoulders made Frankenstein's monster look like a pinhead.

The Troggs never played at Alice's, unfortunately, we couldn't afford them, however Reg had the last laugh when Wet Wet Wet recorded a version of his song 'Love Is All Around' which was used in the popular film *Four Weddings And A Funeral.* The record was released and went to number one where it stayed for months on end. Reg Presley made an absolute fortune; the publicity he received was great for The Troggs and the cash he used for further research into his beloved crop circles.

Clive and I flew out to New York again to set up another Alice In Wonderland night at The Danceteria. We met up with Ruth Polski again and she introduced us to the management of the club who agreed to put on another gig. We planned the second show for 29th November 1985.

We arrived back in London, delighted that we could have another go at New York, and carried on with our London activities until it was time to return for the show. We flew out together this time and managed to enter America without being given the third degree by the customs and immigration officials, unlike the first visit. We had become friends with the bands that played at the first New York show, Certain General and Band Of Outsiders, they even offered to put us up at their apartments. We didn't take them up on their offer but stayed at The Washington Square Hotel which was fine apart from the cockroaches, they were everywhere. *I'm a celebrity get me out of here!*

This time a band called Jad Wio played live, but I have no recollection of them whatsoever, so its pointless talking about them. The night went well, once again, and the New Yorkers were beginning to get the hang of what we were about. Madonna, just as she wasn't on our first night, wasn't the coat check girl that evening either.

The New York club scene in the mid eighties was very different than the London scene, there was no MTV or Internet and long haul travel was considerably less affordable than it is these days. Just as it was in the sixties with the original psychedelic movement and in the seventies with punk, there were different scenes, both coming from the same direction but arriving at slightly different destinations. New York had little idea what was going on in London and vice versa.

After the Alice show we hung around in New York for another couple of days, checking out some of their clubs. We went to The Milk Bar, a super cool trippy bar with white Perspex walls and seats with coloured lights behind. We also went to The Trash Bar where there was a resident tramp who lived in a pile of cardboard boxes in the middle of the club, people would give him food and drink and he was literally part of the furniture. Rumour has it that one night someone dropped a tab of acid in his drink and he totally freaked out and he just disappeared.

With the tramp gone, The Trash Bar soon closed down.

One night Clive and I went to this totally bizarre club on the lower east side called WGAF, an acronym for Who Gives A Fuck. It was in this warehouse in a totally dodgy industrial estate, even the seasoned New York cab driver was a bit worried taking us there and kept radioing into the office with his latest position. The club had sloping floors and ceilings that narrowed at one end, the walls were painted with black lines that counterbalanced it therefore giving the optical illusion that it was totally normal. It wasn't, it was totally freaky. Very clever, I wish I had thought of it myself. At the very end there was a tiny door manned by a dwarf who decided whether or not you were cool enough to be allowed into the VIP area. Luckily we were. It really was like something out of *Twin Peaks.*

Joey Ramone, the singer of the magnificent seventies punk band, The Ramones, was there that night. I had met him before at The Roundhouse in 1976 or '77 and I asked him for his autograph, he signed the back of my fag packet with a pencil, which I still have to this day. Joey suffered from some growing disorder and he was another guy not far off seven foot tall, seeing him stooping at the end of this bizarre room trying to persuade the dwarf, who was less than half his size, to allow him into the VIP area was a sight I shall never forget. Clive and I got talking to Joey that night at WGAF and they fell out over something. Clive has absolutely no recollection of why they fell out, in fact Clive has absolutely no recollection of ever having met him, which is odd because its not the sort of thing you'd forget. But meet they did, and fall out they did, I remember.

Joey Ramone died in April 2001 so if he knew what it was they fell out over he took the answer to his grave and seeing as how I can't recall the reason and Clive can't even remember the night I guess we will never find out.

As for Ruth Polski, the promoter who instigated the whole Alice In New York thing, she too died, ploughed down by a taxi outside a nightclub whilst queuing to see the band she managed, Certain General.

As I am writing this book, reminiscing about those halcyon days of the mid eighties it's beginning to dawn on me just how many people are now dead, and those are just the ones I've heard about. And, I'm afraid to say, there's more to come.

The Surfin' Lungs

Ring Of Roses

CHAPTER ELEVEN

SARDINES IN WONDERLAND

Alice In Wonderland grows from strength to strength, a band gets re-named 'Sweet Gone Wrong', we meet the Cigar Smoking Girl. Zodiac Mindwarp join the Alice gang and we find out what made the Angriest Plumber In The World so angry. Alice In Wonderland is voted Nightclub Of The Year.

As 1985 drew to a close, Alice's was by now so popular we would turn away more people than we could let in. The official capacity was 400 and we probably had 500 every Monday night, week in, week out. The really dedicated fans would hang around outside and as two people left, we allowed two more in. It was great news for us as we could squeeze another hundred paying customers in through the doors.

It was commented on more than one occasion, that a night at Alice's was akin to being packed into a sardine can, our friend and patron, the journalist Jane Simons, used every opportunity to drop another plug for Alice's into her articles and often mentioned it. The sheer volume of punters caused a few minor problems for us DJ's. It could take fifteen minutes to get served at the bar as the thirsty punters were five deep and two hard-working bar girls were run ragged. We had only 3 minutes before the record ended so we had to arrange for a special DJ serving station where we would get preferential treatment. What divas we were.

The other problem, made worse by the frequency of the first problem, was the toilets. 500 odd people and just two loos resulted in major congestion. One night it was noticeably worse than usual and a queue outside the girls loo was beginning to snake around the club. The cause of the queue was a teenage Alice girl who had had far too much to drink, had fallen asleep on the loo and then fallen forward knocking herself out when she hit the door. Trouble is she was then wedged between the loo and the door and was completely stuck.

The lock on the door was always broken so I managed to push it open wide enough to squeeze my hand through and tried to move her out of the way so I could get her out. As I managed to open the door a few more inches I realised, (duh, it should have been obvious) that she was not exactly decently dressed at that time. I quickly called Penny and Janine to witness as I pulled her out and they covered her modesty. Phew, last thing I wanted was to be accused of some bizarre sexual toilet incident when I was just trying to sort out a problem. The girl sobered up and was mortally embarrassed, she didn't have to be, this was Alice In Wonderland.

Vince was the owner of Gossips, he didn't come down that often but when he did you certainly knew about it. By his own admission, he couldn't manage the club as no one would remain working for him, so he left the day-to-day stuff to Mick Collins. Vince was well impressed with the success of Alice In Wonderland and referred to me as his white brother. Let's not forget, he was making more money on a Monday, historically the quietest night of the week, than he was on a Saturday night, supposedly the busiest. I had a lot of respect for Vince, as scary as he was, but was quite glad that he didn't come to Alice's that often. One day some complete unsuspecting idiot decided to burgle Vince's flat whilst he was in it. He only just lived to regret it.

Mick gave us the chance to start Alice's in 1983 and stuck by us through thick and thin. In the early days he would often contribute towards the light show or the decorations, and if we were struggling to find enough money to pay the sound guys he would offer to pay half. Mick was there at the beginning and he was there at the end and we never fell out once. As Alice's had now become so ridiculously over crowded, for a moment I almost got greedy. I was approached by a nearby club, Fouberts, who asked me to move Alice's to their venue, which could hold 1000 people.

I have to say I was tempted, so Clive and I went to check it out. It had a much bigger and better stage area, a considerably better backstage area and DJ box, smarter bar area and dance floor, but it wasn't Gossips. We dismissed the idea and decided to stay at Gossips, the place we had come to love, the place that was so familiar to us and the place that was spot on for Alice In Wonderland. This was mainly due to our loyalty to Vince and Mick but also to our following who were confused enough without having to get them to change a habit of a Monday night lifetime. Good job we did stay, Fouberts closed down a few months later.

At Alice In Wonderland we always tried to put on entertaining bands, some were great, some not so good and some were downright rubbish. When Sexagisma came to town they put on a show that I, for one, will never forget. I received a tape and a publicity photo of an over-the-top glam rock band, they looked like Sweet gone wrong, but the tape sounded good so I booked them to play. When they turned up for the sound check a seventeen stone bloke came up to me, shook my hand and said "Hi, we're Sexagisma." I thought he was their roadie but he wasn't, he was, Jez (or whoever), their singer/guitarist.

Now, either the publicity shot had been seriously air brushed or he had subsequently gone berserk in a pie shop, but he didn't look like the guy in the photo at all. An hour before they were due on stage the band got changed in the dressing room (which was basically a narrow corridor to the side of the DJ box.) That in itself was hilarious, a seventeen stone bloke squeezing into spray-on gold lamé trousers and a pair of platform boots with five-inch heels in a space not much bigger than a telephone box.

At twelve, Clive introduced the band, cackling through his echo box and as they walked towards the stage, the singer tripped and one of the heels on his platform boots snapped off. "Shit!" he exclaimed, "I can't go on like this!" Clive announced over the microphone "Sorry, ladies and gentlemen, we have a technical hitch, Ralph, can we have some gaffer tape back stage please." Ralph, the P.A. guy arrived with the gaffer tape and the boot was temporarily fixed. As the band struck the opening chords of 'Teenage Rampage' and Jez reached for his fuzzbox the gaffer tape gave way and the heel fell off. Like a true professional he carried on balancing on one foot while Clive and I, watching from the DJ box, giggled like schoolboys. It was hilarious.

Half way through the set, they played a cover version of Showaddywaddy's 'Hey Rock'n'Roll', and part of their stage show was that they would all stamp their feet in the chorus. By this stage Clive and I were virtually wetting ourselves as Jez hopped from one foot to the other. "Hey Rock'n'Roll!' (stamp stamp stamp.) Clive turned around to me and said; "It looks like he's got a club foot!" Now I don't wish to mock the disabled, but this guy wasn't disabled, he was just a seventeen stone glam rocker in tight gold lamé trousers with his belly bulging out over the top and a pair of massive platform boots with one heel missing.

Still, it was a comedy moment that, were it not recorded in this book, would have been lost forever. Thank you Sexagisma, you make me smile just thinking about it.

Doctor And The Medics had been asked to record a live show for the *Old Grey Whistle Test* at The Bristol Bier Keller. I organised a small group of coaches for the Alice crowd and we set off for the West Country. Doctor And The Medics gave yet another rousing performance and live they sounded great. However the BBC messed up that night and when the gig was shown on TV the sound was rubbish. It didn't stop The Medics though and their rise in popularity continued.

On one of the coaches on the way back to London there was a girl sitting on the back seat smoking a cigar. It's hard to imagine these days people smoking in such a confined public space but a girl and a cigar? It gets worse. Nania wasn't smoking the cigar with her mouth. People gathered in utter disbelief and amid the cries of "Surely she's not..." and "I don't believe it!" Someone piped up: "Can you blow smoke rings?"

Nania was quite discreet with her 'smoking trick' but one thing that puzzles me is how the hell did she know she could do it anyway? Was she at a dinner party when someone handed out the old Che Guevara specials and she said: "Well actually I don't smoke but I'll see what I can do." We'll never know.

The light shows, laser shows, slide shows and film shows were part of the Alice night. It was another reason why we were so very different from any other night. But as always, we wanted to improve on things and make the evening more exciting. What we need is a bubble machine and a cage for people to dance in, I thought. Oh no we didn't, this was another Alice accident just waiting to happen.

Joe helped me to make the cage, which was made out of wood but painted silver to look like metal. We set it up on the stage and Clive babbled something over the microphone about the cage and invited anyone who felt like it to go into it and dance. We started up the bubble machine and the stage looked fantastic, psychedelic oil wheel projections shining through the bubbles and toilet paper to the white backdrops beyond.

A girl in a paisley mini dress was the first into the cage and others joined in on the dance floor. Wow, this was excellent, this was what we always wanted Alice's to be like. The bubbles were flowing and the atmosphere was amazing. Clive then switched on the smoke machine and played the classic Doors record, 'L.A. Woman,' Now, this must have been a record written and recorded for the benefit of DJ's. It was seven minutes long, which was usually enough time to get a drink or have a wee and it was always guaranteed to get people onto the dance floor.

Problem was, as the bubbles hit the floor and burst, after about five minutes the dance floor was a death trap, covered in slimy fairy liquid. People started falling over, but as they disappeared under the hovering smoke cloud no one really knew what was happening and dozens more flocked to the stage, unaware of what was going on, and promptly fell flat on their backs. It was utter carnage.

One person fell against the cage and fell backwards pulling it on top of them with the girl in the paisley mini dress inside. If that had happened in America they would have sued the pants off us, but this was Alice In Wonderland and no one gave a fuck. Although there were probably a few sore bums and some nasty psychedelic purple bruises the next morning.

I put the success of Alice's down to a number of reasons, apart from the fact that we were quite simply the best nightclub in town, we were also fortunate that our main fan base were the second generation of the baby boom, which happened after the Second World War.

The plethora of kids born in the years after the War finished, the sixties kids who had 'Never Had It So Good', had children themselves, who had now reached their early twenties just as Alice's was kicking off. There were more twenty to twenty five year olds (our target audience) out on the streets than ever before, so we had a much larger customer base than we would have had if we had started the club, say, five or ten years later. So it's a historical fact, Alice In Wonderland was crap but there were so many young adults out there desperate for entertainment, Alice's was better than nothing. Only joking.

Greasy biker (without a bike) Mark Manning was the first ever person (apparently) who turned up at Alice's on the first night other than friends and family and people we knew. As the first official customer we let him in free that night and he never paid to get in from there on. He came virtually every week for the first three or four years of Alice's and in future years would still show his face from time to time.

One night he told me he had formed a band called Zodiac Mindwarp And The Love Reaction and asked if they could play at Alice In Wonderland. So that was it, mild mannered Mark Manning from Bradford became the monster Zodiac Mindwarp from Planet Freakout.

I booked The Zodiacs (as I called them) for their first ever gig, although they subsequently booked a warm up gig elsewhere. In those early days they were more of a psychedelic garage punk band than the heavy metal stadium band they aspired to be in later years. There was nothing quite like them around at that time, their pseudo Hells Angel look was quite unique and their raw powerful thrash made them a great live act. They played a number of times at the club as well as some of the special events and we also got them some support gigs with The Medics.

Zodiacs drummer, Chris, or Slam Thunderhide as he was re-named, was a good friend of mine and it was me who introduced him to Zodiac. He was the drummer of Ring Of Roses before joining The Love Reaction and his then wife, Cathy, was one of my designers at the soon to be opened, Planet Alice. Chris deliberated long and hard about joining Zodiac and asked my opinion. I told him that I thought that if Ring Of Roses were going to make it they would have done so by now. So Zodiacs it was. Who could say whether it was the right decision or not? Cathy, his wife, would have said not. It wasn't long after Chris joined the band that he began to stray, he was having a fling with this 'it' girl and Cathy got to read about it in *Tattler* of all places.

However, she got her revenge by pissing in a bucket for a week whilst Chris was recording in Oxford and when he returned to find that she had changed the locks, she opened the upstairs window and poured the bucket over his head. Hilarious. I've told the story in one paragraph, but if you want the full story, Zodiac tells it in his own book, *Fucked By Rock,* available from the top shelf of all good newsagents.

When The Zodiacs weren't playing at Alice's they would hang out there, standing by the bar chatting up the girls, Zodiac, Cobalt, Evil Bastard, Kid Chaos and Slam, and then, in later years, Flash Bastard and Trash De Garbage. The bands roadies also graced Alice's with their presence, Gimpo and then later, Smiffy came to the club virtually every week providing they weren't touring.

With Chris and Cathy splitting up I was stuck in the middle, Chris was a friend of mine as was Cathy, Cathy was also designing clothes for the soon to be open Planet Alice. I didn't want to take sides but after the bucket of piss episode even Chris would have to admit that he deserved it. And fair play to Cathy she didn't carry out any of the other surprises she had planned for him. Even so, not everyone can say that they poured a bucketful of piss over someone's head. However, I can.

One morning I woke up and knew instantly that something wasn't quite right. I looked out of the window and saw that overnight there had been an unexpected heavy fall of snow and the whole of London was completely frozen over. I went into the bathroom and discovered that there was no running water. Realising that the pipes were frozen I then found out that the loo wouldn't work and, worse than that, the sewage was backing up and coming up through the plughole into the bath.

I monitored the situation over the next few hours but the pipes showed no signs of thawing and the sewage level was rising quickly, it wouldn't be long before the bath would overflow onto the carpet. I had to do something about it so I went and got a bucket and started to bale out. Unable to use the loo and living on the second floor I realised that I had no alternative but to empty the bucket out of the window. The bathroom window was frozen solid so I opened the one in the kitchen and looked outside. There was a rough patch of ground below so I then filled up a bucket with the disgusting slurry and threw it outside.

I then heard this loud shout and I rushed back to the window and peered out. There below, blinking up at me, drenched through and with toilet paper stuck in his hair, was the angriest plumber in the world. Someone else had called out a plumber to sort out the problem and, after battling through the snow to get to us, he was rewarded by having a bucketful of raw sewage thrown over him.

Inadvertently I had scored a direct hit and falling from the top floor it must have hit him at quite a force. "You bastard!" he screamed, "What the fuck did you do that for?"

Just then the phone rang, it was *Honey* magazine who were ringing for a previously arranged telephone interview. After doing the introductions they started with the usual question: "So why do you think Alice In Wonderland is so successful?" Before I had a chance to answer I heard the heavy footsteps of the angry plumber who had got into the block and was out to get me. He shouted every swear word in the book as he thumped on my door. "It sounds like you're being burgled." Said the interviewer. "No it's nothing like that," I replied, "It's an angry plumber." "Why is he so angry?" she asked, "Do you owe him money?" "No it's not that," I replied "He's pissed off because I've just poured a bucket of sewage over him." The girl was stunned by my answer. "Oh, is this something you do often?" she stuttered. "No," I replied, "It's my first time."

It was at Alice's that Zodiac met Smiffy, who had been working for The Damned until they sacked him after he threw a hammer at the lighting bloke and nearly killed him. He was a seriously scary person who, given half the chance, could put the wind up a silver back gorilla. He scraped his hair back into a ponytail, which made him look even more frightening. You never really knew where you stood with him but you didn't want to upset him. Whilst Smiffy may have been a competent roadie he was an absolute liability and a complete and utter psycho.

After receiving numerous complaints from some of the regulars at Alice's about his intimidating behaviour I confronted Smiffy. I gave him the ultimatum, either he behaved himself or he would be banned for good. He got the message and calmed down and was no more trouble, really. Sometimes I would talk to him and he would be quite normal, almost nice, other times he would stare at people as though he was going to kill them. If Zodiac's book is to be believed he not only looked like an animal, he actually was one.

In the early days of Alice's, Zodiac was going out with another Alice regular, a girl called Sandra. She was also the sister of Gimpo (Zodiac's tour manager) and, I think, the mother of one of his children. Zodiac's that is, not Gimpo's, they were weird but not that weird.

Sandra was working as a stripogram girl and had just finished work, turning up at Alice's with her police woman's outfit in a carrier bag. I persuaded her to participate in winding up a couple of the other regulars, Kris Needs and Jeffrey Lee Pierce from the band, The Gun Club. A few moments later she strolled up to the alcove where Kris and Jeffrey were deep in conversation dressed in her uniform and after showing a fake I.D. demanding that they turn out their pockets as she was led to believe they were carrying drugs. (They weren't of course.)

They fell for my childish prank hook line and sinker, they both stood up and emptied their pockets, pulling out fag packets, keys, bits of paper, old tube tickets etc. Their faces turned a whiter shade of pale and were an absolute picture. It was hilarious. It didn't seem to occur to them that real policewomen didn't wear short skirts and high heels, but then they were totally pissed, as usual. They did see the funny side and forgave me for my trick.

Jeffrey Lee Pierce was yet another one who died too soon of too much. A talented artist with lots more to achieve died of a brain haemorrhage in 1996 aged just 37.

In the ten years that Alice's ran I can only remember a few occasions when we experienced any violence, and these were isolated incidents. Fights just didn't happen at Alice's for two main reasons. Firstly the Alice crowd weren't violent people, to be honest, none of us could be bothered, we were far too laid back. Secondly, the immense presence of our bouncers, Bigger and Leroy, two of the biggest, blackest guys you could ever meet, made any potential trouble makers think better of it.

My God they were huge. Bigger could fill a barn doorway but was almost dwarfed by Leroy who was built like a block of flats. You really wouldn't want to mess with them and most people realised that. Except for one complete arsehole, a South African tourist, pissed and leery, started shouting his mouth off and after being asked to leave by Leroy decided to shout unnecessary racist abuse. He really shouldn't have done that. Leroy, despite his phenomenal size (we once worked out his chest measurement was 5'10") was actually a bit of a teddy bear, jovial and a really nice bloke he wouldn't willingly hurt a fly, he didn't have to, he had nothing to prove, he was Michael Watson, the boxer's, minder for God's sake. But like I said, that South African really shouldn't have done that. I think he might have realised that now.

Another night, one steamy evening in August, I had been getting complaints from some of the regulars about this bloke who was going round the club helping himself to other people's drinks when they put them down on the table. He was pointed out to me and I went to speak to him in the far corner of the club by the toilets. I told him that if he carried on like that I would have him chucked out. All of a sudden he turned on me, pulling a flick knife out of his pocket and pointed it towards my throat. I didn't know what made me do it, but I grabbed his wrist, twisted it behind his back and frog marched the knife wielding maniac towards the door.

The place was packed but people just dived out of the way, it was like being Moses parting the Red Sea. Luckily Smiffy, Zodiac's roadie, saw what was happening and helped me bundle the bloke to the reception area where Bigger and Leroy took over. "He's got a knife," said Smiffy. Leroy squeezed the bloke's wrist and the offensive weapon fell to the floor. "Its only a comb, Its only a comb!" bleated the comb wielding maniac, and sure enough it wasn't a knife capable of slitting someone's throat, but a plastic flick-comb hardly capable of back combing an eighties hair-do. Oops. Leroy looked at me as if to say, what do I do now? " Chuck him out anyway," I said, "He's just pissed me off"

On another night, a few years later, another bloke seriously pissed me off. A couple of girls had complained to me about some pumped up body builder type bloke who was strutting round the club sticking his hand up girls skirts as they stood at the bar. Now just because maybe, fifty percent of the girls at Alice's wore short skirts it didn't give anyone the right to take advantage. This arsehole obviously thought differently. He wasn't a regular and looked totally out of place, most Alice blokes were far too laid back to work out at a gym. When I saw him sidle up to an unsuspecting Alice girl, slide his hand up her skirt and pinch her bum I had seen enough. It was early in the evening and there were only a few dozen people there, I was standing at the bar having a drink with Clive and when he strutted past I stuck my leg out and tripped him over.

He crashed onto the floor but quickly got up and swung round to Clive, his eyes blazing and said, "Did you just trip me up?" I butted in, "No he didn't," I said. "I did." He was a bit taken aback and looked me up and down, sizing me up "Do you wanna make something of it?" he said, puffing out his chest like a peacock. I looked him in the eyes and said "Yeah okay. Outside." We both walked towards the door and when we got to the front desk I said to Bigger and Leroy, "Get him out, he's pissing off my punters." "But, but, but..." the idiot stuttered, looking back at me as he was shoved out into the cold London night. Ha!

Jayne County has been around for donkey's years and I used to see her perform when she was a he called Wayne County, playing at the punk venue The Roxy in 1977 with his band The Electric Chairs. She was well into sixties psychedelia and I booked her, as she was now after his treatment, to play at Alice's.

They played in December 1985 under the name 'Jayne County And The Manson Girls (The Shangri-La's On Acid') and I thought she was great, just as Wayne had been when I saw him at The Roxy. She-he, him-her, God this gets confusing. I have to say that not everyone agreed with me, an ageing transsexual dressed in a baby doll nightdress, ripped fishnets with a toilet seat round her neck singing songs like 'Cream In My Jeans', 'Toilet Love', 'If You Don't Want To Fuck Me, Baby Fuck Off' and 'Man Enough To Be A Woman' was not everyone's cup of tea. Tough, I booked her again, a couple of times I think.

I liked Jayne County, we got on well, she had lived a pretty tough life coming to terms with her confusion over her gender and having to explain to her elderly Redneck parents why their little boy was now their grown up woman. She told me she was planning to write a book and I've just discovered that she has, I managed to find a copy and it's worth reading, although I did feel she held back a lot of great stories.

In December 1985 my search for shop premises reached a fruitful end. I had found the perfect place, 284 Portobello Road, London W10. It was on the sunny side of the street just past the Westway, and consisted of a fair sized ground floor sales area with an office at the back and a large basement. It even had a garden. I signed a new twenty-year lease and picked up the keys on the day my grandmother died. That night I went out and got completely off my face.

With the premises secured I now had to find my Personal Assistant. I didn't get the tall leggy blonde I had originally imagined; I did however get Kim, a small, short-legged brunette. Kim Evans was an Alice In Wonderland regular and had been on all of the trips and stuff so far. She was the girlfriend of James Vane, the singer of Ring Of Roses and, being slightly older than most of the Alice crowd was regarded as a bit of an Earth Mother type.

Rather than give her a formal interview I decided to suss her out first to see if she was up to it. Under the pretence of talking to Jim about band stuff, I dropped round to their flat in Notting Hill, a short walk from the new shop. I asked Kim if she had any retail experience and she told me she was currently working at Hyper Hyper on Kensington High Street and had previously worked at Debenhams department store. So far so good.

She then proceeded to tell me a story of how, as a young girl she was heading back to her hometown of Chelmsford by train after the Debenhams Christmas party. She had had far too much to drink and, rushing to catch the train, had forgotten to go to the loo before starting out on the long journey from London. She was alone at one end of the carriage with half a dozen people sitting at the other end. She could hold it in no longer and promptly wet herself. She wasn't that bothered at first as no one could see her. However, what she didn't realise was that there was an electric heater under her seat and as the liquid flowed a huge cloud of steam accompanied by a loud hissing sound filled her end of the carriage. The fellow travellers turned around in unison to see her little face grinning at them over the seat with the steam surrounding her like a halo.

Interview over, Kim had got the job. The way I saw it was that not only had she had a career in retail, anyone who would tell a story like that at an 'interview' deserved to be given the chance. I didn't regret my decision, Kim ended up working for me for the next four years or so and as the Alice 'empire' grew and more challenges were thrown at us she was an invaluable asset.

With Kim now on board we started to get cracking on getting the shop sorted, my plan was to be open for Christmas. Not a chance. Apart from all the mundane stuff to organise like security grilles, alarm systems, telephones, etc. there was a sign to be made and the shop had to be painted in a style befitting to its' Alice heritage. The original colour scheme was purple, black and silver. The whole shop including the loo was painted in a combination of these colours, as was the signage, the carrier bags even the vacuum cleaner.

If someone had to hoover the shop every day they may as well have a cool vacuum cleaner to do it with. Introducing J. Edgar Hoover Cleaner, a purple icon with a patchwork bag cover and eyes with false eyelashes. He became a legend in his own lunchtime and even featured in magazine articles and photo shoots. My dad made the counter, Joe helped with various DIY jobs that needed doing and dozens of Alice regulars would drop by as we were getting everything ready and offered to help. It was a great team effort all round but there was no way we would be ready to open until after the New Year.

Meanwhile we were hastily getting the stock together, various designers including Kathy Renshaw, Wendi Annadin and Emma Flower Child made the clothes, Jon Brodel made holograms, Jeremiah made exclusive Planet Alice incense and Jenny the Belt Lady made belts (of course). We had exclusively designed posters printed and I bought a whole load of selected records from a wholesale warehouse in the East End. We were almost there. Miss Selfridges in Oxford Street were having a re-fit and I bought all of their shop fittings, hangers, mirrors, rails etc. for next to nothing.

I found this amazing place in Kings Cross that sold second hand shop mannequins. It was totally weird, a whole warehouse full of mannequins piled up to the ceiling, there were thousands to choose from, some with all their limbs intact, some with arms and legs missing, this was the place where shop dummies went to die. I picked half a dozen 'girls' that looked sort of sixties-ish and painted them silver with black swirls to match the rest of the décor. I was adamant that Planet Alice was going to be like no other shop in London and that was exactly what it was.

1985 ended with an Alice In Wonderland special party at Heaven in Charing Cross Road. Doctor And The Medics, Ring Of Roses, Apple Mosaic and Zodiac Mindwarp And The Love Reaction were on the bill. Zodiacs were on first and it was, up to that point, their biggest gig to date. They were excellent as were all of the bands. The Medics finished off their show in usual Medics fashion and were joined on stage by The Cult's Ian Astbury who sang a superb version of Van Morrison's 'Gloria'. I taped that gig from the PA decks; I must dig it out one day and listen to it again.

City Limits magazine phoned me to say that Alice In Wonderland had been voted 'Nightclub Of The Year' by their readers. Wow, an award. Clive and I went to the 'ceremony' at our old haunt, The Scala Cinema, to receive it, Ken Livingstone got man of the year and a bemused Indian bloke got the restaurant of the year, so we were obviously among good company. Still, an award is an award, whichever way you look at it and I was flattered, it was a great way to end the year.

Sardines in Wonderland

Zodiac Mindwarp And The Love Reaction on stage at Alice's

CHAPTER TWELVE

SPIRIT IN THE SKY

Alice's very own shop, Planet Alice opens for business, the album, A Pretty Smart Way To Catch A Lobster is released, the Nappy Twins and Captain Rainbow arrive on the scene and The Mission play their first ever gig at Alice In Wonderland. Against all the odds Doctor And The Medics have a number one hit single.

On Monday 13th January 1986 Planet Alice, 284 Portobello Road opened its doors to the public for the first time. With loud sixties music pumping out of the sound system and psychedelic light shows projected on the walls, walking into Planet Alice was more like entering a nightclub than a shop. The Flower Children, Emma and Louise, got dressed up from head to foot in Planet Alice gear and danced in the shop window. Dozens of other club regulars turned up on the opening day to be the first to pick up a pair of Planet Alice hipsters, a hologram, some Planet Alice incense or whatever.

Ian Astbury was there signing copies of the *Love* album, Zodiac was there signing copies of his new single, 'Wild Child' and The Damned, Lemmy and The Medics also showed their faces. So the Alice organisation now had their very own head quarters. No more phone calls from bank managers whilst I was still in bed, no more boxes of merchandise cluttering up my flat and now I had my own group of 'Alice's little helpers' on the payroll. The latter turned out to be particularly useful in the light of what was around the corner for Doctor And The Medics.

Napoleon once said that Britain was a nation of shopkeepers, I don't think that Planet Alice with its loud music, lightshows and go-go dancers was quite what he had in mind.

Staffing the shop was an easy task, there was no shortage of club regulars who were queuing up to be given a job, and as one girl left another would quickly step in. One such girl that came and went was Ian Astbury's girlfriend at the time, Jacqui. Jacqui didn't work there long as she and Ian split up and she then went out with Kid Chaos. Kid Chaos was originally Zodiac Mindwarp's bass player who had been poached by The Cult after meeting through Alice's. Phew. This goes to show just how incestuous the whole scene was becoming.

Working at Planet Alice was more of a vocation than a job, we didn't open until ten o'clock so there was plenty of time for a lie in after the previous night, although working on a Tuesday, the morning after Alice In Wonderland, was the least favourite slot on the rota. Luckily for them, I was one boss who could hardly complain if my staff turned up for work with a hangover. Most of the time the girls just hung around the shop modelling our latest designs, chatting to friends who were always dropping in and drinking copious cups of coffee.

When they weren't doing that they were re-filling the rails, marking up stock, packing mail order parcels, dealing with the fan mail and serving customers. Dozens of other girls came and went but Kim and her sidekick, Tony (who wasn't a girl), stayed until the very end.

In early 1986 The Damned had their biggest ever hit single with a cover version of the classic sixties song, 'Eloise.' Inspired in part by their association with Alice In Wonderland, they dressed in sixties style clothes for the video and TV appearances, even Rat Scabies reluctantly took part and wore what he described as "poncy clothes." When asked in interviews where they got their outfits, The

Damned would say "Planet Alice." Truth of the matter was they weren't necessarily clothes from Planet Alice but they used the opportunity to give us a plug. That was how it worked.

We had the club, the film, the single, the film festivals, the mystery trips and now the shop. What about an Alice In Wonderland album? We were approached by an Alice regular, Frenchy Gloder of Flicknife Records to release an album featuring some of the bands playing at Alice's at that time. Six bands were chosen and they played at Alice's over a six-week period in the spring of '86, each band's entire set was recorded and a track or two from each act was to be included on the album.

Frenchy was called Frenchy, not necessarily because he was French, but because he had a seriously strong incomprehensible French accent, despite living in England for most of his life. I remember asking him if his accent was for real and he just grinned at me knowingly. We got on well, me and Frenchy, and spent many an evening gibbering away at Alice's, him not being able to hear me over the noise, and me not being able to understand him. "Great band tonight!" "Thanks mate I'll have a pint." "I really like their drummer!" "Go on then I'll have a tequila slammer as well!"

Doctor And The Medics were the obvious choice to kick off the recordings, although because they were signed to another label, they had to be listed under their pseudonym of Gwyllym And The Raspberry Flavoured Cat. The Damned, under the guise of Naz Nomad And The Nightmares, were keen to be involved but couldn't play under either of those names for the same reason as The Medics. They asked me to come up with a name and I called them The Spooks. (I had previously called a Medics spin off band 'Bad Acid And The Spooks.')

Zodiac Mindwarp And The Love Reaction who were playing at Alice's regularly since the Heaven show also agreed to take part, they recorded an excellent set which sadly wasn't included on the album in the end as their management, or maybe Zodiac himself, decided that it may not be in their interest long term if they became too associated with Alice In Wonderland. They loved Alice's, make no mistake, but after us giving them a leg-up they didn't want to be always known as an 'Alice Band.'

Voodoo Child, Webcore and Underground Zero made up the rest and the album was produced and set for release. Unlike the Alice In Wonderland 'live' single this album was totally live and none of the bands went anywhere near a studio for the recordings. In between the tracks we added live psychobabble courtesy of Clive to try and capture an authentic night at Alice In Wonderland.

I designed the record sleeve which consisted of a purple psychedelic lobster hidden among random famous faces and hidden messages. Kris Needs was enlisted to write the sleeve notes, which he did admirably. Problem was, no-one proof read the notes and the sleeve went straight to print, non-existent words, spelling mistakes and everything. Frenchy apparently couldn't read Kris Needs hand written scrawl so just put down what he thought it said.

Live At Alice In Wonderland (A Pretty Smart Way To Catch A Lobster) was released and sold moderately well, we launched the record with a 'Lobster Party' at Alice's and even tried to hire a tank of live crustaceans for the event but no-one would let us. Apparently, lobsters freak out when subjected to loud music. I couldn't see the problem with that personally but with respect to lobster welfare we gave up on that idea.

The *Lobster* album has just been released on C.D. for the very first time on Clive's Madman Records, almost a quarter of a century since it was recorded. It's been tarted up a bit and sounds as good now, if not better than it did all those years ago.

Whilst promoting the *Lobster* album I did an interview for a Radio 4 programme, they talked about the club, the events, The Medics and the record and asked me what was next for Alice In Wonderland. Without thinking I said that we were planning to go into politics, (which we weren't.) "That's an interesting idea," said the interviewer "What are you going to call your party?" Stumped for a reply I lied: "Err, the Alice In Wonderland Lets All Have A Party party."

They asked me what our policies were and I winged it babbling on about the first things that came into my head, painting coloured lines on London roads, red for north, green for south etc. so that people could stagger out of nightclubs, gigs and parties and easily find their way home by following their colour. Hmmm.

After the interview I received numerous phone calls from all sorts of people, mostly from complete nutters who just wanted to talk but also from others who had various ideas that I may wish to consider getting involved with. Someone wanted to discuss the possibility of me doing something at the Rio carnival in Brazil, someone else wanted to release another Alice In Wonderland album, another person wanted to take the Alice thing to Iceland (brrrr) and then there was Captain Rainbow.

Captain Rainbow, George Weiss, was the founder of an alternative political party called The Rainbow Alliance and having heard my interview and believing my story about our so-called political aspirations, asked whether Clive and I would be interested in standing as candidates for his party. I asked him who else was involved and he told me that the legendary comedian Peter Cook and Madame Whiplash, Cynthia Payne had agreed to stand. On that basis we agreed to meet up with him and discuss it further.

We arrived at his flat in Hampstead and Captain Rainbow opened the door, looking exactly like you would expect someone calling himself Captain Rainbow to look like. I don't remember an awful lot about what happened next other than the fact that actually, nothing happened. I seem to recall that he was basically trying to get the maximum number of weirdos to stand as candidates as he possibly could. Me and Clive weirdos? No way!

For a few years in the eighties I used to dye my hair blonde, don't ask me why, I just did. My grandfather also struggled to understand why, when I explained it was an image thing, he just shook his head, "You mean like Jimmy Saville?" he said. "Well I suppose so, sort of." I replied. I never intended to emulate Jimmy Saville but if it placated my granddad I could live with it.

I used to go to a trendy hairdressers in Kensington called Antenna, and the girl that did my hair was called Becky. She was at the front of the queue when they handed out attitude and hardly spoke to me at first. "So what is this weird club you run?" she asked me one day. "It's called Alice In Wonderland," I replied "You should come down." "Nah," she replied, "I can't be bothered." "Oh well" I said, "Never mind." "What night is it on?" she asked, "Mondays" I replied "I'm always busy on Mondays," she said. "That's a shame," I said "It's great fun." "Is it on next Monday?" she asked "Of course" I said, "I'll put you plus one on the guest list if you want." "Maybe I'll come, maybe I won't," she pouted.

Becky turned up the following week with her friend, Alison and they became Alice regulars from there on. The new Flower Children on the block were quickly nicknamed the Nappy Twins by Cathy Renshaw, referring to their young age as opposed to their relationship or choice of clothing. Becky still had the attitude of a camel but mellowed after a while and then she even began to smile. Alison ended up working at Planet Alice and Becky eventually worked at Gossips as the cloakroom girl, she also modelled clothes for Planet Alice. When she could be bothered.

I have just found out that Becky, hairdresser with attitude, is these days the aunt of the gorgeously talented Leona Lewis, The *X-Factor* winner and superstar diva. Wow!

Wayne Hussey, the guitarist of the popular goth band, The Sisters Of Mercy, came to Alice's regularly, so when The Sisters split and he formed his own band, initially called The Sisterhood it was only natural that they should play their first gig at the club. Andrew Eldridge, the original singer in The Sisters Of Mercy objected to Wayne using a similar name to his band and threatened to "blow up" Alice In Wonderland if they played under the name of The Sisterhood. They did and Andrew didn't carry out his hasty threat.

However he won in the end and they changed their name to The Mission. 'The Sisterhood' played a great gig which was favourably reviewed in the music press, Wayne continued to show his face at Alice's and a few months later The Mission played on the same bill as The Medics and The Damned at the San Siro stadium in Milan. The Medics were by far the best band that day and I have a vivid memory of Clive jumping off the stage during a guitar solo, doing a complete lap of honour around The San Siro before returning to the stage just as the solo was finishing not even out of breath.

Some of the members of The Mission took exception at something Clive said that day and later that night, after drinking copious amounts of alcohol, decided to have it out with him. The problem was that Clive had, on this occasion gone to his hotel bed early that night leaving The Mission to bang on every other hotel door demanding to have a fight. They never found Clive who was snoozing away quietly in an adjacent building.

In the early days of Alice In Wonderland we were pleased to get any publicity from whatever magazine or newspaper that was interested in writing about us. After all, the more people that heard about it the better, when the first TV crew, a production company from Denmark, turned up to document the club we were seriously impressed. However, a few years down the road and a few dozen film crews later it was getting a bit tedious, worse than that, it was pissing off the punters. The Alice people came down to the club to have a good time, not to be gawped at and filmed as if they were freaks in a nineteenth century circus.

Crunch time came when no less than three Japanese TV crews turned up on the same night. The crews themselves weren't the problem, they were only little and hardly took up any space, but the tripods, cameras, lighting equipment and the bright glare of the spotlights were killing the atmosphere and with the punters crammed in shoulder to shoulder it was all a bit much.

When one of the cameramen put the camera on the floor and pointed it upwards as the groovy young chicks danced on the stage that was the final straw. A few of them complained to me that this guy was virtually shoving his camera up their skirts so I politely told all of the TV crews to leave. I gave them my card and suggested they came to Planet Alice and filmed there instead.

Doctor And The Medics recorded their first album, *Laughing At The Pieces* in early '86. Miles Copeland, the boss of IRS was less than impressed saying that there was no obvious hit single on the record. Hit single? This was Doctor And The Medics and that was never going to happen. The Medics weren't a pop band but a cult indie band with a loyal following who had released a couple of credible records to date but chart fodder was not in their remit.

I remember meeting Clive in Clerkenwell, we were doing a photo shoot for *The Observer* magazine about the top ten most influential DJ's in London. Apart from Clive and I, included in that list was an up and coming DJ called Tim Westwood, soon to be a star of Radio One. After the shoot Clive told me that unless The Medics could come up with a hit they would be dropped from the record label. Clive told me he was going to do a cover version but couldn't decide between Thunderclap Newman's 'Something In The Air' or Norman Greenbaum's 'Spirit In The Sky.' He decided on 'Spirit In The Sky.'

Miles Copeland wasn't the only one pissed off with The Medics, Annadin Brother Sue, who had been in the band for years decided enough was enough and it was time for her to hang up her wig and concentrate on her career working for EMI records. The story according to the press was that Sue had run off to join the circus, sorry, I lied.

Wendi started out on her search to find a replacement for Sue and decided on Colette Appleby. Colette worked for the promoter, John Curd, and was of course, a fully paid up member of the Alice In Wonderland fan club. Perfect.

Colette was fast tracked into The Medics, Wendi taught her the songs and the synchronised dance routines and within a week she joined the other members of the band in the studio to hastily record the new single.

The single sounded great, produced by Craig Leon who had produced The Ramones excellent first album, it was certainly more commercial than anything The Medics had done previously and the record company were right behind it. Next came the video to accompany the record, costing the princely sum of just £5000, which, considering that most bands would spend several hundred thousands and the record still wouldn't necessarily chart was pretty good going.

The video consisted of some deliberately tongue in cheek special effects (early Batman style) like appearing to walk up walls and stuff. The stage set was painted in black and white psychedelic swirls, which sprung to life courtesy of a painted disc attached to a Black and Decker electric drill.

The pluggers promoting the record toured round the country in an ambulance with two bimbos in nurses' outfits handing out bottles of vodka (with The Medics logo printed on it) to the Radio One DJ's as they left their houses for the BBC. The record and indeed the video started to get a lot of exposure and all of a sudden a hit single seemed possible after all.

Planet Alice staged a major promotional campaign for the record and we had two mannequins in the shop wearing the original Annadin Brothers white dresses from the *Spirit* video with authentic make-up painted on their faces by Wendi herself.

And so it was in May 1986 the unthinkable was happening, Doctor And The Medics were about to have a hit single. 'Spirit In The Sky' entered the charts at number seventeen and after more radio and TV plays, the following week rose to number five. We could not believe it. All of the members of the band and all of us involved with the band thought the whole thing was hilarious. The next week the record climbed to number three and The

Medics were booked to do *Top Of The Pops*.

Filming *TOTP* was a real hoot and despite the producers complaining about Wendi and Colette wearing short skirts and no knickers everything went fine. (They were wearing tights by the way.) The week after the *TOTP* performance Doctor And The Medics reached the magic number one slot. Doctor And The Medics were number one in the U.K. charts! Unbelievable! They knocked the dreadful *Spitting Image* record; 'The Chicken Song' from the top spot where it had been for a painful three weeks.

Another *TOTP* performance and the dressing room was awash with champagne. A crate from the record company, a crate from the agents, a crate from the distributors, even the manufacturers of the tape that the record was recorded on sent a crate. There was champagne everywhere. Wendi and Colette decided to fill a bath with the stuff and dived in, after all it's not every week you are at number one in the UK singles chart. No complaints from the TV bosses about no knickers this time, we had some g-strings made with The Medics logo printed on them. Ha!

A third consecutive *TOTP* appearance followed and then the video was shown on the fourth week. Eventually after three weeks at number one they were displaced by George Michael's Wham! With 'Edge Of Heaven.' They had kept the very popular chart act from the coveted top spot for a week or two which was ironic as Wham! were trying to sue The Medics old record label, called Waam to get an injunction to stop them releasing any more records under 'their' name.

It was great fun for everyone whilst it lasted, after all, at the very least it would be something else to tell your grandchildren about one day. With Wham! now top of the hit parade, 'Spirit In The Sky' gradually slipped down and out of the charts. Wham! were eventually replaced at number one by Madonna's 'Papa Don't Preach' and then consequently Chris de Burgh's 'Lady In Red' not exactly my favourite records but classics nonetheless.

Amazingly The Medics getting to number one didn't have too much effect on Alice In Wonderland, we couldn't get any more in the club anyway, and as most of the teenyboppers who bought the single were safely tucked up in their beds at ten o'clock they didn't attempt to come down.

Clive continued to DJ at Alice's and fair play to all of The Medics, none of them let their new found number one status change them, unlike dozens of other bands I came across who suddenly found themselves propelled into stardom and then set out to explore their own backsides.

It was great news for Planet Alice which was still pretty much in its infancy, being the ideal location for TV interviews and photo shoots we were featured in magazines and journals that previously wouldn't have gone anywhere near us.

'Spirit In The Sky' was not just a number one hit in the U.K. but in eighteen other countries as well, selling almost two and a half million copies worldwide. Doctor And The Medics were the band of the moment, however, some people slagged them off accusing them of being some joke novelty band put together just for the single. The pervy pop mogul Jonathan King took a particular dislike to the band and dissed them at every opportunity until it was pointed out to him that they had been gigging for about five years.

'Spirit In The Sky' had been originally recorded in 1970 by an unknown hippy, Norman Greenbaum, it was a surprise hit then and Norman was given a huge advance of cash to record an album of similarly styled songs.

However, Norman used the cash to buy a goat farm and with the few hundred bucks left over recorded a crap low budget album, which he filled with songs about milking goats and life on the farm. He disappeared into obscurity and sold the publishing rights to his song just months before The Medics recorded it. Oops.

The search was on in the media to find Norman Greenbaum and he was eventually tracked down working in a café as a waiter somewhere in the states. The irony of this story is that the owners of the café, fed up with their 'star' waiter constantly being hounded by the world's press sacked Norman Greenbaum for being a disturbing influence on their business.

Back to the future with Doctor And The Medics and after recovering from their post 'Spirit In The Sky' hangover it was back to business. Touring, TV stuff and working on a suitable follow up single.

Doctor and the Medics filming 'Spirit In the Sky' video

A busy day at Planet Alice, 284 Portobello Road, London W.10
(Colette in the foreground learns to count)

Psycho punks invade the stage at Alice's

CHAPTER THIRTEEN

THE ROCK'N'ROLL FRIDGE

Another film festival, a rock'n'roll refrigerator and the fourth Alice In Wonderland Magical Mystery Trip.

Alice In Wonderland was still packing in the punters and through popular demand set up another film festival at The Scala cinema. This time *The Magic Christian, I Keep Thinking It's Tuesday, For A Few Dollars More, Dougal And The Blue Cat, Danger Diabolic* and *Gimme Shelter* were the films. The Medics had by now outgrown the film festivals and we didn't need a big band in order to sell all the tickets, so Another Green World played live and, sure enough, the show sold out and all went well.

When the sample album sleeve for *Laughing At The Pieces* came back from the printers for approval, Clive and I looked at it and both said in unison "But it's brown!" The sleeve consisted of photos taken at the *Spirit* video shoot and the background should have been black and white psychedelic swirls, instead they were brown and white. Not very psychedelic is brown. I couldn't understand it, I took photos at that shoot and my prints show black and white backdrops so why was the professional photographer's brown?

Apparently nothing could be done about it so brown it was. Clive then had this great idea that we would send out a press release saying that if anyone didn't like the sleeve they could send it back and we would replace it with a sleeve hand drawn by The Medics themselves. Nice one Clive. We expected maybe a dozen or so would be returned, instead there were hundreds. They were arriving at the Greek Street office by the sack load.

It was an administration nightmare and had it not been for the Planet Alice girls we'd probably still be dealing with it now.

Among the sack loads of record sleeves was a letter from a fan, which took a while to filter through the system before eventually arriving at my desk. The letter was from a young goth girl from up North somewhere who said that she was being bullied at school for being 'different' and that the other girls at school thought she was a freak because she liked Doctor And The Medics. She went on to say that she had begun to self-harm and that the only thing that made her life worth living was The Medics. If she didn't get a reply to her letter from Clive soon, she would kill herself.

I handed the letter to Clive when I saw him later that week and suggested he wrote back to her as soon as he could. Clive looked at the letter and noticed that the postmark was dated two months previously. Oh dear. We were in the tour bus travelling to a gig somewhere and spent the rest of the journey imagining what had happened to the poor young goth girl.

Was she hanging from the rafters in a barn somewhere with a rope around her neck clutching her copy of 'Spirit In The Sky' as she swung gently back and forth in the breeze? Was she lying in a bath with her wrists slit whilst 'Happy But Twisted' was playing loudly in the background? Did she fill her pockets full of rocks and walk into the sea gurgling 'Love Peace And Bananas' as she drowned? Clive wrote to her that day and the letter was posted.

Meanwhile we hoped for the best. We got a reply from her a couple of weeks later, she hadn't killed herself, and in fact her life had taken a turn for the better. She had a new Boyfriend who was an Iron Maiden fan, and she was now no longer a goth and, whilst she still quite liked The Medics, they were not her favourite band anymore. All that worrying for nothing. Whenever I hear Eminem's 'Stan' being played, which tells a very similar story, I think of that girl.

Right from the beginning we replied to all our fans correspondence personally, whether it was Doctor And The Medics, Alice In Wonderland or Planet Alice mail, everyone had a hand written letter from 'Alice'. Initially I responded to the letters myself, but as the amount of mail increased to such unbelievable proportions we had to invent more 'Alice's'. I trained the girls at the shop to write 'Alice' style, which was childlike lower case script with different sized letters and back to front t's and s's.

Dogs d'Amour never played at Alice's but were often seen hanging out there, the lead singer, Tyla, once played in the same band as me, The Lollipop Sisters. He was the guitarist until his girlfriend made a pass at me. The singer in the band told Tim (as he was then) on his 21st birthday whilst we were all out celebrating. Tim went ape and we fought, it was handbags really and Tim walked away, kicked a rubbish bin over, left the band, kicked his girlfriend out and formed Dogs d'Amour. In that order. They went on to be quite a credible band, got a record deal, sold some records and eventually moved out to L.A.

Tim sort of forgave me for the girlfriend incident, even though I was the innocent victim, and came down virtually every week to the club for a while, even posing for a photo with his new girlfriend (who didn't make a pass at me) for the inside cover of the *Lobster* album.

Before Tim left The Lollipop Sisters he gave me his fridge. He said that it had a bit of a history. His girlfriend (the one that made a pass at me, although he didn't know it then) used to be married to Mott The Hoople's former guitarist,

Mick Ralphs. He happened to be walking down the Portobello Road when he saw Aerial Bender, his successor on guitar with Mott, selling his possessions on a market stall. Mick Ralphs bought the fridge from Aerial Bender, gave it to his wife who gave it to Tim who then gave it to me.

The fridge was, over the years, passed around various members of my family, if anyone had just moved into a new flat and needed a fridge; I had exactly what they were looking for. Eventually the fridge ended up, back to where it had been sold from all those years previously, the Portobello Road, only this time at Planet Alice.

Virtually every week at Alice's a live band played, sometimes two, they would come on at midnight and play for about three quarters of an hour to an hour. The stage was in the corner of the club with pillars blocking the view from most of the other areas of the club, so unless you were directly in front of the stage or, like me, in the DJ box actually on the stage, you hardly saw the band. Maybe the odd glimpse of a guitarist between the pillars if you were lucky. However that was the way it was and no one ever complained.

Alice's became a much sought after place to play and became a launch pad for new talent and a place where various larger, well-known bands could get back to their roots and play a club gig for a change. For the new bands starting out they had the chance to play in front of a ready-made crowd of some 400 plus people, great exposure.

I worked it out once that one in every ten bands that played at Alice's then went on to have a top twenty hit record. Not bad odds. If an unknown band with little or no following managed to get a gig in a London club during the mid-eighties they would be lucky if they got paid a penny, however at Alice's we paid quite well regardless of how many people the band brought with them. One or two bands complained about their fee, thinking that because the place was packed they should have got more, but it didn't work like that, people came to Alice's for the club, not necessarily to see the band. Anyone that complained never got booked again.

Some bands even offered to pay ME to allow them to play, but it never came to that, over the ten years that Alice's ran for hundreds of bands played, some excellent, some average and some were downright crap. Some of the better bands ended up playing more than once, some were particular favourites of mine, and some were favourites of the crowd. A lot of the bands that played also became club regulars and that often helped their cause.

However, having said all of that, the bands were an essential part of the mix that made Alice's the phenomenal success that it was and without them Alice's would not have survived.

As well as some of the bands already mentioned a few other groups also went on to have hit singles after playing at Alice In Wonderland. A band called Timbuk 3 had a surprise hit with 'My Future's So Bright I Have To Wear Shades,' and The Shamen had a hit with 'Ebenezer Good.' I have to say I can't remember either gig so they can't have been that good and particularly in the case of The Shamen, I don't know why I booked them in the first place.

I came across some of the members of Sigue Sigue Sputnik at various times during the course of my life. I first saw bass player Tony James when he was with Generation X at The Roxy Club and in the early eighties he responded to an advert I had placed in *NME* when we were looking for members for our new band, The Lollipop Sisters. Tony James came along for an audition but didn't bring his bass with him. We didn't realise it at the time but it wasn't so much that we were auditioning him but more to the point, he was auditioning us. He was just putting together his Sigue Sigue outfit and thought myself and our singer may fit the bill. We didn't.

A few years after that audition I bumped into Sigue Sigue Sputnik again, this time at *Top Of The Pops*, one of their singles had just been hyped into the top twenty as The Medics were riding high with 'Spirit'. We met in the corridor by the dressing rooms, they glared at us and we glared back.

A few weeks later and some of their members started hanging out at Alice's, one of their drummers beat up his girlfriend after a night at my club and the story was widely reported in *The Sun* and other tabloids. *The Sun* mentioned that 'they had started arguing at top London nightclub, 'Alice In Wonderland.' We had had some serious publicity over the years but being written about as the place where an argument started between a C-list drummer in a soon-to-be-has-beens band and his girlfriend seemed fairy puerile to me.

It was the promoter, John Curd, who told me about an Irish band, The Golden Horde, that he was somehow involved with. They had released an excellent record called 'Chocolate Biscuit Conspiracy' and he asked if I could put them on at Alice's. I obliged and they were excellent.

What happened after that I really don't know. Dozens and dozens of superb bands that recorded some excellent material graced the stage at Alice's only to split up for some reason or another and disappear into obscurity before they had hardly got going. Which is a real shame; imagine if the same fate had occurred to, say, Oasis, splitting up before they had really begun?

The Mystery Trips had by now become part of the Alice crowds' calendar. It wasn't a case of whether or not there was going to be a trip this year but rather when was it going to be and who was going to play.

Our P.A. guys, Robin and Ralph, told me about Lowestoft Pier which was even further from London than the Clacton venue was. Once again I went out there with Joe and it took us about an hour and a half to get there. Not too bad, I thought. I tried to charter trains as it worked so well the last time but for some reason British Rail were having none of it. So coaches it was then.

I contacted a coach company who assured me they could provide forty coaches to transport two thousand people from London to Lowestoft and take them all back the following morning. So once again with the venue and transport sorted we were off. Bands booked to support Doctor And The Medics were: Zodiac Mindwarp And The Love Reaction, The Golden Horde, Voodoo Child, Mournblade and Webcore. Another Green World and for the first time, the Brindisi String Quartet, were booked as ancillary acts as well as the Alice In Wonderland, Dead Dog and Taste Experience discos. The usual weird sideshows were organised and things were beginning to come together.

The first problem I had was where everyone could meet. The last time I hired coaches the punters converged at Speakers Corner in Hyde Park but then there were only eight of them, this time there were forty. Still, it would be alright wouldn't it?

If you've ever driven down Park Lane between Speakers Corner and Hyde Park Corner you would have noticed dozens of coaches double-parked along the side of the Park. They'll just have to triple-park, I thought, so Speakers Corner it was.

Out of courtesy I did contact the police to ask their permission and was told quite emphatically: NO WAY. They said something about a gathering of more than ten people was classified as being a mob, it was too late by then, tickets had already been dispatched with Speakers Corner designated as the rendezvous. Oops.

However, I decided to wing it and take the risk. To cover my arse I typed a letter dated one week before the show saying that I thanked the police for their kind co-operation and confirmed that as agreed, two thousand people and forty coaches will be meeting at Speakers Corner on Friday 27th June 1986. I posted the letter on the morning of the show.

And so it was that two thousand hungry-for-it Alice freaks turned up at the given place to await their magical transportation to another mystery place totally unaware of how their evening would pan out. I had organised for stewards to check the tickets and load the punters onto the coaches. However, a number of things didn't go according to plan.

When I timed the journey originally I didn't take into consideration that Joe drove at about 90 miles per hour, knew London like the back of his hand and knew the quickest route to Lowestoft. As opposed to coaches that drove at 60 miles per hour, were driven by people who had hardly ever been to London before and hadn't got a clue where they were going. They would just follow the person in front who also didn't know where he was going. Because it was a Mystery trip the passengers obviously didn't know where they were going and in order to protect the secret I hadn't told the stewards either. Consequently a few of the coaches unfortunately turned up a bit late, still, shit happens, most of them got there in time.

When the crowds piled off the bus into the venue they were greeted by Annadin Brothers, Wendi and Colette wearing Alice costumes. They handed out souvenir badges and sticks of seaside rock, specially made for the event with Doctor And The Medics written through the middle.

The show itself lived up to its predecessors reputations, all the bands were great, The Medics, unfazed by their recent heady heights of number one stardom went for it in excellent fashion, Clive arrived on stage on a pantomime horse and The Zodiacs, second on the bill, bathed in the press coverage that an event like this attracted.

There were the usual peripheral acts, light and laser shows, the Alice disco on the balcony upstairs, alternative performance artists and Another Green World. The Brindisi String Quartet played Hendrix songs in a specially made tent structure that having taken half the afternoon to put up was pulled down within fifteen minutes of people arriving. Oh well.

As the show drew to a close and we were all congratulating each other on another great show Clive came in and told me the bad news. It was another of those: "CHRISTIAN I DON'T WANT TO WORRY YOU, BUT..." situations.

Basically there were about 350 punters hanging around waiting to go home and no more coaches in the car park. I had brought these people there and it was up to me to get them back. The coaches had all left and hundreds were left stranded. Oh fuck.

The next couple of hours were an absolute nightmare, I eventually managed to track down the owner of the coach company who promised to look into what had gone wrong and get back to me with an answer. Apparently half of the coaches had been sub-contracted and some of the subbies had decided they didn't like the look of the lovely Alice folk and having endured the journey there just buggered off back home for an early night. Other coaches left half full because they couldn't be bothered to wait until the end leaving me to deal with the consequences. Thanks.

After numerous phone calls between me and the coach company bloke we were still without a solution and the natives were becoming restless. By this time the police had arrived and having purveyed the motley crew, who by now resembled survivors of a nuclear holocaust, said that everyone would have to leave Lowestoft immediately or they would be arrested for loitering with intent, or something.

It was now about ten in the morning and these people had been partying for some eighteen hours, I pleaded with the police to give me some more time and eventually by about 10.30am we had arranged to charter a train to take the tired and partied out people back to London. Escorted by the police, the bedraggled wasted party animals were led through the streets of Lowestoft to the station where they were herded in and told that a train was on its' way from the depot to take them home. A massive cheer went up.

At about 12.00 noon the train arrived and the punters were loaded into the carriages and the doors were closed. Joe and I breathed a sigh of relief and stood there on the platform waiting for the train to depart. It wasn't moving and I couldn't understand why.

Next thing I was confronted by this petty minded, bigoted, little jobsworth of a station manager who said that there was no way the train was leaving the station until all the litter had been picked up. Whilst waiting for the train to arrive the crowd had been scoffing crisps, guzzling cans of coke and smoking copious amounts of cigarettes, (all purchased from British Rail, incidentally.)

Having taken God knows how long to get these people on the train there was no way I was going to let them off again. "If these people get off this train there will be a riot," I explained to Mr. Jobsworth. He puffed out his chest, put his whistle in his pocket and folded his arms. He had absolutely no intention of being reasonable. "We'll pick up the litter, just blow your fucking whistle!" I said, exasperated.

So with Joe and I left sweeping the floors of Lowestoft station, the train eventually pootled off on its journey back to London. An hour later and Joe and I had finished the job of cleaning up and, totally exhausted, drove back to London ourselves. We still arrived home before the train though; apparently some idiot opened the door of the fast moving train and tried to jump out shouting "Choo Choo, Choo Choo!" Someone pulled the emergency cord, the nutter was wrestled to the ground and the train screeched to a halt. It stayed in the sidings for another hour until the police arrived to take the bloke away.

To make matters worse, Joe, after dropping me off at my flat in West Hampstead drove to his flat in Muswell Hill and, absolutely knackered after 36 hours non-stop, went straight to bed leaving his camera case in the back of his car. He had documented the whole evening from start to finish, taking photos of everything, his car was broken into and the camera and all the photos were stolen, gone forever.

It was after those sequence of events that I decided that Lowestoft would be the last ever Mystery Trip and I meant it this time. Excellent they may have been, legendary they may have become but all good things must come to an end and that moment was then.

Fifteen years later and Clive was at a petrol station somewhere and a guy wearing a suit and driving a BMW walked up to him and shook his hand. "Doctor," he said, "The Lowestoft Mystery Trip was the best gig I have ever been to." Testament indeed, a once spaced out Alice party person, now a respectable grown up but still a human being who was there that night and never forgot.

Two girls who came to Lowestoft with Zodiac Mindwarp's manager, Dave Balfe, Ultravixens Zoë and Charley were on a mission to be the most photographed punters of the trip. Following in the example of the Underwear Girls from the previous Mystery Trip, they dressed to get noticed and appeared in virtually all of the press reviews of the show. Draped around Zodiac in *Time Out,* draped over each other in numerous Japanese magazines, they even got their faces in the local paper, *The Lowestoft Journal.*

The Lowestoft Journal reported the event and were outraged that 'the elite from the smoke' descended on their town without telling the locals, saying that many rock fans from Lowestoft would have loved to have gone to the gig. I don't doubt that, I didn't stop them buying a ticket. I think they missed the point somehow.

One bloke from Lowestoft did go to the gig, having bought his ticket to the mystery destination, he spent half a day travelling to London only to be brought straight back home by coach. "Fucking hell!" he said when the coach pulled into his home town, "I live here!"

In order to make the Alice In Wonderland 'brand' easily recognisable the graphics had to maintain continuity. The original leaflet design for the opening night set a precedence that continued for the next ten years. Initially based around the child like writing of the original logo, which, I confess I ripped off from another great Alice, Alice Cooper. The sleeve for his *Killer* album featured a snake and the childish writing.

The reason why I used that was that I was sick to death of Letraset. Letraset, how crap was that? For those of you who don't know what Letraset is, or was, I will explain. Before computers, artwork lettering had to be typeset by printers, hand drawn or transferred. Letraset was basically transfers, problem was that when you were three quarters of the way through a poster having painstakingly rubbed the letters from the transparent sheet onto the page you would lean on another part and lift all your done work back onto the plastic. Try as you might you could never then put it back properly.

The stuff was a nightmare, so for that reason I developed Alice Cooper's baby writing to suit my purpose, if I was running out of space on a particular line I could do unevenly sized letters to fill the relevant gap. There really was method in my madness. Developing the style further I made it less Alice Cooper and more Alice In Wonderland by adding swirls and symbols.

Apart from the flyers and posters advertising the club nights and the special events I also designed a number of record sleeves for various bands. The Pooterland people who set up their own psychedelic web site have even included a *Christian Paris Art Gallery* where they have downloaded some of my artwork complete with yellowed sticky tape in the corners to indicate that they were once stuck on their walls. Gosh I really am flattered, even though I don't have a clue who they are.

Mystery Trippers at Speakers Corner

Acid punks on the coach to Lowestoft

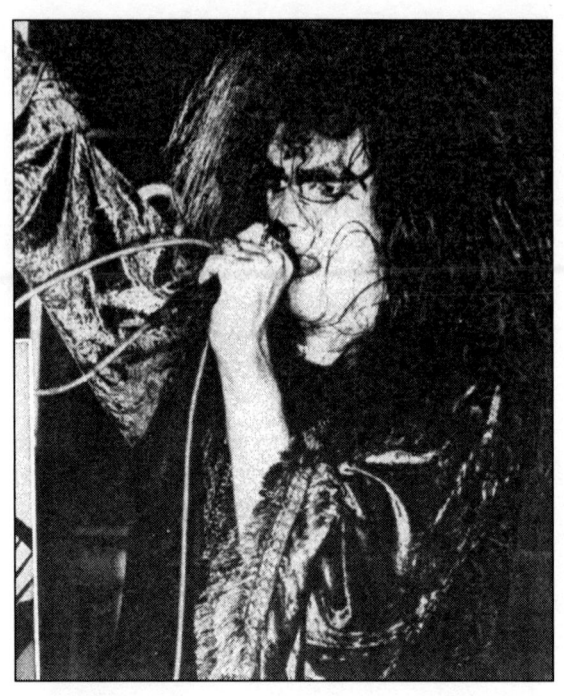

Clive at the Lowestoft Mystery Trip

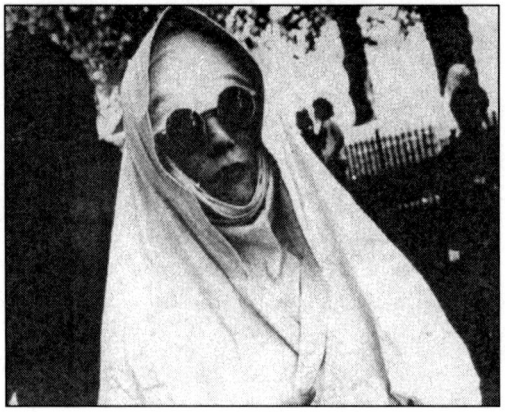

Nuns in shades

Zodiac Mindwarp and Ultravixens Zöe and Charley backstage at Lowestoft

CHAPTER FOURTEEN

BIG IN JAPAN

Screaming Lord Sutch drops in to Planet Alice, Stevie Ray Vaughan plays at Alice's, the Exploding Vicar takes to the stage, Alice Cooper wishes he hadn't invited me to his party, Alice In Wonderland and Doctor And The Medics take their mad show to Japan and Gary Glitter shows his true colours.

The follow up single to 'Spirit In The Sky' for Doctor And The Medics was a track from the album, 'Burn,' a good single, which charted on the back of 'Spirit' reaching number 29. It was never going to be as successful as its' predecessor but 'Spirit' was a tough act to follow. No more *Top Of The Pops* for The Medics although the video was shown. I was in the video dressed as an Annadin Brother with my real brother Julian, so I eventually fulfilled my lifelong ambition of being on *Top Of The Pops!* Sort of.

Screaming Lord Sutch was a really nice bloke, I'm not just saying that because he's dead, I met him a few times and he really was, or certainly appeared to be a genuinely nice bloke. For those of you who don't know who we was, David Sutch was the leader of the alternative political party, the Monster Raving Looney Party, they were the jokers who had candidates at local bi-elections and would get just four votes. Their policies would include stuff like turning Britain's butter mountain into a ski slope.

He was also the singer in his own band who had a few hits in the sixties, the best known was 'Jack The Ripper,' he would arrive on stage in a coffin wearing his signature top hat. Any money David made he ploughed straight into his Monster Raving Looney Party.

One day he called into Planet Alice and introduced himself, he said he was clearing out his garage and found some old sixties stage clothes and would I be interested in selling them on a sale or return basis. I opened up the bag and pulled out a selection of mouldy leopard skin print plastic macs etc. Some of them were child sizes and clearly not his stage clothes at all.

Politely and diplomatically I said that I didn't think there was a market for this sort of stuff. He looked genuinely upset and said that he didn't want much cash for it, anything would do. I felt sorry for him and said I would give it a go. I took the bag and put it in the backroom, I didn't want my shop to smell of mouldy plastic.

A couple of weeks later he came back into the shop and asked how it went, he looked around to see if he could see any of it on the rails. Oh shit, I thought, I'd forgotten all about that, I went to look for the bag and discovered that one of the girls had thrown it away thinking it was rubbish, (it was.) Oh fuck, I thought. I went back into the shop and took £20 out of the till and gave it to him. "Someone gave me £40 for the lot" I lied, "And here's your half." He beamed happily and left.

That night he turned up at Alice In Wonderland and didn't even try to blag his way in on the guest list, I bought him a drink and he asked if he could play at the club. I would have loved to have booked him to play at Alice's but due to the size of his stage show he needed too much money so unfortunately it never happened.

A few years later we met again, he had a joint birthday party at another venue with a mutual friend, the Page Three girl, Sam Kirli, he played live that night, the same set he'd been playing for thirty odd years. He even arrived on stage in a coffin wearing a top hat.

In June 1999 I read that David 'Screaming Lord' Sutch had hung himself, he had been suffering from depression since his mother had died the year before and I guess just couldn't face carrying on anymore. That was a really sad day.

Sometime in 1986 the brilliant guitarist, Stevie Ray Vaughan, played a special gig at Alice In Wonderland. I'm afraid I have a bit of a confession to make here, firstly, I can't remember how he came to play at the club, and secondly I had no idea who he was. It wasn't until the night of the show when his entourage arrived and he started sound checking that I realised he was a bit more special than the average Alice band. Years later *Rolling Stone* magazine listed him as number seven in the top 100 guitarists of all time and there he was playing at Alice's. I do remember the gig though, the club was packed to the gills and hundreds were turned away that night.

The band were superb and I was slightly embarrassed when I admitted to Colette of The Medics, who was there that night, that I hadn't got a clue who he was.

Despite years of rock'n'roll excess and a history of drink and drug addiction, Stevie Ray Vaughan was another one who died from an unrelated cause just a few years after gracing the tiny stage at Alice In Wonderland. Whilst on tour with Eric Clapton a helicopter taking him to his next gig crashed in fog and he was killed.

You may remember the Exploding Vicar from the beginning of this book. Let me explain: After The Medics 'Spirit In The Sky' hit, rumours were flying about that the band had found God and were now a Christian Rock Band. This was simply not true and something had to be done to dispel these falsehoods. One wild weekend in Glastonbury I was with my brother Julian staying in his

Volkswagon camper van when we came up with the brilliant idea of making a vicar who would literally explode. When we got back to London, Julian set about the task of creating our latest monster.

He made his first appearance at The Town And Country Club where The Medics were headlining. He consisted of a mannequin's body dressed in full vicar's garb with a papier-mâché head which we packed full of pyrotechnics.

At the sound check we tested it out using a cardboard box and set it off just as the singer of the support band was walking past, I can't remember who the band were, but they were not an 'Alice' band but someone whose record label had paid for the band to have the privilege and the exposure to support The Medics on their UK tour. He complained bitterly about constant ringing in his ears and accused us of ruining his singing career forever. Personally I think he knew deep down he didn't stand a chance and was just looking for an excuse as to why he was so crap.

For the live performance we set up the Exploding Vicar and positioned him in the centre of the stage, his head was ram packed with as much gunpowder as we could fit in and for added effect we added a bag of flour. The idea being that because the explosion would happen so quickly, first he would have a head and then a split second later he wouldn't, we thought that a big puff of flour would make for a better show. This was probably the piece de resistance as far as Alice In Wonderland Health and Safety Nightmares go.

As The Medics played their set to the ever rapturous crowd, the vicar was detonated, his head blew up exactly as planned but fired melted globules of boiling hot flour in all directions. The first few rows of punters were showered in flour shrapnel, which even melted the tights of Annadin

Brothers, Wendi and Colette. Amazingly no one appeared to be seriously hurt and to my knowledge no one was blinded or anything.

However, I did notice that the singer of the support band who witnessed the explosion in rehearsal, was singing dreadfully out of tune, and kept putting his hand over his right ear Joe Cocker style. Their record company subsequently dropped them once the tour was over, and of course the band blamed our vicar.

A few months later and The Medics were booked to perform live on *The Tube*, which was a popular Channel 4 music TV show hosted by Jools Holland, Paula Yates and Muriel Grey. They had somehow got to hear about our legendary vicar and wanted him on the show, so Julian made another one. Being considerably more sensible than us and with a much higher regard to the safety of their audience they filmed the vicar being detonated in a warehouse with everyone hiding behind barriers and with fire officers standing by, extinguishers at the ready just in case. It was nowhere near as much fun.

The Exploding Vicar re-surfaced recently when Julian was clearing out his loft and came across the original clay mould used for the papier-mâché head. It was Julian's daughter, Dolly, who found it. "Oh my God what's this?" she screamed, staring at the scary head. Julian explained that it was used as a mould for the exploding heads. Dolly looked confused and asked; "Why would you do that?" "It's a long story" replied Julian, "Ask your uncle Christian."

Gossips was always a special place and I cannot think of another venue in London that would have been more suited to host Alice In Wonderland. With a different theme each night it was clubs within a club. Monday night, traditionally the quietest night of the week was always

Alice night and we made sure that it was always the busiest night of the week.

Tuesday night was rock night, either The Pipeline, The Gutter Club (run by Tyla of Dogs D'Amour) or Buttz and Spikes. Buttz was in a band called the Babysitters and Spike was the main man with The Quire Boys who themselves had a hit with 'Hey You'.

Wednesday night was always difficult to make work. I tried it a couple of times myself with a couple of Alice spin-offs, The Magic Roundabout and a surf club called Wipe Out. Alan McGee of Creation Records had his night, The Trip (until I insisted he was closed down), and comedian Vic Reeves (way before *Shooting Stars*) together with one of Jonathan Ross's brothers ran a comedy club for a short while.

Thursday night was Gaz's Rockin' Blues, run by Gaz Mayall, son of the blues guitarist John Mayall. I bumped into Gaz years later in the most unlikely of places. I was living in a tiny village in the middle of nowhere (west Wales actually) and one night in my local pub who should I see playing darts? Gaz. No matter how huge the world is I constantly find that it's not actually as big as it thinks it is.

Friday night at Gossips was hip-hop, and the man on the decks? A certain Mr. Tim Westwood, now a radio one DJ In one of my scrapbooks I have a photo from *The Observer* magazine of myself, Clive and Tim (among others) being heralded as the up and coming DJ's in London.

Saturday night was always reggae night with DJ Dave Rodigan. So there we have it, Gossips, as small as it was had a certain magic of its' own and it wasn't just Alice's that it rubbed off on.

I have always loved Alice Cooper, I bought all of his early albums up until *Go To Hell* and saw him at the Wembley Arena on the *Welcome To My Nightmare* tour in 1975. I was well impressed when The Medics were booked to support him eleven years later and totally enjoyed the whole gig. Alice Cooper is a real rock star so he can be forgiven for being a bit prima-donna-ish. He never came to speak to The Medics even though his people borrowed Wendi's hairdryer to keep his snake warm.

The backstage party after the show was quite fun, there were lots of people in the music biz that I knew there that night so there were plenty of people to talk to. One person who was missing was Alice himself. I was chatting to Colette whilst perched on the buffet table laid out with sausage rolls and vol-a-vents and stuff when Alice eventually arrived. Alice walked in surrounded by his entourage and everyone's eyes turned towards the door. At that point I stood up from the table, I didn't realise it at the time but earlier in the evening I had sat on some chewing gum and was consequently stuck to the tablecloth. As I stood up I took the tablecloth with me sending dozens of drinks, sausage rolls and vol-a-vents crashing to the floor.

Everyone in the room swung round to see what was happening, including Alice Cooper and his entourage who just glared at me. I had stolen the thunder from Alice's great entrance and I couldn't even pretend it wasn't me as I still had the white tablecloth stuck to my backside like a bride's wedding dress train. Sorry Alice, it wasn't deliberate. About five years after the table cloth incident Alice Cooper turned up at my Planet Alice shop in Hollywood, I wasn't in that day so I've yet to actually meet him.

The Medics latest single, 'Burn,' didn't enjoy the major success that its predecessor, 'Spirit In The Sky,' had had and the record company wanted another hit. They, not the Medics, came up with the idea of doing a cover version of Abba's 'Waterloo'. At that time Abba were totally un-hip, they had not had the renaissance they were to enjoy in the forthcoming years so the idea was too much too soon. I was not happy about it at all and thought that The Medics were about to commit commercial suicide. However, I was talked into accepting the idea at least, even though it pained me to be enthusiastic about it. Roy Wood of Wizzard was roped into playing sax and producing the track and it was recorded at Mickie Most's studio in St. John's Wood.

When Roy arrived the first thing he did was open his sax case, the second thing he did was pull out a full bottle of vodka and the third thing he did was drink it, all of it. The record itself is quite a good version with Wendi and Colette singing the vocals and posing as Abba girl look-alikes.

The video was a pastiche on Abba's *Eurovision Song Contest* performance and even featured the original compere, Katie Boyle. Katie took a shine to me and even joked to her ancient husband that she wanted me to be her toy boy. Oh great, it could have been Joanna Lumley or Lesley Anne Down but it wasn't. It was Katie Boyle. Clive pretended to play the sax (my sax incidentally) and Roy Wood also performed looking like he's always looked. Captain Sensible and Lemmy also made cameo appearances and the record was ready for release.

The record company had posters printed with a question and answer theme. 'What have Napoleon, Abba, Roy Wood and Doctor And The Medics got in common?' To which someone dryly wrote underneath: 'None of them have had a hit record recently.' Cruel, but fair. The record wasn't a hit and I was right in my original reservations.

However, just because The Medics couldn't repeat their number one achievement, which they weren't really meant to do in the first place, it didn't mean they were finished. Far from it, the die-hard fans forgave them for their brief flirtation with pop mainstream and they still pulled as big a crowd as ever whenever and wherever they played. 1986 had seen them play all over the place, they were supporting Simple Minds at The Milton Keynes Bowl at the very same time when the England football team were knocked out of the World Cup by Argentina thanks to Maradona's 'Hand Of God', they also played the Glastonbury and Reading festivals.

Planet Alice had become designer fashion. What? I had absolutely no idea about fashion as such and this was not what we set out to do. Yeah we sold clothes, but fashion? However suddenly we were approached by the top style magazines who wanted to feature our clothes in their photo shoots. Planet Alice in *Vogue?* My mum read *Vogue*. Were we in danger of becoming mainstream? Fact of the matter was; our clothes were so outrageously colourful amongst the drabber collections of many of the fashion designers at that time we made good copy.

I bought a job lot of flared hipsters for next to nothing and Kim's brother, Graham, sewed on the off-cuts of material from our other designs in a haphazard fashion. This was the birth of the popular Planet Alice patchworks, which, for a while, everyone had to have.

We turned the flares into straight legged trousers as even our off the wall customers weren't quite ready to venture back into flares just yet. Next came patchwork mini skirts, hot pants, waistcoats, jackets and coats. It became such a hit in the fashion press that proper fashion designers (as opposed to us who were just pretending) started copying our designs, John Galliano and Italian giants, Fiorucci to name just two. But a pair of patchworks had to have the

Planet Alice label stitched onto the back pocket or they didn't count.

Jenny, the Belt Lady, bought a crate of original Mary Quant flower buckles and started making wide leather belts that ironically became known as Planet Alice belts. Mary Quant was none too pleased and quite rightly put a stop to us selling them. By a strange quirk of fate she ended up using our designs of wrist and ankle swingers, borrowing our patterns from our manufacturer Wanda who lived in Wandle Road, Wandsworth. Try saying that if you have a speech impediment, unless you're Jonathan Ross of course.

Anyway, as Mary Quant is recognised as the inventor of the mini skirt, I was hardly in a position to complain.

When we did *The Tube* show a couple of coach loads of Alice regulars were transported to the gig. With free transport and free entrance the tickets were snapped up in minutes. Some of the Alice crew were interviewed and our legendary Exploding Vicar (with a new head, obviously) made his second and last appearance. The Medics were great, however, their performance was ruined by the uninvited stage invasion by seventies pop star, the soon to be disgraced, Gary Glitter.

Gary Glitter jumped on stage without any prior warning as The Medics were doing their penultimate song, 'Spirit In The Sky'. Clive didn't really know what to do so basically ignored the ageing embarrassment we know to be Gary Glitter. It got worse. The Medics were called back for an encore and Gary Glitter came back on again. The Medics played 'No-one Loves You When You've Got No Shoes' and Gary Glitter, not knowing any of the words, just preened and posed in front of the camera punching the air with his fist and doing his passé eyebrow movements. It makes me cringe just thinking about it. Clive was visibly not happy with the situation at all but like the real trouper that he is, carried on regardless.

Big In Japan is a well-used rock'n'roll cliché that basically means that a band is finished in the UK and the record company who had splashed out thousands on advances is trying to recoup some of their losses by promoting them in Japan. The Japanese love most things English so it's a done deal that they would get maximum press exposure and sell a few more records into the bargain.

Having said all of that, when The Medics and the Alice organisation were asked to go out to Japan that was not the case at all. A Japanese promoter called Koichi was a regular at Alice's and after going on the Lowestoft Mystery Trip wanted to promote the whole thing in Tokyo and Osaka. As well as setting up a couple of shows for The Medics, he wanted the Alice In Wonderland disco to fly out to Japan and do a Mystery Trip. He also negotiated a deal with Sony to release the *Lobster* album and he organised a small franchise outlet of Planet Alice clothes in the massive Seibu Department Store in Tokyo.

When we first arrived at the hotel we stepped out of the limo and there was a solitary Medics fan waiting outside, when she spotted the band she threw her arms in the air and scuttled off to the nearest phone box. By the time we had checked in, the hotel lobby was full of young girls clutching records for the band to sign taking the obligatory million photos.

The Thompson Twins, a fairly rubbish eighties band who had a reasonable hit with 'We Are Detectives' were staying at the same hotel but their fans switched allegiance to The Medics as soon as they saw them arrive. One night we invited The Thompson Twins to join us out drinking but they declined preferring to have a quiet night in drinking tea. I rest my case.

The first couple of shows in Tokyo and Osaka went down well and one of the highlights has to be the all girl Japanese band who were supporting The Medics. During her solo, the female guitarist suddenly stopped and as the drums and bass carried on she walked up to the front of the stage, pulled out a comb and started back-combing her hair. That was part of their act. Fantastic! Only in Japan.

After the Tokyo show we all went back to the hotel to party. This time it was party in Richard's room. A whole group of Japanese fans followed us but most of them couldn't fit in the room so they waited outside in the corridor, happy just to be close to their new favourite band. Steve McGuire felt sorry for the fans and went out to speak to them. He said in broken English: "And now we play Ancient English Game, ya?"

The Japanese ensemble giggled and replied "Ya! Ya! Ya!" "Now you do this" said McGuire facing the corridor wall with his hands above his head. A group of about a dozen girls followed his example. "And now you wait" said the McGuire monster. The girls were lined up along the corridor, facing the wall with their arms above their heads chattering away wondering what this 'Ancient English Game' was all about.

McGuire went back into the hotel room, stripped down to his underpants, put on a shower cap and with a hairbrush in his hand he then ran down the corridor slapping each girl's backside with the brush. "Ah so." He said, "Ancient English Game!" The girls thought it was hilarious and kept chanting "Ancient English Game, Ancient English Game!" This was the country that earlier that day on TV was advocating the 'Tree Religion' where people would wake up in the morning and hit themselves with a twig. I loved Japan but Christ was it bizarre.

It amuses me to think that those girls have now grown up and probably have children of their own who now go to gigs, hanging around hotel corridors outside their latest favourite bands room wondering if they might get to play 'The Ancient English Game.'

The Mystery Trip was organised entirely by the Japanese promoters, they asked me what sort of things went on and I gave them a long list of what our UK punters would be subjected to and left them to it. The mystery destination was just outside Tokyo at a fairly large hall, which apparently was the headquarters of the Japanese mafia. The promoters had set up a moveable scaffold tower to hang toilet paper from the twelve metre high ceiling. Even with the scaffolding these tiny Japanese guys had to stand on their toes to stick the loo roll up, it was a hilarious sight.

The coaches arrived to take the polite sober Japanese punters to the gig, dressed in their new Planet Alice creations they quietly took their seats, The journey was spent playing bingo and when they arrived they walked in to the venue and immediately started taking photos of the toilet paper fluttering from the domed ceiling high above their heads. The gig went well and the Japanese crowd loved it, but it went to show just how culturally apart the UK and Japan were.

We were treated like royalty throughout our stay in Japan and were at times embarrassed at the way we were regarded with such awe. Vom and I were at a nightclub in the VIP room behind glass and dozens of Medics fans were lined up on the other side, their faces pressed to the glass just staring at us. We spotted a table football machine in the 'public' area and asked our host if we could go and have a game. He was a bit nervous at letting us mingle with the Japanese kids but reluctantly agreed and told the two lads playing at the table to go away. Obediently they abandoned their game and left the table, our host then beckoned us over. We felt sorry for the two guys who had been turfed off the table so invited them for a doubles match, England versus Japan. They could not believe it and checked with our host that it was okay and so it was game on.

As their friends took hundreds of thousands of photos, Vom and I totally thrashed them. One bloke had his camera focused on our opponents goal and snapped away rapidly trying to photograph the goals. How bizarre was that? Some Japanese guy must have an album full of photos of a little plastic goalkeeper staring blankly as yet another ball was thumped into the back of the net. Maybe they let us win or maybe they were just totally crap at table football, either way they didn't give a shit, they had something to talk about with their mates for years to come.

Whilst in Japan we did numerous magazine, TV and radio interviews and the whole tour was a great success, there was the usual hotel party madness, trashing someone else's room and raiding their mini bar. Richard Searle, The Medics bass player was totally pissed off when he saw his room bill and Vom then told us of his clever trick. He had this great idea of putting the empty bottles back into their dispensers in his mini bar so the hotel wouldn't realise they had been drunk. Duh, the mini bar was connected to a computer, which monitored every time a bottle was removed. Poor Vom, totally unaware of this he had had a hell of a job to push the bottles back in and each time he tried it he clicked on another 'sale'. His bill was phenomenal, zillions of Yen I don't doubt.

I have never been a great food person, eating to live rather than living to eat, and I have in the past been accused of being a food philistine. I'm getting loads better these days, and recently found out that there's more to prawns than prawn cocktail crisps. However, in Japan, the food was virtually inedible, unless warm monkey brains drizzled with congealed elephant's blood is your thing.

Whilst in Tokyo, it was my birthday and Clive and Wendi took me out for a birthday breakfast in an authentic Japanese restaurant, served by real life Geishas and everything. The breakfast consisted of a fish head with real seaweed floating in salty seawater. It really was disgusting; I felt like a contestant in the bush tucker trial on *'I'm A Celebrity Get Me Out Of Here!'* It's a very kind gesture, Clive and Wendi but can I pass on this one?

A full English breakfast was available at the hotel but finished at nine o'clock when we were all still in bed, sleeping off the previous night's party. On our way by coach to the Mystery Trip gig, Colette and I saw in the distance the famous golden arches of McDonalds. I know McDonalds is the pits, but after eating nothing but rice for nine days it was like an oasis in the desert. "Stop!" we shouted at the coach driver, and we all got off the coach and ran towards the counter. A double cheeseburger and fries, an apple pie and a chocolate milkshake had never tasted so good.

The promoters were so thrilled with the shows that they wanted to do Alice In Wonderland in Tokyo once a week. I gave it some thought and talked to Clive about it, perhaps we could all take it in turns to fly out there and DJ. However, the flight home, which seemed to take months, put me off it. I loved Japan but it's a bit too far out even for the seasoned Alice crew.

As 1986 came to an end we had the usual Alice In Wonderland / Doctor And The Medics Christmas party, this time at The Hammersmith Palais. I had this idea that we could have a giant Doctor And The Medics devil face spitting out evil red laser beams from the stage. Clive agreed it would be great and I set about making the face out of the largest piece of hardboard I could buy.

I had a hell of a job getting it to Hammersmith but proudly set it up on the stage and helped Jim to fix his lasers so they shone out of its' eyes and mouth. I went to the back of the hall with Clive and Richard to admire my handiwork. It looked ridiculous, like the Stonehenge sketch from *Spinal Tap.* Whilst an eight foot high devil face may look quite scary when you're standing right in front of it, from the back of the Hammersmith Palais you hardly noticed it. Oops. Clive and Richard fell about laughing whilst I felt just a tad embarrassed.

For a short while Doctor And The Medics shared the same tour manager as Gary Glitter, and Glitter, having heard about Alice In Wonderland hired my oil wheel projectors for his show. A few months after that and he booked Clive to DJ at a New Years Eve gig in Bournemouth. With nothing else to do I tagged along with Clive and Wendi to help him on the decks. The last time we had come across the former glam rock pop star was when he jumped up on stage to join The Medics when they performed on *The Tube,* Gary Glitter was totally embarrassing that night, but that was now water under the bridge.

After the show we knocked on Gary Glitter's dressing room door to say hello. He wouldn't open the door at first and we heard lots of whispering and shuffling about. He clearly had someone in the room with him so we turned away and walked off. No great loss we thought. As we reached the end of the corridor Gary Glitter opened the door and called us back. We went into the dressing room but there didn't seem to be anyone else in the room. Very odd. I realised many years later that one of the reasons why it took him so long to open the door was that he must have just taken his wig off. Gary Glitter a rug head. Hilarious!

We then all went back to the hotel and hit the bar where we stayed drinking until the early hours, Gary Glitter was not a nice person and had the sort of arrogance typical of a so called rock star. He said something to me that night which I completely forgot about until years later when it was reported that he had been arrested for child sex crimes. He seemed to think I was a Mr. Fix-It (his words) and he asked me if I could find him some young girls, I remember at the time that shocked me and I thought maybe I had misheard him.

Reflecting on those events many years later it occurred to me how desperate he was. Did he honestly think that someone could turn up with some random under-age girls in Bournemouth of all places? Bournemouth is renowned as a retirement town, maybe someone could have found him a few random grannies, but not me that's for sure.

The disgraced glam rocker is now out of everybody's gang and after hearing about his activities I haven't played any of his records since.

1986 took us all by surprise. It was an amazing year, no doubt about it. Alice In Wonderland continued to be THE place to go to, Planet Alice got off to a roaring start and Doctor And The Medics against all the odds reached the magical Number One spot in the UK singles chart. Spacemen 3, The Milk Monitors, Rose Of Avalanche, My Bloody Valentine and The Bomb Party all played at Alice In Wonderland that year, all of them hoping to emulate the success of The Medics. Still, 1987 is coming up and who knows what will happen next.

The good Doctor

CHAPTER FIFTEEN

YOU'RE NOT BIG AND YOU'RE NOT CLEVER

In which the final Film Festival takes place, Planet Alice opens its second shop in Kensington, Gaye Bikers On Acid play at Alice In Wonderland, The Medics and the Alice crew go mad in Europe, Kylie Minogue buys Planet Alice gear and a few more punters become casualties.

Saturday 10th January 1987 was the day of our final All Night Film Festival at the Scala Cinema. *Godzilla Vs. The Thing, Forgotten Planet, The Party, Morgan,* and *Fistful Of Dollars* were the films and live on stage were The Brindisi String Quartet. The all girl foursome of accomplished, classically trained string players had previously played at Alice's and also as a side act at the Lowestoft Mystery Trip. My brother Julian arranged a selection of Monkees, Hendrix, Doors, Beatles and Stones songs and the girls were great. The show sold out once again, but for some reason that I really can't remember, we never did another Scala.

Such was the success of Alice In Wonderland that other people tried to jump on the bandwagon and every week another psychedelic nightclub would open up. Usually they would close down again a couple of weeks later but one or two lasted a bit longer. The Crypt, The Pigeon Toed Orange Peel Club, The Taste Experience, The Chistlehurst Experience and The Trip were clubs that came and went but none had the staying power of Alice's.

Likewise with Planet Alice, once other clothes shops realised that people were wearing 1980's style psychedelic clothes, they would try and emulate our designs and other little shops were opening up quickly (and closing down even quicker.) Sweet Charity, Thunderpussy and Dolly Daydream, were some that I can remember, but as with the clubs, they didn't have the following that we had, so soon disappeared.

When I first started Planet Alice I decided the logo should have a sixties feel to it and settled on a typeface (these days a font) called Arnold Brocklyn and, using the old favourite Letraset, painstakingly transferred the letters to create the artwork that would be used for signage, letterheads and the all important label. Walking through Highgate in North London one day I saw a laundrette called: Wishy Washy Squishy Squashy Cleanie Knickie Very Quickie. After laughing to myself at the laundrette's name I realised that the typeface was Arnold Brocklyn, the same typeface I had used for my shop, Planet Alice. I can't have the same logo as a fucking laundrette I thought to myself, and when I got home, I set about designing a new one.

I was so busy at the time that I employed someone to take my design and draw it out properly. Now we had a logo that was unique to us and I then arranged for a new shop sign, new labels and new stationery with the new logo. The new labels were stitched instead of being printed and would now be proudly sewn onto the outside of the clothes instead of discreetly stitched to the waistband or the inside pocket. The logo stayed with Planet Alice until the end.

Voltaire once said of the Holy Roman Empire: "(It is) neither Holy, nor Roman nor an Empire". The same could be said for Gaye Bykers On Acid, who, to my knowledge were neither gay, nor bikers nor were they on acid. They were however a great band who played a few times at Alice's. Jumping on the Zodiac Mindwarp bandwagon, they signed a £100,000 record deal and released a couple of good records. Led by the charismatic lead singer, a bloke called Mary, they were always good entertainment and always went down well. As well as playing at Alice's the band members were also regulars at both the club and the shop. We sold Gaye Byker tee shirts and Mary modelled some Planet Alice clothes for a TV shoot. "I feel like a Womble." He said, as he tried on one of our bright green fake fur jackets.

Planet Alice had become fairly well established by now, the unprecedented amount of press exposure kept up our profile and I researched the possibility of expanding. I looked at Camden, Kensington and Covent Garden as likely places for another Planet Alice when I received a phone call from the new manager of Kensington Market who virtually begged me to take on a unit there. This was ironic seeing as how a couple of years previously when I first started planning Planet Alice they wouldn't give me the time of day. Not unless I gave them a backhander of course.

I was able to negotiate a knock down rent and choose from a selection of already occupied units, who I was assured would be re-located elsewhere. Kensington Market was a large building set on three floors containing a hundred or so small shops within. I chose a little lock-up unit in the basement and set about putting the Planet Alice mark on the otherwise dull nondescript shop. Painting the walls purple and black just like Portobello Road and filling it with our unique colourful collections, we were set up and ready to open within two weeks.

The new shop opened on 27th March and was an instant success making a profit from day one. The overheads were fairly minimal and stocking the shop was no problem, we just upped our manufacturing and spread the goods between the two premises. We had been open less than a week when a wholesaler placed an order for one a 45-degree angle with me still in it and then left the room.

The following morning the hotel manager arrived at work and as he drove up to the hotel saw the beds sticking out of the window with the linen strewed all around the gardens and he went absolutely loopy. He ran up to my room, past all the furniture in the foyer and the lift and burst in through the unlocked door. The angriest man in the world then saw the state of the room with me still asleep, my bed still propped up against the wall. Someone had to pay for all this damage, and once again it was the perpetrator, Jeff. If his credit card had any more credit on it, it was disappearing fast.

The gig itself was excellent, the Medics played well and went down well, the Alice disco was going great and the crowd were doing their thing on the dance floor. All of a sudden the music stopped. Power cut? Machine failure? No, Alice In Wonderland Pissed DJ Syndrome. Clive thought I was DJing I thought Chris was and Chris thought Clive was. Actually no one was, it wasn't the first time this had happened and it wouldn't be the last. As usual it took a while before any of us realised what was happening and as the punters waited patiently on the dance floor, Clive, Chris and I all arrived at the DJ box together to get the music going again, I thought you.... But you said... It was.... Oh well, shit happens.

We ended the tour in Paris. The Medics had a small following in the French capital and Alice In Wonderland was also quite well known. The place was packed and the evening went superbly. So finishing the tour on a good night it was back to the UK to nurse our hangovers.

1987 was the year that Kylie Minogue wore my hot pants. Don't worry it's not what you think! Many celebrities and well-known people bought Planet Alice clothes over the years but my favourite customer has to be princess of pop, the diminutive antipodean Miss Kylie Minogue. It was after *Neighbours* and around the 'I Should Be So Lucky' time, and way before she became the nations favourite that she is today.

Kylie's people, and apparently even Kylie herself, came into Planet Alice and bought dozens of outfits for photo shoots and stage clothes. I had an appointment with my bank manager that day, so I missed her. When I heard about it, to be perfectly honest I wasn't really that bothered, at that time Kylie was not that credible and it was a long time until she would be. These days I'm with the rest of the universe, totally besotted by the small but perfectly formed Sheila and if I knew that she was going to visit my shop my bank manager would just have to wait.

Kylie was perfect for Planet Alice clothes; we only did girl sizes in eight, ten and twelve and didn't cater for anyone or anything larger. There are photos out there somewhere of Kylie wearing clothes from Planet Alice, multicoloured patchwork hot pants, black leather patchwork mini skirt and whatever else she bought that day.

Alice In Wonderland had its fair share of casualties among its regulars, some were injured or died from accidents or natural causes and others suffered as a result of their own actions. One such person was a guy called Nidge. Nidge was a manic speed freak with a ginger Mohican who hung out at Alice's from the very early days.

He was the son of a wealthy upper middle class family and dropping out and tuning in to Alice's was what many middle class rebels did for a while, just as the hippies did in the sixties and the punks did in the seventies, in fact every middle class family had to have one. There was always one freak sticking out like a sore thumb at the back of the family wedding photo, I know because I was one of those freaks.

Nidge was photographed during the poll tax riots kissing his girlfriend silhouetted in the foreground as London burned behind him, the photo appeared on the front page of some of the broadsheet newspapers. Ironic seeing as how his family had bought him a three-storey house in Fulham. Speed turned to heroin and it was heroin that killed him.

Nidge's legacy was that it was him who first shortened the Alice In Wonderland name to 'Alice's' and from thereon it stuck. I hope he's now at peace.

Another bloke, whose name escapes me, was at Alice In Wonderland every week without fail, he went to all the film festivals, mystery trips, picnics and everything. One day he just disappeared and no one knew what had happened to him, not even his housemates, he left his room one day and didn't come home, all his belongings, his clothes, his records, his passport everything was left in his room. After a couple of days his parents were informed and they called in the police. The police came down to the club and asked a few questions but none of us could shed any light on his whereabouts. Eventually we just forgot about him.

Six months later he turned up at Alice's and told his story. Apparently he had taken loads of LSD and ended up naked in a park in Hampshire lying under a bush absolutely convinced he was John Lennon. A dog walker who called the police eventually found him, they took him in for questioning but were unable to get any sensible answers out of him. After a couple of days of putting up with hearing him calling out for Yoko from his cell they had no alternative but to section him. They didn't believe that he was 'the walrus' and he was taken away in a straight jacket.

Six months he was in care and still had absolutely no idea who he was or where he lived. As far as he was concerned he was John Lennon and he lived with Yoko Ono. As well as Yoko he apparently also ranted on about someone called Alice, the specialists eventually realised that it was not a person he was going on about but a place: Alice In Wonderland. This was a breakthrough in his recovery process and bit-by-bit they pieced his life together and eventually worked out who he really was, where he really came from and what he was really about.

Blackie Lawless, the lead singer of the outrageous metal band, W.A.S.P. hung out at Alice's for a while. W.A.S.P. written as an acronym, usually means: 'White Anglo Saxon Protestants' although Blackie swears in their case it stands for 'We Are Sexual Perverts'. Either way, it was always good news to have a well-known rock star standing at the bar and as he had previous links to The New York Dolls that was fine by me. He mentioned Alice In Wonderland a few times in press interviews, citing it his favourite London club. Apparently it reminded him of the Cathouse in L.A.

Me by the European Tour Bus

Me and Colette working on tomorrows hangover, Amsterdam 1987

Voodoo Child

CHAPTER SIXTEEN

SNAIL FARMING

Clive tries his luck at snail farming in Wales, Vic Reeves sleeps through the hurricane and Cindy Beale and Dollar get kitted out in Planet Alice clothing.

In 1987 Clive and Wendi moved to Wales to get married, have loads of kids, walk the hills and make jam. Not necessarily in that order. The Medics career had ground to a halt, with no current record out and just a few university gigs booked, there was not a lot promising on the horizon. Clive loved his new life in Wales and looked at ways at how he could make a living there. He decided on alternative farming. First he looked into llamas, then Angora rabbits before finally settling on snails.

Clive read up about l'escargots and bought the necessary equipment, poly tunnels, vegetation, all the things that you need to be a snail farmer. He bought four thousand snails to set up his farm, the first thousand died of old age and a mole that broke into the tunnels ate the second thousand.

Another thousand were killed by the frost and the remaining snails escaped. Clive's brave attempt at trying to breed molluscs, fatten them up and sell them to restaurants wasn't the success he had hoped for. Still, it made for a good press story.

In the summer of 1987 I was approached by the promoter, John Curd, to get involved in a large gig he was organising in Finsbury Park that he called *Acid Daze*. Hawkwind were confirmed as headliners with Doctor And The Medics, Naz Nomad, Pink Fairies, Gaye Bykers On Acid, and Pop Will Eat Itself as the support acts. Alice In

Wonderland, of course, provided the disco.

I had worked with John Curd a few times before and although he was a league or two above me in the promotions game we had a mutual respect for each other. I had met him some ten years previously when he put on a show at The Roundhouse in Camden. An all-girl teenage band called The Runaways were over from California to play a couple of London gigs, I was totally in love with their guitarist, Joan Jett and travelled to London for the show. Afterwards I tried to get into the backstage party where I was turned away by John Curd. Not to be defeated I went round the back and tried to get in through the fire escape. I was spotted by John who once again told me to go away. I pleaded with him and eventually he said. "Go on then, I would have done the same when I was your age."

I was allowed into the back stage party where I met the band, including Joan Jett who gave me her guitar plectrum. She wrote out her address on a bit of paper and said I should write to her. I couldn't believe it, okay, so she didn't give me her phone number, but better than that she had given me her address! I wrote her a letter as soon as I got home and posted it the next day. I didn't realise that the address she gave me was her fan club address but fair play, she replied personally to my letter and I still have it.

Ten years later and, working with The Medics, I came across John Curd again. I had to meet him somewhere to pick up tickets for a show that I would sell at Planet Alice. "Are you John Curd?" I asked. "No," he replied, "I'm his brother, who wants to know?"

I did a radio interview for some station and the day it was aired I received a phone call from an A and R man at a major record label who wanted to discuss an idea he had.

We arranged to meet and he said that he wanted me to find another band capable of producing hit records. He took note of my claim that one in every ten bands that ever played at Alice's then went on to have a hit single and wanted me to identify the next one.

The Flying Tractor Band were four sixteen year old lads who, although too young to go to Alice's in the early days had, however, bunked off school to go on one of the Mystery Trips. (They were the nuns in shades, by the way.) They played their own instruments, looked good and had some good material. I thought the idea of a young boy band who were actually fairly competent musicians might just work. I wasn't sure about the name, but that could be changed and if they didn't have an obvious hit record in their repertoire there was always the option of a good cover version. The A and R man went to see them play and was impressed.

So, with the prospect of a major record deal up my sleeve I decided to manage them. After shelling out a few grand on equipment and rehearsals I was beginning to regret my decision, the record company A and R man was sacked from his job, the good looking guitarist was replaced with a bloke with no chin, and the singer fell in love with a woman more than twice his age and started writing romantic poetry.

With no record deal, a lovesick singer and a guitarist with no chin, The Flying Tractor Band didn't seem such a good prospect after all. Still, they played at Alice's a few times and I got them a few support gigs at The Town and Country Club with The Pink Fairies and the Clarendon where they played with Naz Nomad And The Nightmares.

After a few months I decided to cut my losses and we went our separate ways, they split up soon after and joined the list of bands that never made it.

The *EastEnders* actress, Michelle Collins, who played the blonde vamp, Cindy Beale, came into Planet Alice one day. She absolutely loved our stuff and tried on virtually everything in the shop. I recognised her straight away even though, up close I noticed that she was ginger and not the blonde she was on the telly.

I had to explain to her when she failed to squeeze into a size ten mini skirt that there had been a mistake at the manufacturers and the wrong labels had been stitched on. I handed her a size twelve and said "Try these, they're really a size ten." She did, and the skirt fitted perfectly so she bought it.

Now I was seriously worried about Cindy Beale and Planet Alice. Not because I was concerned about my sizing and trading standards, not because she had tried on virtually every item in the shop and not because she was ginger. But what if she told Ian about Planet Alice? What if her on-screen husband at the time, Ian Beale came into Planet Alice and bought a pair of patchworks and wore them at the chippy? I would never have lived it down. Luckily he didn't, I would never have lived it down.

Seventies pop duo and *Eurovision Song Contest* entrants, Dollar, were photographed for a session in *The Sun* newspaper wearing Planet Alice clothes. Oh dear. Under the banner headline of *Hippy Days Are Here Again* they posed dressed from head to foot in our gear. All publicity is good publicity so I didn't really mind too much, but I wished it were someone just a bit more credible.

Luckily for us the good looking girl half; Theresa, got Planet Alice gear whilst the male half; David Van Day, got kitted out in Thunderpussy stuff. Theresa looked great, David looked both embarrassed and embarrassing. Tough luck Thunderpussy.

David Van Day gained a certain amount of TV and press coverage recently whilst trying to re-kindle his career by appearing on *'I'm A Celebrity Get Me Out Of Here!'* There appears to be a pattern forming here. He's the second person slightly attached to the Alice thing who has appeared on that programme. Who's next? Lemmy? Captain Sensible? Or perhaps even Doctor Clive himself. Now there's an idea, Clive would be brilliant. He's funny, intelligent, likeable and will do anything for a laugh. He also has the constitution of an ox.

One night after a gig in Birmingham we went to an Indian restaurant that boasted the hottest vindaloo in the world ever. They were so confident of 'Death Curry's' potency that if anyone could finish a whole dish of the lethal stuff they would get a voucher for the same again free of charge. Clive ordered a plate of Death Curry and ate the whole lot. Not only that, he cashed in his voucher and did it all again. I took a tiny taste of it and I thought I had spontaneously combusted. I had to drink five pints of beer to cool down. So after that performance Clive would have no problem eating a witchetty grub.

Alice In Wonderland celebrated its fourth anniversary and still showed no signs of fatigue. Week in, week out we were still packed out every single week and it didn't look like ending. This was no mean feat, one-nighters at London nightclubs rarely lasted a full year, let alone four.

The wholesale business at Planet Alice was growing, with one set of fixed costs as well as the retail sales and the mail order sales, the bulk orders were what drove the turnover up. Our clothes were being sold around the world, America, Japan, Italy, France and Germany among other countries. One day I had a visit from a buyer for a small chain of boutiques in Iceland who placed an order for, among other items, fifty pairs of hot pants. Hot pants to Iceland? Brrrr. That amused me no end and it was a story I would tell often in press interviews over the following years. I suppose there's no reason why the girls in Iceland shouldn't have worn hot pants or mini skirts, it's just that I didn't want them to die of hypothermia.

In October 1987 I promoted a show at The Astoria in London's Charing Cross. Doctor And The Medics had always sold out at a 2000 capacity venue and I couldn't see any reason why they shouldn't have sold out this one. It was the night of the great hurricane that ripped through London and the southeast causing absolute mayhem, turning Sevenoaks onto One Oak and causing untold damage to cars and buildings.

Being a promoter is a risky business, people have lost their homes over a show that failed to sell the anticipated number of tickets. The bigger the show the more you stand to gain or lose. I was expecting to sell 2000 tickets but I only sold 1000. I could have made £10,000 instead I lost £5000. Whether the weather had anything to do with it or whether it was The Medics decline in popularity, I will never really know. Perhaps it was my skills as a promoter that was the problem. I advertised in all the music papers and paid for fly-posters to be stuck all around London. However as soon as my posters were stuck up, another promoter would cover it up with a poster advertising his show.

However, a bloody hurricane? How was I supposed to have seen that one coming? The weather forecaster, Michael Fish, didn't and it's his job. Anyway the show must go on and it did, The Medics did their best to create an atmosphere among the half full venue, but already the signs were showing, Clive talked about The Medics being a failed former number one pop group in between each song as if to highlight the fact that their glory days were coming to an end.

Vic Reeves, an unknown comedian at the time, was booked to act as compere for the show. He was constantly booed by the audience, probably the same people who in future years would laugh their socks off at him, and nothing he could say or do could stop the jeering. He just wasn't funny. The evening had a very strange atmosphere about it right from the start and was totally unlike any of the previous Alice events, or indeed an ordinary night at Alice In Wonderland. The brewing hurricane seemed to get into peoples senses and the show was basically an all round disaster.

After the show, Clive and a few other Medics, Vic Reeves, and myself all went back to the hotel in Bayswater where the PA crew were staying to drown our respective sorrows. As we arrived at the hotel the wind was by now really picking up but we paid it no notice and set about some serious drinking, after all, thankfully it's not every day I lose £5000 on a show that goes wrong. We drank and we chatted and Vic joked, but try as he might he couldn't put a smile on my face.

A good few hours later we phoned for a cab to take us back to Clive's place in Blackheath, South London. It was now about 4.30 in the morning and the storm was in full force. As we left the hotel the hurricane was at full strength and nearly knocked us over, we virtually had to carry a seriously pissed Vic as we bundled into the back of the cab and headed off for Blackheath.

The journey took forever, London looked like it had just been bombed, there were fallen trees everywhere blocking roads, scaffolding had come crashing down on top of cars and buildings and there was litter and debris everywhere. We narrowly avoided being hit by a flying sheet of corrugated iron as we weaved our way across London on the few roads that were still accessible.

Eventually we arrived in Blackheath outside Vic Reeves modest terraced house (something tells me he doesn't live there now.) Vic had crashed out in the cab and had slept through the entire journey and had absolutely no idea what had been going on that night. We woke him up and he stumbled out of the cab and looked around at the devastated scene, there were fallen trees, crushed cars, broken fences, dustbins and bits of twisted metal everywhere you looked.

Newspapers and plastic bags swirled in the air and a tree had fallen onto his garden wall reducing it to a pile of rubble. "Fookin' Hell." Said Vic. "I don't fookin' live here!" For the first time that night I laughed. So it's official. Vic Reeves really is funny.

The Medics were asked to record a version of Elvis Presley's 'Burning Love' that was to be used as the soundtrack for a US film about the witches of Salem. Clive dressed up as a comedy Las Vegas Elvis for a hilarious video, which for some reason hasn't shown its face on YouTube, yet. The record wasn't released as a single but appears on their second album.

I have never really liked being interviewed on camera or on radio, but it was something I couldn't shy away from, it was expected of me and if I was to continue to promote my enterprises I just had to deal with it. However I still didn't like it.

The well known jazz musician, George Melly, came into Planet Alice one day looking for an unusual hat. I think he lived in the Portobello Road area and it didn't take him long before he made sure that everyone in the immediate vicinity knew who he was, if they didn't already. He must have tried on every hat in the shop before settling on a purple crushed velvet floppy top hat. The hat was designed with a cool and funky psychedelic chick in mind, not an ancient short chubby jazz legend. However a sale was a sale and what could I say. Are you sure about this George?

A few weeks later and I was being interviewed by a TV company and they asked me what sort of people came into Planet Alice. "All sorts really," I replied, "George Melly came in the other day." "Really?" said the interviewer. "Yes, really." I replied. At which point everyone in the shop burst into laughter. "Cut!" said the director "Let's do that again, isn't there anyone more fashionable you could name?" "Of course," I replied. So we started again. "What sort of people come into Planet Alice?" asked the interviewer. "All sorts really" I replied, "Kylie Minogue came in the other day". "Really?" said the interviewer. "Yes, really." I replied. Once again everyone burst into laughter and once again the interview was stopped. It really was quite funny; I guess you had to be there. Every time I ever saw George Melly on TV I remembered that interview. Really? Yes really.

Towards the end of 1987, IRS, The Medics record label, fulfilled their contractual obligation by releasing their second studio album, and two more singles. The album was called *I Keep Thinking It's Tuesday (Two Pieces of Cloth Carefully Stitched Together)*, the same title as the Alice In Wonderland film from 1984. And the singles were 'More' and 'Drive.... He Said.' A video was recorded for 'More' but despite a bit of air play and a few showings of the video on TV, the record didn't chart, neither did the follow up and the record company decided that enough was enough and dropped The Medics like a sack of potatoes.

That was it, The Medics had had their brief time as a number one pop group and now it was over. You could say that it was better to have had success once and to have lost it than to have never had it at all. And after all, let us not forget, the Medics weren't necessarily supposed to have had that success in the first place, but you try telling Clive that.

But they were still a great live band, no doubt about it, and there are thousands of bands out there who would wish that they had a front man capable of getting an audience going like Clive could.

1987 had been another amazing year and everything seemed to be going from strength to strength. Although The Medics may have peaked, it seems that Planet Alice, with two shops so far and the possibility of opening more, seemed to have a great future ahead. Alice In Wonderland was as busy as ever, Jayne County played there a couple more times that year as did Voodoo Child, The Surfin' Lungs, Mournblade, The Incredible Zombie Rockers, The Grizeldas, Bone Idle And The Layabouts, Underground Zero, The Eight Track Cartridge Family and the winner of the best name of the year: The Junior Manson Slags. However with everything being so cool for so long, maybe things won't be quite so fantastic in 1988....

Madeleine models for Planet Alice

Tony, Kim and Me at Planet Alice, Portobello Road (Beer cans on the counter?)

Webcore on stage at Alice In Wonderland

CHAPTER SEVENTEEN

THE CURSE OF THE GREEN DRAGON

In which I go off the rails for a while, Nigella Lawson props up the bar at Alice In Wonderland and Planet Alice continues to be the weirdest shop in town.

One night after Alice's Clive was back at my flat and we were talking, drinking and listening to music when for no apparent reason the video recorder suddenly switched itself on and the tape constantly fast forwarded and rewound itself completely on its own. Clive and I watched in amazement as the video machine went mental, whirring away, backwards and forwards completely unaided. We switched it off from the mains and Clive said, "That's always happening around me, machines just switch themselves on and off for no reason at all." Clive eventually crashed out on the sofa and I went to bed.

The next morning we were still talking about the weirdness of the video recorder the night before and Clive went home. After he had gone I looked around for the TV remote control and eventually found it under the cushion of the sofa. The same cushion on the same sofa that Clive had been sitting on the previous night. Mystery solved, Clive hadn't been using his magical electro psychic powers to manipulate machinery, he was totally unaware that he had been sitting on the remote control and as he rocked back and forth inadvertently pressed the buttons making the video recorder operate.

I had a huge green Chinese dragon tattooed on my arm to cover up some other tattoos I had done as a teenager.

When Clive saw it he told me that he had bad feelings about the tattoo, he reckoned it signified evil and would bring me untold bad luck. I listened to what Clive said but after the video remote control incident I couldn't quite take him seriously. What does he know? I thought.

1988 started badly for me and I had a whole load of crap in my personal life to deal with. My sister, Deborah, and her unborn child died suddenly and a few weeks later I found out that my mum had got cancer and wouldn't be too far behind her. Everything that could have gone wrong did. I had a car crash, my new flat I had just bought in West Hampstead got burgled, I then had my American Express card stolen and someone went on a major shopping spree at my expense.

Next I got mugged of my takings after a night at Alice's, and the next day was taken into a police station (although released without charge) for drinking in an un-licensed bar. Virtually every day for a month something bad happened.

A few days after my sister's funeral my shop was terrorised by a wild five year old Portobello Road street urchin who caused absolute havoc. The girl was totally out of control and ran around the shop pulling all the clothes off the rails and pushing the mannequins over. Kim and I ran after her trying to stop her but she was fast and slippery. Eventually we managed to bundle her out of the shop. We locked the door behind her and she kicked the toughened glass which cracked and slid down to the pavement like a guillotine. The five year old managed to pull her leg away just in the nick of time as the deadly shard crashed to the ground. She ran away laughing.

I made some enquiries and found out where she lived, I called round to speak to her parents and her father answered the door. I asked him whether he knew that his five-year-old daughter was running around the Portobello Road causing mayhem and he just shrugged his shoulders and said he really didn't give a fuck. I told him about the glass door and he told me that I was lucky she didn't lose a leg or else he would have sued me. Unbelievable.

During this seriously horrible period of my life I arrived at the shop one morning to find Kim in tears, the shop had just been looted by a gang of thugs from Brixton. They had just walked in and started helping themselves to the stock. Kim told them to put the stuff back and they just laughed and walked out carrying their booty. I told Kim to sit down and went over the road to the café to get her a cappuccino.

Whilst I was queuing for the coffee the looters came back and helped themselves to another few rails of clothes. They had taken virtually everything in the shop and my insurance didn't cover it.

After that incident and the countless other bad things that had happened I told Kim that if I was a character in a soap opera, people would think that the storylines were a bit too far fetched and all of those things couldn't possibly happen to one person in such a short period of time. "If I wake up tomorrow and discover that a bomb had just gone off outside my house," I said, "It wouldn't surprise me."

The following morning I awoke to the sound of sirens and I looked out of the window of my flat to see fire engines, police cars and dozens of people in fluorescent jackets. The whole area outside my flat was two foot under water, the street was cordoned off and it was total chaos. A bomb hadn't gone off, it was nothing quite so sinister. Apparently British Telecom were digging up the road to lay new cables and had hit a gas main. When the gas board arrived to sort out the problem they dug through a water pipe. Even so, it looked like a bomb really had gone off.

Kit, or Suzy Creamcheese, DJ'ed at Alice In Wonderland and also put on the lightshow along with her boyfriend Wizz. They worked on the Mystery Trips and Kit also worked part time at Planet Alice. She started arriving late for the club and sometimes didn't bother turning up at the shop on her day to work either. I called her into my office and asked what was happening and she burst into tears and said that she had been diagnosed as having cancer and had only a few months to live. Kit was a bubbly Mancunian with dreadlocks and leather patchwork trousers (from Planet Alice of course.) and was good fun to have around. I was devastated, especially having just lost my sister and being told that my mother was also on her way out, both due to cancer.

Kit and Wizz split up and Kit came to me in a flood of tears and said that it was upsetting her having him working at Alice's and that if he didn't leave, she would. I broke the news to Wizz who got really upset. "You don't understand," he said, "You don't know what problems she's got." "Actually, I do, and I'm sorry Wizz but that's the way it is." I replied, thinking he was talking about the cancer.

A couple of weeks later I started to notice that the till was always under on a Thursday, the day that Kit and Claudia, Vom's girlfriend, worked. I questioned Kit about it and she said: "I didn't want to tell tales but Claudia is always making mistakes and can't work the till." The petty cash box was also missing money after a Thursday and so putting two and two together felt I had no alternative but to let Claudia go.

A week or so after Claudia's untimely exit, and with Kit still either turning up late or not at all, the penny suddenly dropped. She wasn't dying of cancer, she was a heroin addict who was stealing from the till, stealing from petty cash, forging my signature on cheques taken from the back of the chequebook and basically ripping me off rotten. She had used my own personal grief to hide her addiction, playing on my vulnerability at a time when I was at my lowest ebb. I told her to leave the shop and the club and we never saw her again. That is what heroin does to people, they become so desperate they don't care who they rip off or how they do it. Claudia I am so sorry.

Unable to cope with what was going on in my life I decided the best way forward was to drink. I'd wake up in the morning and drink, I'd go to the shop to work and I'd drink, I'd go home to get changed and I'd drink. I would go out to a gig and I'd drink, I would then go onto a club and I'd drink and I would then go onto a party and I'd drink. I would then go home and drink, sleep for a bit and then start all over again. I went on a bender for thirteen days and have virtually no idea what happened during that time.

I do remember ending up one night at five in the morning in this strange place with these strange people and after going down two flights of stairs to the loo thought to myself, what the fuck am I doing? I had left my cigarettes upstairs but who cares? I had to get out of there. I ran out and flagged down a taxi to take me back home to West Hampstead. When I got there my key wouldn't open the entrance door and I then realised that that was my old flat which I had moved out of a couple of weeks previously and I couldn't remember where I had moved to.

I walked up and down the neighbouring streets, I knew my new flat was in West Hampstead somewhere but I couldn't remember where, everything looked the same, rows and rows of Victorian houses converted into flats, all of them identical but none of them looking familiar. I couldn't even remember the road name let alone the number.

Eventually I gave up looking and remembered I had a shop in Portobello. I then flagged down another cab and asked him to take me there. I arrived at Planet Alice and let myself in; I headed straight for the stock room where I fell asleep on a pile of bright pink, phosphorous green and electric blue fake fur jackets.

That was how Kim and Tony found me when they opened the shop a few hours later. They let me sleep for another couple of hours and then Kim told me that I really had to sort myself out. I responded by walking out and going to the Frog And Firkin pub around the corner where I drank beer and tequilas for the rest of the day, buying drinks for complete strangers, anyone who would talk to me got a drink. At about ten o'clock I staggered out and got a cab home via the off license where I bought a couple of bottles of vodka.

When I arrived at my flat I put on a record and proceeded to work my way through the vodka. A couple of hours, and another Velvet Underground album later, and I started feeling really weird. I had been seriously drunk before, more times than I cared to mention but this was different and although I hadn't slept properly for weeks I was wide awake but still kept drifting in and out of consciousness. I felt myself slipping away, somewhere I had never been before. I saw my dead sister above my head reaching out for me and I held out my hand and closed my eyes.

I nearly went to whatever the place I was destined for but at the last second fought against it, snatching back my hand and shaking myself back to reality. I managed to stand up and staggered into the kitchen where I poured the rest of the vodka down the sink. I wasn't ready to die yet; I had more stuff still to do.

That incident was so vivid and was like nothing I had previously experienced or have done since. I am absolutely convinced that that night I came very close to drinking myself to death. This was a big wake up call for me, I was in serious danger of self-destructing and I realised I had to do something about it. After my near death experience I calmed down considerably, and knuckled down to running my businesses without the interference of copious amounts of alcohol.

One thing that didn't suffer from the curse of the Green Dragon was the club. It carried on as usual, as popular as ever, packed out week in week out whoever was playing. Clive had given up working at Alice's and Chris was now the main DJ The style of music played had developed and changed over the years and Chris was forever bringing in new stuff to play.

As Planet Alice's reputation continued to grow hardly a week went by when we weren't featured in one fashion publication or another. We had maybe twenty different designers working under the Planet Alice umbrella with all designs exclusive to us and available nowhere else and each item proudly carried our new purple and black or silver and black label.

Talking of umbrellas we even had our own collection of psychedelic rainwear, mini macs with matching umbrellas designed to be worn with very little else. They went down a storm. Hah!

One night at Alice's a slightly chubby brunette was chatting me up at the bar. I asked her what her name was and she said it was Nigella. "That's an unusual name." I said. "Yes," she replied I was named after my father, Nigel. What's your name?" "Christian." I replied. "I like the name Christian." She said. "Yeah," I replied. "I was named after my father, Jesus Christ."

Okay so it wasn't the best chat up line but remember, she was chatting ME up. Later that evening someone told me she was the daughter of Nigel Lawson, the Chancellor of the Exchequer. There were a few Alice regulars whose fathers' were politicians but none so high profile as Nigel Lawson at that time, second only to Margaret Thatcher as being the most important politician in the Country. However, these days if you did a survey more people would have heard of celebrity chef and domestic goddess; Nigella Lawson, (not so chubby but still very curvy), than her father, Nigel Lawson, the former Chancellor of the Exchequer in Maggie Thatcher's Tory government.

Stiv Bators, punk legend and former singer with The Dead Boys and Lords Of The New Church came to Alice's a few times. He was with Johnny Thunders on our second anniversary, he got in, Johnny didn't. Stiv was another one who died too soon, pipping his former band members (from The Whores Of Babylon), Johnny Thunders and Dee Dee Ramone to the post. Despite decades of needle abuse, unlike the other two, it wasn't the drugs that got him in the end. He was run over by a taxi in Paris in 1990. Vom, The Medics drummer, played with Stiv for a while.

Planet Alice was getting quite a reputation for itself, in the fashion press, in the tabloids as well as among the people who bought the clothes, whether it was the clubbers and party people or the wholesalers. Because the shop was so different from any other shop and the clothes were like nothing else available anywhere, people would come from all over the country to visit. Tourists visiting London who had read about Planet Alice would also make a special pilgrimage. If they couldn't find an outfit that they liked or that fitted, they would buy a tee shirt, a poster, some jewellery or maybe just a badge.

Some people would come into the shop and just hang around to soak up the atmosphere, I have to say, those people weren't exactly my favourite customers, even the people who just bought a badge after trying on half the clothes in the shop at least contributed towards my turnover. Still, I just had to accept it.

Occasionally we would get people with no intention whatsoever to buy anything and would just come in to gawp. "My mum says this is a weirdos shop." Said one teenager to her friend as they looked around the place.

One day my mum was in Leeds visiting relatives when she picked up a rather large goth punk girl hitch hiker. My mum noticed that the girl was wearing a tee shirt with a distorted Planet Alice logo stretched across her ample chest. "My son is the owner of Planet Alice." Said my mum to the chubby young thing. I don't know who was the most surprised, my mum coming across a Planet Alice fan so far from London or the fat goth who was given a lift by the mother of the owner of her favourite shop.

The girl then told my mum how much she loved the stuff at Planet Alice but after making a special trip to London couldn't find anything in her size other than the extra large tee-shirt with the logo on which she wore to death. Remember we only did sizes eight, ten and twelve for girls. My mum took down the girls' details and said she would have a word with me and ask me to make a special item of clothing in her size just for her, she also said that she would pay for it and send it onto her. That was the sort of thing my mum did. Thanks mum.

The girl, then gave my mum her address and said she would really like a mini skirt in a size 22. Size 22? When the skirt came back from the manufacturers I thought there had been a mistake, it was the size of an average village and I dread to think what the girl looked like when she proudly wore it out clubbing on the following Saturday night. Still she was happy and I can't knock that. That was precisely why we were so sizeist, they were Planet Alice clothes that had to be worn by people who could carry it off.

We were constantly being asked by people from all over the world to send them a catalogue, problem was, we didn't have one. I couldn't expand the mail order business without one so I booked a studio and photographer and organised a photo shoot. I roped in a bunch of Alice regulars to be models and the low budget catalogue was printed and sent out. A girl from Leicester ordered every single item on the list, I was a bit suspicious at first, thinking she was going to copy them, especially as a few weeks later she asked us to send anything else Planet Alice that wasn't in the brochure.

She spent a small fortune with us, but I was not about to argue. I needn't have worried about her intentions, though, she was just Planet Alice mad and sent me a photograph of her in her bedroom, the walls were covered from floor to ceiling in Alice In Wonderland and Planet Alice posters and a rail stretched from one wall to another completely full of Planet Alice clothes. Wow, what a collection, I wonder if she has still got it today, or whether she sold it on E-Bay. Maybe she just chucked the whole lot in the bin once she'd got bored of it all. Who knows?

*Despite the curse of the Green Dragon;
I still manage a smile*

Planet Alice psychedelic rainwear

CHAPTER EIGHTEEN

DROP KICK ME JESUS THROUGH THE GOALPOSTS OF LIFE

The Osmonds don't play at Alice In Wonderland but Crazyhead do. The Skateboard Party is a great success and Wayne Sleep is spotted pirouetting at the club.

Choosing the bands that played at Alice's was always a challenge and I was inundated with demo tapes of all sorts of different bands and from that I had to choose who would play and who wouldn't. One band got so fucked off that I wouldn't give them a gig that they took to phoning me up at the shop threatening to kill me. Now let me get this straight, I won't give you a gig because your band is crap, you write crap songs and you can't sing, and you want to kill me?

For every thirty tapes I received (I'm guessing), only one band would get a chance to play at the club. Being a regular helped, so did having a good name. Alternatively having a cute girl in the band usually did the trick.

One band that approached me and managed to get through the red tape, were a group called Victims Of The Pestilence. They were really nice people, looked sort of rock'n'roll and their music sounded great. They were from out of town somewhere and had quite a following, they told me they usually brought a couple of coaches of fans with them, all of whom would pay to get in. All good news so far.

On the night of their gig when the doors opened at ten a long string of punters filed into the club. Normally people didn't come to the club until eleven or twelve so it was fantastic to be so busy so early.

I began to notice that the crowd didn't quite look right. A bit too fresh faced and a bit too tidy. There seemed to be a lot of skipping going on and I was getting a bit concerned. Mick was beginning to get worried that he would run out of soft drinks and as the usual leather jacket spiked hair brigade of Alice regulars started filing in they too looked around at this new influx of happy smiling people and started to wonder what was going on. "Who's playing tonight?" asked one of the psycho punk Alice people. "The Osmonds?"

I decided to put the band on early so the coaches could take the band's fan club back to Welwyn Garden City or wherever they had come from. As the band launched into their first song: 'Jesus Gave Me Rock'n'roll' and the group's disciples started swaying and clapping the penny eventually dropped. The name should have been a big enough clue and when they played their second number: 'Pray For Their Souls' I realised that they were a God squad band. Still, never mind, the good little boys and girls left as soon as the band finished allowing the usual reprobates to reclaim their club.

The well-known ballet dancer and future *'I'm A Celebrity Get Me Out Of Here!'* contestant, Wayne Sleep, came down to Alice's one night. I don't know why or how he came to be there, he was not our normal Alice punter but there he was as small as life standing up at the bar with a bunch of his friends. He was quite pissed when he arrived and as the evening wore on got even more so. The drunker he got the camper he got and for no apparent reason started doing his ballet poses. Next thing he was pirouetting and in a packed club was causing a bit of a stir.

Smiffy, Zodiac Mindwarp's roadie, asked me if 'that bloke' by the bar was part of the entertainment, "No." I replied. "That's Wayne Sleep, God knows what he's doing here." Smiffy glared at him and said to me "Can I deck him?" "No." I said. "You leave him alone and behave yourself."
A well-known character in the music business, a bloke called Strangler, was a regular face at Alice's for a while. Apart from being Ian Dury's minder, he also used to do the odd bit of work as a roadie or security for various other bands. He was introduced to the Alice scene through Andrew and Jenny, who apart from working with The Medics also managed the superb Ian Dury And The Blockheads.

Strangler was a big scary bloke with a mop of curly hair and a badly scarred face. He looked like he had only just survived a train crash. Such was his beauty he was on the books of the Ugly Agency and landed a part as a freak in the classic Peter Greenaway film, *'The Cook, The Thief, His Wife And Her Lover'*

After I had split up with my long-term girlfriend, various people tried to set me up with suitable replacements. "I know this cracking bird," said Strangler, one night, "She's about six foot tall, blonde, drop dead gorgeous with legs up to her armpits. I'll bring her to Alice's next week." The following Monday and Strangler turned up with this stunning looking blonde, even taller than me in her heels, wearing black leather studded hot pants, a leather crop-top and thigh length high heeled boots. Rod Stewart would have thought it was Christmas every day with this one. "Christian," said Strangler, "Meet Trixie."

I chatted to her for a while but soon realised what her nocturnal occupation was. The name kind of gave it away. "Why are you called Trixie?" I asked, my tongue firmly in my cheek, "Are you a magician?" Trixie looked at me blankly. "No," she said, "Do I look like a magician?"

Thanks, Strangler, but I think I'll pass on this one.

Another Monday night and Strangler was at Alice's with Lemmy from Motörhead. They were standing at the bar next to Clive and I chatting up two young girls. When Lemmy turned around to talk to us the girls decided to seize the opportunity and escape from the veteran rockers. "Lemmy they're getting away from us!" said a worried Strangler. Lemmy responded in his familiar gravelly rock'n'roll-battered voice; "That's because we're a lot older and a lot fatter." Brilliant.

No one really knows how Strangler died. He was arrested for being drunk and disorderly and thrown into a police cell. The next morning when the police went to wake him up they discovered he was dead. There have been all sorts of conspiracy theories surrounding this unfortunate death, but with a lack of proper information I'm not saying anything.

The Mutoid Waste Company were an alternative arts group, for want of a better description, formed by Portobello local, Joe Rush. They made sculptures out of bits of old cars and other scrap materials and put on exhibitions and parties at warehouses and other disused places that they squatted.

Joe Rush would often hang out at Planet Alice and from time to time came down to Alice In Wonderland with some of his crew. After smashing up the front of my Triumph Spitfire sports car, I had this idea that it would be really cool to customise it and turn it into a Mad Max style vehicle, it was a bit of a hairdressers car anyway. I wanted to convert the car into a giant purple lobster with snapping claws on either wing and the Planet Alice logo painted on the sides. If anyone could do it, The Mutoid Waste Company could so I spoke to Joe and he was well up for it.

We planned it all out and he gave me a price of which I agreed. Unfortunately the lobster vehicle was one idea that never reached fruition. I sold the car and abandoned the lobster idea for the moment at least.

In October 1988 we decided to celebrate Alice In Wonderland's fifth anniversary with a special event at The Town and Country club. We had planned the usual birthday party at Gossips with The Medics playing under a pseudonym as usual but wanted something bigger and different in another venue.

I had this idea that it would be really good to build a huge skateboard half-pipe on the stage and in between the bands have professional skateboarders doing their stuff. I had previously thought of doing something similar with surfers but the logistics of tons of water and wave machines was just a bit too adventurous even by Alice standards.

I co-promoted the show with John Curd and we set up a full size half-pipe on the stage at The Town and Country club, which took the best part of a day to construct. In the interest of health and safety (see how sensible we had become these days?) we had a net draped in front of it to catch low flying boards before they knocked the heads off the audience.

For the first time (other than at *Acid Daze*) on an Alice event, The Medics didn't headline, by then their popularity had declined and were unlikely to sell out a two thousand capacity venue. Gaye Bykers On Acid were the headlining act with The Medics, under the name of Gwyllym And The Raspberry Flavoured Cat supporting. Bone Idle And The Layabouts were also on the bill as well as the obligatory Alice DJ's, lights and lasers. It was an excellent show, the likes of which had never been done before and probably never since. And despite skateboards flying around and skaters crashing to the ground no-one was seriously hurt.

In the wake of Zodiac Mindwarp, a number of bands appeared on the scene in a similar psycho-metal vein, Gaye Bykers, The Batfish Boys, and a great band called Crazyhead.

Crazyhead played a couple of times at Alice's, including a fan-club party, and were beginning to get a strong following. Ian Astbury had swapped his flares and hippy image for a leather jacket biker look and The Cult were on that same bandwagon. They booked Crazyhead to support them on tour and for a while there was a bit of a buzz about the band.

Me and DJ Chris Duffell at the Skateboard Party

Another crazy night at Alice In Wonderland

Mary from Gaye Bykers On Acid with Tony at Planet Alice

CHAPTER NINETEEN

THE WEIRDO TERRAPIN GIRL

In which I am accused of being the Godfather of Acid House, the Bangles pose in Planet Alice kit, Bob Geldof comes to Alice's by mistake and we get to meet the Weirdo Terrapin Girl and Lady Posh Knickers.

Acid House was sweeping the nation and the tabloids were full of it. Raves were happening every weekend where thousands of people would travel to some warehouse or a tent in a field to take drugs and party all night. Ravers started coming in to Planet Alice to buy our psychedelic tee shirts, they weren't the usual Alice types, but a new breed of chavs that had nothing to do with Alice's whatsoever.

One day a couple of young hoodies walked into the shop and one said to the other: "This is the original Acid House shop, the bloke that owns it is the bloke that started the whole thing." No I fucking didn't, I thought to myself, I don't even like Acid House.

Various newspapers and journals including *Rave* magazine, came up with a similar story, citing the Mystery Trips as the forerunner of raves and Planet Alice as the only shop dedicated to selling 'rave clothing.' I was quite flattered in some ways that I was regarded as being so influential. The Mystery Trips were, indeed, long before raves and Acid House parties, but they were totally different.

Whereas on an Alice trip the punters were taken to the event by coach or train, at a rave you had to make your own way there. Also raves were highly profitable gigs for the promoters, our Mystery Trips were always planned to be non-profit making.

I went to a rave once, and it was crap. After spending an hour or so driving round the M25 and queuing outside telephone boxes dialling a constantly engaged number, we eventually heard a recorded message that gave the whereabouts of the party. It was of course in the opposite direction and we eventually arrived at a hastily erected marquee in a muddy farmers' field. Dodgy looking spivs were at the door, demanding £50 admission. The show had been advertised at £20 entrance, but with a captive audience who had travelled half the night to get there, they thought they could charge what they liked.

We refused to pay their prices, so turned around and went home. The Alice In Wonderland Mystery Trips were memorable events for those that experienced them, many saying they were the best nights of their lives. My rave experience was memorable but only because it made me realise what rip-off merchants there were out there. As for Planet Alice, I never set out to cater for chavs that's for sure.

I happened to see a banner headline on BBC's Teletext saying: *The Godfather Of Acid House*. I clicked on the story and was amazed to find a ten page 'in depth' story about me, Alice In Wonderland and Planet Alice. I wasn't interviewed for the article, but someone had researched the story and somehow thought that I started the whole Acid House scene. I didn't, I can assure you. However, sales of tee shirts increased considerably (as did shop lifting) so I sat back and let them think what they wanted to.

The Bangles were sort of label stable-mates with Doctor And The Medics. They were signed to MCA who distributed IRS records, and were managed by IRS boss

Miles Copeland for a while. The all girl group from the States had a few massive hit records in the eighties, but after various internal disputes, went their separate ways. Whilst promoting their latest single, (don't ask me which one,) they bought a whole load of Planet Alice gear and posed dressed from head to foot in patchwork jackets, trousers and mini skirts. I'm afraid I can't remember much about it but I came across a photo in my press cuttings book. Blimey, how vague is this story?

Nutmeg became one of the new Alice house bands, playing every three or four weeks for a couple of years. They were one of the best bands that ever played at the club, and had they been around a few years previously could have possibly gone on to much bigger and better things. Their amazing lead singer, Tom Dalpra, led the four lads from Cambridge. Tom was a sheet metal worker by day and a kamikaze performer by night; he looked and acted like a young Iggy Pop circa The Stooges 1969.

One reviewer likened him to a sixties Mick Jagger with a feather stuck up his backside. A poetic description indeed and one not far from the truth. Whenever they played at Alice's they went down a storm, with people coming specifically to see them. With his long greasy hair, the bare-chested Tom would thrash around the floor to songs like 'In England They're Going Mental', 'Real Live Wire' and 'I'm In The Mood.'

One night I was at a Nutmeg gig in Finsbury Park when Tom, during a guitar solo, shinned up the lighting rig by the side of the stage and climbed out of a skylight window above. He then ran across the roof, slid down a drainpipe and ran back into the venue through the front door where he tore through the audience back to the stage. He then jumped onto the stage, turned around and dived over the audience's heads to the bar area beyond where he crash landed into a trolley full of empty beer bottles. He really didn't give a fuck and had a total reckless regard to his safety and of those around him. But what a performer.

They released an album on their own label that whilst the songs are all there, unfortunately the production lets them down, still, it's bloody good. Despite being managed by Hawkwind's manager, Doug Willis, and being courted by a string of major record labels, Nutmeg split up. Apparently the untimely death of founder member, Matthew Hobbs was the deciding factor. Their bass player, Simon, ran off with Alice's door girl, Marcella and I heard that Tom went back to the foundry to return to his proper job.

In recent years Tom returned with a new band called The Lonely and has released a video called *Live Wire Or Wasted Soul?* a documentary about his career. Check them out on YouTube; there are some great clips.

In the very early days of Alice In Wonderland I had this idea that it would be a bit of a wheeze if the Alice regulars could write a series of fairy stories. Yep, not my best idea admittedly, I was going through a Marc Bolan Tyrannosaurus Rex thing at the time. So a few of our groovy Alice folk humoured my not-so-brilliant-idea and came up with a selection of psychedelic tales mainly about pixies and wizards sliding down rainbows and stuff and I would print the stories and leave them around the tables for the other punters to read. Like I said, not my best idea that's for sure. However, no other club was immature enough to do it so what the hell. The lovely Alice punters loved them, or so they said. And then there was Glen's effort.

Glen was one of the original members of The Medics Essex contingent and came to the second night of Alice's when The Medics played there for the first time. I spoke to Glen that night telling him how pissed off I was because his hair was longer than mine. It seemed to matter then, these days I guess we should all be thankful that we actually still have hair.

Glen became an Alice regular from then on and moved to London to be closer to the scene. He participated in my 'fairy story' idea and caused even the broadest minded Alice regular to raise an eyebrow. No pixies or wizards sliding down rainbows in Glen's world, his story consisted of every dark side of his personality thrown into a bag, shuffled about and then scattered over the page. I can't print this, I thought, when I read it. But in the true spirit of Alice In Wonderland everything-goes, I went along with it. Publish and be damned.

A few years later and the Alice regulars looked aghast as Glen turned up at the club dressed as a woman. Not as a comedy pantomime dame woman in drag, but as a fairly convincing girl. In metro-sexual eighties London boys wearing make-up was not un-common, but Glen took it one step further: Mini skirt, tights, handbag and everything. Smiffy even went to chat him up before he was told that underneath the make-up, blouse and false tits was a very confused Glen.

He soon became known as Glen or Glenda after the cult sixties B-Movie of that name which was about an equally confused cross-dressing Glen who had a penchant for pink fluffy cardigans. Blimey, Alice In Wonderland seemed to attract the oddest people. Excellent, that was what was supposed to happen.

Planet Alice clothes were always bizarre, but with the arrival of our new designers, Dolly Daydream and Anne Delaney became even more so. Mini skirts and tops made out of discarded telephone cards and satin tops with risqué see-through plastic love hearts or fake fur love hearts strategically positioned on the front. The new collections received copious amounts of fashion press and TV coverage, including a spot on a Saturday morning kids show on BBC1.

A few weeks after that TV show I was walking down Oxford Street and noticed that Top Shop had dressed their mannequins in rip-off Planet Alice gear, including the furry heart top. What a fucking cheek. I guess I should have been flattered that Top Shop thought our designs were that good that they had to be copied but I wasn't, I was fucked off, they were making cheap money out of our hard work. I was beginning to get the measure of this fashion business.

An Alice regular called Sparky approached me one night with his own idea. He wanted to be a human joke-box at Alice In Wonderland. I welcomed any intuitive ideas, after all I had nothing to lose, so I agreed. He turned up with this large cardboard box that he set up in a corner by the fire escape and he climbed inside. I tried the joke-box out before the club opened by pushing a coin in the slot and pulling the cord. "What's yellow, looks like a banana and tastes like a banana?" squeeked a muffled voice. "I dunno," I replied "What is yellow, looks like a banana and tastes like a banana?" I waited as Sparky shuffled about in the box before replying: "A banana!" I thought for a moment and said: "But Sparky, that's just not funny." "It gets better," he replied. It didn't.

The night Sparky decided to launch his joke box the club was packed to the gunnels and poor Sparky was stuck in the corner in his cardboard box. It was only a matter of time before the marauding punters, crammed into the confined space of Alice's, knocked his cardboard box to the ground and he was left waving his legs about, unable to get up or out. It was hilarious, Sparky's joke box really was funny, but not in the way it was intended.

Apart from The Bootleg Beatles, The Counterfeit Stones and Bjorn Again, there didn't seem to be tribute bands around in 1989. Roman Jugg, guitarist of The Damned and Naz Nomad, Alice regular and good friend came up with the idea of doing The Romanes: a Ramones tribute band. With Roman on guitar and I think the former Volcanoes front man, Jan, was on vocals, as for the rest of the band, I have no idea. They were brilliant, almost as good as the real thing, and although my cheeky advertising might have suggested that the real Ramones were playing and the club was packed solid, no one complained or asked for their money back. So I did it again.

After the success of The Romanes, we decided to organise a Sex Pistols tribute act, called The Sox Pastels. They were basically the band members of a group that played at Alice's regularly at the time, Los Bastardos. They dressed for the occasion, 'Johnny' wearing a bondage shirt, 'Steve' wearing a knotted handkerchief on his head, 'Sid' with a leather jacket and bloodied chest and 'Paul' wearing a union jack vest. By a complete coincidence, a real Pistol, former bass player Glen Matlock was at the club that night. He had been to Alice's a couple of times before but said he had no idea The Sox Pastels were playing live. He thought they were quite good, I thought they were excellent.

I guess it was inevitable that just as I got into punk and later became inspired to start the Alice thing, original punks would now come down to Alice In Wonderland. As well as those previously mentioned: The Damned, Siouxsie Sioux, Jayne County, Glen Matlock, Johnny Thunders, Chrissie Hynde, Stiv Bators, Jeffrey Lee Pierce and Charlie Harper, there were a whole bunch of others that I remember. Mick Rossi from Slaughter And The Dogs was a regular, Ten Pole Tudor came a few times and then there was Gene October. Gene October was once the lead singer of Chelsea and he came to Alice's virtually every night in the early days, the gay predator hanging round the bar looking out for his next victim. A bit of a sad case really, he got a job working at MCA records who were the distributors for IRS, Doctor And The Medics record label. He said that he was employed as a talent scout but when we bumped into him at the MCA head office he was actually the cleaner.

Steve Ignorant of Crass also used to come down, usually with his mate Charlie Harper of UK Subs fame. Blimey, I've just had a thought. Was he the shoe bloke ("You've got to let me in I'm a friend of Charlie Harper's!") from the first Scala Film Festival? Surely not.

When I was a punk in 1977 I used to love to go and see a band called The Adverts who released a couple of great singles, 'One Chord Wonders' and 'Gary Gilmore's Eyes'. So when I was approached by their singer, TV Smith, to play at Alice's I jumped at the chance.

What goes around comes around, they say, and recently I have been in talks with TV Smith's partner and the former Adverts bass player, Gaye Advert about an art exhibition. The exhibition called 'Punk And Beyond' features various punk musicians from back in the day, including me.

Another female bassist; the majestic Patricia Morrissey of The Gun Club, Fur Bible, Sisters Of Mercy and The Damned used to hang out frequently at Alice's. She was a good friend of a Planet Alice designer, Cathy Renshaw, and occasionally came back to my flat with Cathy and a bunch of others to party. She went on to marry Dave Vanian of The Damned and together they had a baby girl.

Shane MacGowan of The Pogues could also be spotted at Alice's in the early days and turned up at one of our film festivals at the Scala in his native King's Cross. I guess as a person who was always known for his outlandish recklessness, Alice In Wonderland was perfect.

Animal from the Anti Nowhere League showed up one night. Zodiac Mindwarp before Zodiac Mindwarp. These are just some of the punks I remember and I am sure there were dozens of others I didn't hear about. Anyway, I hoped they liked it.

In October 1989 Alice In Wonderland celebrated its sixth anniversary. The Medics played of course and Clive returned to the decks to DJ. for the first time in what seemed liked ages. I think Clive was beginning to realise just how much he missed Alice's. He had been engrossed in Wales for a couple of years now, starting a family and messing around with his snails and somehow Alice's was no longer a priority.

After the night a whole bunch of people came back to my flat in West Hampstead to carry on partying. We put on some music, opened some bottles and chatted away as was the norm. There was a strange girl there who seemed to be very interested in my terrapins that I kept in a tank in the sitting room. An hour or so later and I became aware that someone was constantly flushing the toilet at the other end of the flat. I asked DJ Chris who the girl was and he said, "I've no idea, I thought she was with you." "Nothing to do with me", I replied, "I thought she was with you!"

It transpired that some random girl gate-crashed one of the cabs going back to my flat and just tagged along. Everyone thought she was with someone else. When she returned from the bathroom she stared at me with a glazed look in her eyes and said, "He's free now, he's free." I escorted her out of the flat and made sure she left for good. Puzzled by her comment I went to check on my reptiles and sure enough one of them was missing.

The bitch had flushed my pet terrapin down the bloody toilet.

One Monday evening Bob Geldof and his then wife, Paula Yates, came down to Alice's.... by mistake. They walked up to the reception desk and peered into the club at the lovely Alice freaks having fun among the fluttering toilet paper hanging from the ceiling. Wherever it was they wanted to be that night it wasn't the weird, wild and wonderful world of Alice In Wonderland that's for sure. "I told you this was the wrong place!" snorted Paula as she spun Bob round and pushed him back up the stairs, much to the amusement of the gathered Alice regulars.

It's a shame they didn't stay, they would have had a great time. The place was heaving; The Medics were playing that night and were brilliant as always. Bob and Paula's marriage was reportedly on the rocks at that time, and Bob's lousy sense of direction and wrong choice of club may have been the straw that broke the camels' back as a few years later they separated.

Unlike previous fashion and style moments, the Alice crowd never really got a collective name. Punks, hippies, goths, glam rockers, bikers, acid punks, psycho punks, rockabillies, psychobillies, beatniks, psychedelics, whatever, they were all there but there was no label. Loosely we called them Alice people. I heard a tape recently from an interview I did on Radio 2.

I had never heard it before but vaguely remember doing the interview. As part of the programme about the New Hippy scene of the eighties the producers also interviewed the man behind the book *Encyclopaedia Psychedelica*. In the interview the bloke gave the 'new brand of hippies' a name: Zippies. This was at the time when Americans loved the grouping of people and came up with names such as: Yuppies, Dinkies, Gappies, Nimbies etc. And they decided to call us Zippies. It never caught on. I didn't want to be called a Zippy and nor did anyone else.

For a few weeks, sometime in 1989, a Marilyn Monroe impersonator, calling herself Marilyn (obviously) hung out at Alice's. I first met her some eight years previously when she used to come to see the band I was playing in at the time, The Lollipop Sisters. Even then she was on a sharp decline and I remember at the beginning of the gig she would pass for a reasonable Monroe look-a-like but by the end of the show as the drink took its' toll she resembled more of a Diana Dors circa Adam Ant's *Prince Charming* video.

Now, another eight years down the line, she was well past her sell by date. I saw the original publicity photos from 1970 and she looked great, but now after years of serious drink and drugs addiction and God knows how many face lifts and plastic surgery operations she was just a fraction of her original self. In 1989 as the bookings for personal appearances as the real Marilyn had dried up she was reduced to working as a hostess at a seedy Soho strip joint. I guess under dim lighting and with layers of make-up a pissed randy middle-aged businessman found her acceptable and that was how she now made her living. After her shift she would come down to Alice In Wonderland but no one could take her seriously.

One day she decided enough was enough and she booked herself into a smart hotel, and after having a seriously expensive 'last supper' went up to her room, put on a pink satin nightdress, took a couple of handfuls of barbiturates and lay on the bed in her last dramatic pose to die. After spending the last twenty years impersonating Marilyn Monroe, she even had to impersonate her death.

She was found the next day by hotel staff wanting their bill settled. She died penniless, unloved and lonely, just like a few other Marilyn look-a-likes before her and I guess a few more Marilyn look-a-likes in the future.

Planet Alice was taking up a lot of my time during the last years of the eighties, I had taken on a few new designers and we continued to get lots of publicity in the fashion press. The wholesale orders were fantastic, although a bit of a strain on cash flow. We decided to exhibit at the Earls Court Show during London Fashion week. We got a few collections together and set up our stall so that we couldn't be missed. I had originally intended to park my 'lobster car' (had I got round to having it converted) outside Earls Court on double yellow lines and filming it as it got towed away.

The show was a phenomenal success for Planet Alice and the orders we received surpassed our expectations. Next problem was actually getting the orders manufactured in the agreed time scale. Our designers and manufacturers had to work flat out over the next few months and I even roped in my sister Nibs to bash out a few dozen pairs of patchwork trousers. We had orders from all over the world, including Iceland again, who this time ordered a hundred pairs of our Salvador Dali hot knickers, which were like hot pants only smaller, therefore even colder for the Icelanders.

Whereas my brothers Joe and Julian were regulars at Alice's, my parents weren't. It wasn't quite their thing. However they supported it right from the beginning and were quite proud of their sons' achievements. They usually showed up on the anniversary nights and mingled among the usual bunch of reprobates and no one gave them a second look. That was what Alice's was all about. On one occasion they even bought some friends down with them. I had to apologise for the dreadful smell in the toilets that night as the Smeg Monster decided that he too should come to the party.

Whilst writing this book my Dad died sort of unexpectedly. It's a shame he never got to read it even though he knew I was writing it. Apart from supporting me with his very large presence he also helped me by editing the *I Keep Thinking It's Tuesday* film as well as helping me with shop fittings and stuff.

One extremely busy night at Alice In Wonderland the club was packed to the gunnels and the punters were queuing five deep at the bar. I went to my special serving hatch by the cigarette machine to get a drink. The Alice DJ's were the only people allowed to be served there as this was the busy thoroughfare for the glass collectors. Unwilling to join the long queue, a stunning looking young girl with a black Clara Bow haircut wearing a black patent leather mini dress, matching thigh length stilettos and fishnets was pleading with the barman, Pedro, to serve her from the side hatch.

Pedro was having none of it but much to the annoyance of the patent leather beauty he poured me a pint. I felt sorry for the shiny young thing and feeling flush from an anticipated monster door takings I bought her a vodka and tonic. Later on that evening I bumped into her again and she reciprocated by buying me a drink and we got chatting. It turned out that she was Lady Arabella Whoever, a member of a highly eminent aristocratic English family.

I've changed her name in respect for her high profile family, but Arabella, Annabella or whatever, she was soon re-christened Lady Posh Knickers by Leo of Los Bastados and the name stuck. She hung out at Alice's for a couple of months before vanishing one day, we lost touch and I never saw her again.

Many years later I read in the press that she had got married to a guy, let's call him Hugh, who was from an equally important family. Lady Posh Knickers was barely recognisable in the wedding photo, not a scrap of patent leather in sight and I thought to myself: I bet Hugh has absolutely no idea what his delightful English rose got up to at the wild and wacky Alice In Wonderland in the late eighties.

As the eighties faded and gave way to the new decade we could look back at another great selection of bands that rocked out at Alice's. Los Bastados, Sonja Kristina (again), The Babysnakes, The Earthmen, (Boys Wonder in disguise,) and Groovy Chainsaw and an excellent band called 638-938.

Nutmeg

Multi-coloured, multi-cultural Alice In Wonderland

The Bangles wear Planet Alice
(We didn't sell shoes)

CHAPTER TWENTY

OOPS I'VE JUST SOLD MY SHOP

The Doctor returns to Alice In Wonderland, the Portobello Road shop gets sold by mistake, The Sex Bitch Goddesses pull off the worst performance ever and another club regular bites the dust. I meet Beatle daughter, Lee Starkey and together we make plans to open a Planet Alice shop in Los Angeles.

Alice In Wonderland had by now been going for over six years and had sold out every night for as long as I could remember, but over the last few months I had noticed that it was gradually quietening down, and Monday nights were now only two thirds full. I hadn't advertised since the very early days, no leaflets, nothing, I didn't need to, but now things were changing and I had to do something about it.

Clive was by now seriously concreted into his new life in Wales and had virtually given up on The Medics, he hadn't been to Alice's for the past couple of years, with the exception of the birthday parties, and we missed him terribly. I rang him up and suggested he came back to Alice's to DJ He agreed. I sent out press releases, bleeding the snail farm story dry, I distributed loads of leaflets, heralding the return of the Doctor, and it worked. Clive returned on top form, continuing his much missed psycho-babble over his echo box and Alice In Wonderland was happening all over again after a minor blip.

Another great band that played at Alice's in the early 90's were Hippies With Muscles. They had a strong blues influence that every now and again exploded into rock'n'roll. Apart from a hippy or two (neither of which had muscles incidentally,) they had an Indian girl backing singer who used to give it loads on her tambourine dressed in full national costume; Sari, red spot on the forehead, everything, just like a Kumar from Number 42. She used to work for the Nationwide Building Society and would turn up at Alice's for the sound check in her smart blue uniform before changing into her Sari for the show.

During their set she would roll around the floor going loopy, what a sight. Something tells me that her strict religious parents had absolutely no idea what their daughter was up to in the evenings, neither I guess did the Nationwide Building Society. I once recorded one of their gigs on a mobile four-track for an album that never got released, it's good stuff.

By 1990 the UK was deep into a recession, Maggie Thatcher had pushed things just a bit too far and now we were all left to suffer the consequences. Consumer spending was down, no doubt about it, but at Planet Alice I was confident we could weather the storm. One day an Italian hairdresser approached me out of the blue and asked me if I would be interested in selling him the remainder of the lease on the Portobello Road premises, I said I wasn't, but he persisted and came up with an idea whereby I could sell him the lease but keep the basement area, which he would convert, and I'd also get to keep the front display window. I could then stay there rent-free. It was a tempting offer.

Another Italian hairdresser got wind of what the first guy was up to and came in with an even better offer, he didn't want another Italian hair salon on 'his' patch and would do everything he could to stop him. It was scissors at dawn and I was holding all the cards, able to negotiate a deal that would suit me.

In the end I sold the lease to the second guy for more than I could have possibly hoped for, (bear in mind I paid nothing for it in the first place,) I kept an office there rent-free and received a years salary paid monthly. It was too good an offer to turn down, I still had Kensington Market, and so I could shift the stock over to there and with the money from the sale of the lease I could look at buying my own premises.

Whilst our respective solicitors were dealing with the lease sale, I noticed that retail sales at Kensington had plummeted, they were less than a third of the normal turnover so I drove over there to see what was going on. They had moved the staircase that led to the basement further back right by the main entrance. What was happening is that people didn't see the staircase so didn't venture downstairs.

Simple as that, the upshot of it was that despite putting up signs (which unit holders on the ground floor kept taking down) the basement became deserted and there was nothing I could do. I tried to re-locate to the ground floor but there was nothing available, I was stuffed and faced with the prospect of losing money week in week out I had no alternative but to close it down.

All of a sudden I had gone from having two retail outlets, with the prospect of opening others, to having none, apart from my office. I started the search for new premises and in the meantime made Kim and Tony redundant, giving them severance pay to go off travelling. I still had the wholesale side of the business, which I was keen to continue with, but without the presence of retail premises, it would be difficult to sustain.

As Planet Alice in Portobello Road was winding down and I had just a few rails of stock left, I was approached by a girl called Sam Kirli who wanted to borrow some clothes for a photo shoot for her and some of her colleagues. I explained that stock was limited but that didn't seem to bother her at all. I arranged to meet her at the now closed and half empty shop and was intrigued as to who they were and what they were all about. When they arrived, the plunging necklines and silicone enhancements kind of gave the game away.

Sam, Charlene, Charmaine and Sharon were all topless models for *The Sun* newspaper, so us not having matching tops and bottoms didn't phase them at all. As Sam said: "I'm a size eight bottom and a size mega top."

I later found out that Sharon wasn't a 'Page Three Girl,' but a 'Star Bird,' who posed topless for *The Daily Star,* apparently there's a difference, a sort of pecking order. Star Birds aspire to be Page Three Girls and as for *Daily Sport* Girls, they don't count. Their rules not mine. As it happens Sam was a great girl and we became good friends for a while, purely platonic I assure you. I had by now moved to St. John's Wood and she lived just a few blocks down the road. She even performed as an Annadin Brother with Doctor And The Medics on a gig or two.

With Clive back DJing Alice's returned to being the fun place it was originally meant to be, whilst we were unlikely to match the days at its very busiest where we would turn more people away than we would let in, I couldn't complain, especially after six and a half years. Clive was by now missing his rock'n'roll lifestyle and was inspired to kick start Doctor And The Medics again.

Vom had by now left The Medics to go to Germany where he eventually joined Die Toten Hosen, (German for 'The Dead Trousers'), a stadium heavy metal band. Richard had jumped ship for Boys Wonder, who later became acid jazz band, Corduroy. With Chris Renshaw (Slam Thunderhide of the Zodiacs) guesting on drums for a short while, and a new bass player, Gareth Thomas, The Medics dragged themselves back on the scene.

They released a new single, a cover of 'Hi Ho Silver Lining', it was quite a good version but there only really needs to be one version of that song and someone had already done it.

I was approached at Alice's one night by a girl called Grania who was the lead singer of a four-piece all-girl band called The Sex Bitch Goddesses. They wanted a gig but she said they hadn't made a demo yet. I booked them without even hearing them on the basis that their name would probably pull a few punters and Grania was quite cute. Whereas Gaye Bykers On Acid may not have been gay, bikers or on acid, The Sex Bitch Goddesses certainly lived up to their name, apart from the Goddesses bit that is, Grania was alright and I think the guitarist wasn't too bad but the other two were having a laugh.

When they played they were absolutely dreadful, maybe the worst band ever. They couldn't sing or play their instruments, they looked like tarts, spent half the gig tuning their guitars and apart from their version of 'Wild Thing' each song sounded like the last. Dreadful. I think this was their one and only gig, and just like I fell for it in the very early days with Bad Karma Beckons, I was had again. I very much doubt whether they released any records, (although they should have qualified for a track on 'Now That's NOT What I Call Music'.) I dare not search on the internet as I dread to think what would turn up if I typed in: 'Sex Bitch Goddesses'. Still, they get a mention in this book so they did something right.

Over the years at Planet Alice our designers had come up with some amazing designs, however, every now and again they would make clothes that just didn't work and consequently just didn't sell. One of our designers came up with this fabulous looking outfit consisting of a mini skirt and top made out of this new silver material. It really did look fantastic, problem is it was totally impractical, the material wouldn't give and the Planet Alice girl who tried them on said it was like wearing a suit made out of wood. Still, we'd give it a go; we put them on the rails and after selling just one skirt in a month, returned them to the designer.

One night at Alice In Wonderland, in the spring of 1990, I was sitting in one of the alcoves when I got talking to a young girl next to me, she knew who I was and said that she was a real fan of Planet Alice and had bought loads of clothes from there over the past couple of years. She even admitted that she was the girl who had bought the 'wooden' silver skirt, and yes it was un-wearable, but it did look great in her wardrobe. She introduced herself as Lee Starkey, daughter of Beatles drummer Ringo Starr.

I talked to Lee for the next couple of hours and I told her that I had seen her as a young child at her father's studio when I was playing in The Lollipop Sisters. She couldn't remember the occasion but when she later talked to Ringo about me, he remembered. She asked me what had happened to Planet Alice. I told her the story about the hairdressers and the lease and said that I was looking around for new premises to start up the retail side again, but in the meantime was still running the wholesale business from my office at the old premises.

She then asked me if I would consider taking on a partner, because she had always wanted to get involved in fashion and seeing as how Planet Alice was her favourite shop it would be perfect. I said I would think about it, but up until now had always done things on my own and forming business partnerships can be messy stuff.

I became friends with Lee and after meeting up with her, either at Alice's or elsewhere, I began to think that maybe a partnership might not be such a bad thing after all. I looked at the advantages; there was no getting away from the fact that she was Ringo's daughter and even though she was born after The Beatles had split up there was bound to be a certain amount of press interest which is always a good thing. Another consideration was that it appealed to me to have a young apprentice who could come up with new ideas and help towards making Planet Alice an even bigger brand than it was at that time.

The third consideration was financial. I had a fair amount of money to invest in a new business after the sale of the lease at Portobello, however if someone was going into a fifty-fifty partnership with me we would have twice as much cash available which from a cash flow point of view was attractive. I met up with Isaac Tigrett, who was now married to Lee's mother Maureen and was quite keen to check me out. Isaac was a tough business cookie who was the original co-owner of The Hard Rock Café. After a few weeks of thinking about what I was going to do I rang Lee up and said that I was sorry but, all things being considered and due to the current economic climate I wasn't prepared to open another retail outlet at that time, maybe in the future but not then.

Later that evening I met up with Lee at The Hard Rock Café in Marble Arch and she said that she had been speaking to Isaac and had had an idea. How would I feel about opening a Planet Alice shop in Los Angeles?

I never saw that one coming, but the idea intrigued me, I had never been to Los Angeles but loved New York (I later found out they're about as similar as London and Llanddewi Brefi, but how was I to know?) Lee begged me to give it some serious thought and I told her it wasn't that simple, I had to consider my existing business interests in the UK, Alice In Wonderland, The Medics and the Planet Alice wholesale business as well as my home, my family and friends.

Lee suggested I met up with Isaac again and I did so the next day. It soon became obvious that the idea of opening in L.A. where Isaac and Maureen lived for most of the year, came from Isaac and not from Lee. Isaac was under pressure from Maureen to spend more time in the UK close to her children, Lee, Jason and Zak, as well as Zak's kids, her grandchildren. Isaac thought that if Lee and Jason would move out to L.A. Maureen would be happier. Isaac sold the idea to me, saying that he loved the whole concept and as well as the shops he would look into the possibility of helping us to open Planet Alice restaurants, Hard Rock style with a psychedelic theme.

And so it was that I started planning Planet Alice in America. I put Dolly Daydream on the payroll to design a new collection and tried to inspire Lee to come up with ideas and learn about the business. I was becoming concerned about her commitment to the project, but every time I questioned her about it she insisted she was desperate for it to work. I would suggest that she should come to my office in Portobello and learn about budgets, cash flow and all the boring stuff essential for a business to be both viable and profitable. Tomorrow she would say, but the next day the answer was the same and tomorrow never came.

Lee actually admitted to me once that she felt a bit awkward, whereas I had earned my money through sheer hard work, she had been given hers on a plate. But as I said to her, it wasn't her fault she was Ringo's daughter, that was the card she was dealt, but with Planet Alice she had the chance to make something of herself, she could be Lee Starkey, co-proprietor of a high profile successful fashion business as opposed to just Lee Starkey, Ringo Starr's daughter. It was up to her, I was basically giving her half of an established business but on the understanding that she would get her act together and help to make it work. She may have had a substantial trust fund to fall back on, I didn't. For the rest of 1990, Lee and I hung out together, she would come to Alice's every Monday night and I would get her in on the guest list at other venues to see bands like Motörhead and Dread Zeppelin.

She was enjoying the fact that for the first time in her life she could tell people that she was doing something constructive and revelled in talking about the plans for the shop and our intentions to open in L.A. the following year. Meanwhile, I was making it absolutely clear to everyone that this was not going to be just Lee's shop and that I was putting up fifty percent of the capital investment.

A bunch of cocky young kids blagged their way into Alice's on the guest list and hung out every week for a year or two. The Senseless Things were being courted by a few major record labels and eventually signed for Epic. They were okay, but not brilliant, but what they lacked in originality they made up for in attitude. I asked, Ben, their singer, if they would play at the club, but he declined. I think he felt it was beneath them. Maybe it was the fifteen minute sound check or the dressing room the size of a shoebox but they were having none of it.

Now let me get this right, Alice In Wonderland was good enough for The Damned, The Cult, The Mission, Doctor And The Medics, Zodiac Mindwarp, The Shamen, Daisy Chainsaw and Gallon Drunk to name, just a few, but not The Senseless Things. Oh well, suit yourself. Still, they were nice kids and I forgave them. The Senseless Things like so many other bands disappeared into obscurity and then split up, although Morgan, their bass player went on to play with Muse and The Streets.

Towards the end of the year a couple of new characters arrived on the Alice In Wonderland scene. Helen and Kim worked as hostesses in a seedy Soho bar and after their shift they would hang out at Alice's.

Kim was soon re-christened Mad Kim, not necessarily because she actually was mad, although it has to be said there was no smoke without fire, but because there seemed to be a plethora of Kims out there. We already had Earth Mother Kim (Planet Alice manageress,) Gorgeous Kim (Magic Mushroom Band,) Cosmic Kim (Tarot card reader,) and Auntie Kim (sensible peroxide goth who just wanted to take care of everyone.)

Mad Kim was quite nice looking but Helen was something else. Helen looked like a French Barbie doll, long blonde hair extensions, petite in a typical French way with Riviera bust enhancements and a porcelain complexion. After another wild night at Alice's they ended up at my flat in St. John's Wood to carry on partying. It was there that Helen told me her story.

Apparently one day, whilst sitting on the beach in Brighton, a girl suddenly appeared next to her. The girl told Helen that she was visiting earth from another planet and her mission was to tell Helen that she too was from that planet and that she had been living inside the 'Barbie shell' to observe life on Earth. Helen told me this story in total seriousness, she admitted that people did find it hard to believe but she swore that she spoke the truth.

I listened intently and incredulously as she continued, telling me in graphic detail how she was then whisked away in a spaceship to this 'other planet' where she was a sex slave for a community of aliens in exchange for immortality and eternal beauty. This scenario was a script straight out of a sixties low budget B movie, and I don't know what really happened, obviously I wasn't there, but Helen certainly believed that what she said happened really did happen. Who am I to judge?

In case you're wondering what the punch line is, there isn't one. To my knowledge she wasn't the Alien Green Jelly Girl from the Clacton Mystery Trip, she was much prettier, and besides the Green Jelly Girl wasn't French. However, I do wonder where Helen is now, perhaps she's living in the suburbs of Marseilles with a proper job and a family, forever Dolly Parton like or maybe she's back home on the Planet that she was convinced she came from.

In 1990 the circus came to town. Circus Archaos were an alternative group of entertainers who came over from France and put on a show at Clapham Common, which ran for twelve weeks. There were no animals in the performance but chain saw jugglers, fire breathers and bizarre *Mad Max* style metal clowns. Dan Carpenter, the former sax player with Ring Of Roses, Another Green World and Spannerman was in the circus band, The Thunderdogs, and swung from a trapeze playing his instrument.

Dan was an old Alice regular and turned up after a Circus Archaos show with a dozen or so performers. They spread out around the club, mingling with the punters adding even more strangeness to the occasion, it's not often that you go to a club and stand next to a scary seven foot high clown with a costume made out of bits of old cars.

I got chatting to a midget who was whizzing around the club on a child's high chair on wheels driven by an electric motor. Sitting underneath the attached parasol he was dressed in a pin stripe suit with a trilby hat. He may have been paralysed from the waist down but I cannot be sure. I offered to buy him a pint but he declined. "I had better not," he said in a French accent, "I've already had one, and going for zee piss in zis thing is a bloody nightmare!"

Ruby Tuesday, the girlfriend of Rich Josh, used to be a designer for Planet Alice. One night at Alice's I asked her if she would be interested in designing for the soon to be opened L.A. store but she turned me down as she was concentrating on her own ideas in the fashion business. However she told me she'd just formed an all-girl band called The Sling Backs and she'd like to play at Alice In Wonderland.

It was the usual noisy night at Alice's and despite asking her to repeat the name of her band I still managed to get it wrong. I booked them for a gig and sent off press releases and designed a flyer advertising The SLING BATS. I even drew bats all over the leaflet. Oops. The band were none too pleased, it was their debut performance and they had asked loads of people to come and see them. Well, Sling Backs or Sling Bats they never amounted to much so I guess it didn't matter.

Drug use in London nightclubs is commonplace, everyone knows that, but at Alice In Wonderland we had a strict no-drugs policy, after all, we had a license to protect. However, that didn't mean that everyone obeyed the rules, but anyone found taking any illegal substances was thrown out immediately. The favourite spot to take drugs was at the back of the club in one of the cave-like alcoves, people would attempt to have a sneaky spliff but were discovered in no time. It was the first place the bouncers would look. No amount of bleating apologetically would wash with Bigger or Leroy and if you were caught you were out.

Where there's psychedelia there is inevitably LSD and we were powerless to stop those that wanted to drop a tab, tune in, turn on and drop out. One such person who dropped out, quite literally, was an Alice regular for a while, a bloke called Hugo. He loved his acid and seemed to be on it every time we saw him. One day, thankfully not at Alice's, he played out the apocryphal 'chased-by-a-banana' story to the tee. Whilst high on a potent dose of White Lightning he jumped out of the window of his second floor flat believing he could fly. He couldn't and was impaled on the metal railings below. Ouch.

It's not my place to be judgmental or sanctimonious, but if anyone reading this decides they want to try LSD, I can categorically state that no matter what happens, if you jump out of a window you will NOT be able to fly, you will drop like a stone, just like poor Hugo. I have often wondered at what point he realised he had got it wrong and that he wasn't Biggles after all. What was going through his mind as he flapped his arms to no avail? We shall never know. Still, at least he died with a smile on his face which is more than can be said for some. King Henry II died after having a red hot poker shoved up his backside, I bet he wasn't smiling when he met his maker. Thankfully that incident didn't happen at Alice In Wonderland either.

New Years Eve 1990 fell on a Monday. Fantastic. The last time this had happened was in 1984 and it gave us the chance to have a serious Alice In Wonderland party. We didn't have a band playing that night as we knew the place would be heaving and we were right. The club was packed to full capacity and we turned away another hundred or so people desperately looking for somewhere to see in the New Year.

After the club closed at 3.30, myself, Clive, Zak Starkey and a few other people went back to Lee's flat in Warwick Avenue to carry on partying until the sun came up.

One person who didn't come to the after-club party was our old friend Frenchy Gloder. Frenchy, you'll remember, was the owner of Flicknife records who released the '*Lobster*' album. Leaving Alice's at closing time was the last thing he remembered. A few days later he was rushed to hospital in a seriously bad way and they didn't think he would last the night. A priest read him last rites and it was not looking good.

Rumours flew around the industry about what had happened to him and *Sounds,* the music newspaper reported that Frenchy had died of a drug overdose.

A year later and Charlie Harper (from the UK Subs) was at the 12 Bar club and who should he bump into but good old Frenchy. Charlie thought he'd seen a ghost and nearly fainted! We hadn't heard about Frenchy supposedly dying. We just thought he'd had enough and fucked off to Ireland. But very recently, we are back in touch and he filled me in with the true story.

A few weeks before the Alice New Year party, Frenchy was involved in a motorbike accident, and in true rock'n'roll fashion, stuck a bandage on it and hoped it would get better. It didn't. The leg went septic and he was rushed to hospital but despite being seriously close to death he somehow pulled through and after eight months in hospital and a further eighteen months convalescing he was fine.

Becky, nappy twin and hairdresser with attitude, modelling Planet Alice

An Italian Alice girl shows off her new make-up kit

CHAPTER TWENTY ONE

PLANET ALICE GOES TO HOLLYWOOD

In which I move to Los Angeles to open a new Planet Alice shop. Prince and Alice Cooper show up as does the remarkable Hoover Davidson. Gallon Drunk and Daisy Chainsaw play at Alice In Wonderland, Tracey Shaw wears Planet Alice gear on Coronation Street and Planet Alice closes down after my spectacular fall out with Lee Starkey.

As we entered 1991 we were met with the rare arrival of heavy snow in London. I was entrenched in my flat in St. John's Wood working on the business plan for Planet Alice in L.A. Dolly Daydream presented us with her new collection and we organised a photo session with Lee and a group of her friends modelling the clothes. Everything seemed to be going fine, next stop was finding suitable premises.

I didn't know Los Angeles at all, having never been there, but it was somehow decided that Melrose Avenue in Hollywood was where we had to be. Rodeo Drive (as in *Pretty Woman)* was the street where the seriously up-market designer fashion outlets were and Melrose was where the more alternative club and street wear shops could be found. Isaac had a real estate agent on the case who suggested 7223 Melrose Avenue, which was available for rent.

Lee and I flew out to America to check it out, whilst it was at the quieter end of the street, the rent was affordable, the premises in a good state of repair and the right square footage for what we needed. We stayed out there for a week and after looking at a few other options decided it would be fine. We signed the lease and paid for three months rent in advance.

Alice In Wonderland was still trotting along nicely and on the 18th March London based swamp rockers Gallon Drunk played there. At that time they were largely unknown and although they had signed to a record label they had not really taken off. Closely associated with former Birthday Party frontman, Nick Cave and his band, The Bad Seeds, Gallon Drunk released some great material and became the latest in a long line of bands who played at Alice In Wonderland before going on to get a reasonable amount of exposure and success.

Much of the first half of 1991 was taken up with the launching of Planet Alice in America. I also had to sort out my UK affairs: My businesses and my flat. It was a mad rush to tie up all the loose ends, I had to organise who was going to run Alice In Wonderland in my absence and arranged to take three months off my management commitments with The Medics. I organised a party at Alice's (with The Medics playing live, of course), I then got back on the plane bound for Los Angeles to set up and open the latest chapter in the Alice saga.

I had organised for half a dozen or so of our designers and manufacturers to provide the stock and sorted out all the problems with exporting the goods to the US. American law dictates that different tax ratios were payable on different fabrics, 7% on cotton, 2% on man made materials, or whatever. Oh great, and how do I work out the tax payable on a pair of patchwork trousers which consist of a dozen or so different fabrics all taxable at a different amount? Still, I got it sorted and now in LA whilst the elves churned out the stock, it was down to the business of getting the shop decorated, furnished and kitted out.

I had already designed the 'artwork' for the walls, having planned it in advance, even doing a scaled model of the lay out. After sorting out boring stuff like plasterers and waiting for plaster to dry, I set about drawing my designs on the walls ready for colouring in. I had bought this fantastic light projector, which shone moving crystals onto one section of the wall, and things were slowly coming together. Lee and Jason helped to paint the walls and even Maureen put in an hour with the paintbrush. The press reported that Ringo did his bit of painting as well, I have to say though, he didn't.

The first time I met Ringo Starr was at a party at the Tigretts not long after we arrived in L.A. to get the shop together. He arrived late as the hire car ran out of petrol on the way there. It was the first time he had been to his ex-wife's house and the first time he had seen her for many years. Isaac wasn't there that night but we were all on our best behaviour and in respect to Ringo's teetotalism, drinking was kept to the minimum. I was told off for calling him Ringo and he asked me to call him Richard or Rich. That was a difficult one for me, I had known about Ringo Starr all my life and to me Ringo was his name.

Lee, Jason and I went round to his apartment on, or near, Rodeo Drive and he played us some recordings of his latest material and asked me what I thought. Well what was I going to say? He told me an amusing story about Michael Jackson who apparently had an apartment in the same block. One day they ended up in the lift together and Michael Jackson looked at Ringo, knowing exactly who he was, and Ringo looked at Michael Jackson knowing exactly who he was but because they hadn't actually been introduced to each other neither of them said anything. Ringo reckoned it was the longest lift journey of his life. Imagine if the lift had broken down? I wonder who would have been the first to say "Don't I know you from somewhere?"

I met him on a few more occasions, he came to check out the shop as we were getting it sorted and took us out shopping around Melrose. On another occasion he took us out for a meal at the Belle Air Hotel. I had lobster, Ringo had egg and chips. At one point a violinist came to the table playing Beatles songs until an embarrassed Ringo told him to go away.

The psychedelic swirls on the walls had to be the right colours and I carefully chose the different shades of purple, yellow, green and blue. What I couldn't find, despite going to a few different paint shops, was the right shade of red. It needed to be bright pillar-box red, which amazingly didn't exist in America. I went to a specialist shop that mixed up colours to order and I looked at their swatches, there were dozens of different reds but nothing that resembled the red I wanted, London bus red. In the end I had to arrange for someone to buy a large can in the UK and bring it out with them on the plane.

I was at a party at the scriptwriter, Ian Le Frenais' house and there were a few well known faces hanging about, the comedian Mel Smith was there as were the actors Dan Ackroyd and Woody Harrilson. I ended up playing a game of pool with Jeff Lynne of The Electric Light Orchestra and I told him that I had previously worked with Roy Wood, the original singer in ELO, when The Medics recorded 'Waterloo.' Jeff wasn't that impressed by his ex-partner, apparently Roy never could come to terms with the fact that ELO became so mega successful after he left to form Wizzard. Surely Roy Wood has earned a bob or two from 'I Wish It Could Be Christmas Everyday?'

Whilst out in L.A., Lee and I were invited out for a Mexican meal by Joe Walsh, the guitarist in The Eagles. Apparently every year he celebrated that particular day in memory of a bunch of Mexicans who fought off an invasion by the Americans a couple of hundred years previously. The Mexicans, delighted by their victory, celebrated by getting totally legless, as they crashed out on the beach after their party, the Americans came back and, stepping over the drunken Mexicans, walked into town and took it over. The bloke who played the guitar solo on 'Hotel California' told me that story.

When I had the Planet Alice shop in Portobello Road, our purple vacuum cleaner, J. Edgar Hoover Cleaner, became a bit of a star in its' own right. This time for America I wanted to go one better. I commissioned my brother Julian and one of his biker mates to make the Hoover Davidson. This unique vacuum cleaner had ape hanger handlebars, working headlamp and indicators and a black leather bag jacket. It was switched on using the throttle and the motor even revved up when you twisted the handgrip. Apart from all of that, it was actually a working vacuum cleaner.

The Hoover Davidson was made in the UK and was brought out by one of Lee's friends as hand luggage on the airplane. It's hard to believe that America let a vacuum cleaner masquerading as a motorbike, onto a plane bound for their treasured country and through customs without really questioning it. But they did.

Many years later my brother Julian, by then a very successful composer and arranger, was at the backstage party of the first ever *Electric Proms*. After arranging the score for the orchestra that backed Kasabian he was the conductor for the live performance. Zak Starkey, was guesting on drums and had invited Lee to the show and consequently the after gig party. Julian reminded Lee that he had made the Hoover Davidson and asked what had happened to it. Lee said it had been stolen. Where it is now, who knows, in the corner of the thief's sitting room, in a private collection of rock'n'roll memorabilia, or lying unwanted in a landfill site somewhere? Wherever it is I would quite like it back.

Anyone reading this book might be excused for getting a bit concerned about my unhealthy fascination for vacuum cleaners. And you'd be right, especially if I admit to once seriously considering having a vacuum cleaner tattooed on my arm. I even designed it in readiness, but luckily that was one of my ideas that I didn't follow through. Phew. In the mid eighties and early nineties vacuum cleaners were dead boring, Electrolux and Hoover Juniors were so dull and I just wanted to brighten them up a bit.

These days I have a super duper funky Dyson that looks like it's come from another planet. (I absolutely love it, but as my cleaner pointed out, I don't actually have to use it). My latest Dyson is a groovy purple and silver.... Hang on a second: Purple? Silver? Am I getting déjà vu here?

I have this theory that James Dyson was strolling down the Portobello Road, down on his luck, hands in pockets, his boat bike didn't catch on, nor did his ball barrow, he must have been wondering where his next idea was going to come from. He found himself drawn in to the weird and wonderful Planet Alice just as it was due to close. One of the Planet Alice girls was hoovering the carpet with the purple and silver icon, J. Edgar Hoover Cleaner, and all of a sudden Mr. Dyson becomes inspired. So come on James, where are my royalties? You've cleaned up, now cough up!

When I first agreed to go into partnership with Lee it was arranged that I would stay at Isaac and Maureen's house in Belle Air as their guest whilst I set up the shop. They were generous hosts and I was treated well, Maureen would buy me presents and Isaac introduced me to a few of his contacts to help with some of the aspects of the shop fitting. I had designed the purple Perspex counter but I had neither the skills, the tools, nor the time to physically make it. Isaac knew a man who could.

Before going out to L.A. I had worked out a business plan, a budget and a cash flow forecast. The financial agreement I had with Lee was that I would make a capital investment of fifty percent of the budgeted set up costs. We were pretty much coming in on target, and then we hired the P.R. company.

I hadn't allowed a vast sum for the launch in my budget but I did allow for the airfare to fly Clive over to DJ at the party. I was intending to do the marketing myself, as I had always done previously, and assumed that I could do a deal with a club for a low key launch party. The way I saw it was there would be plenty of time for a big show, once we were established and had something to shout about and when the business could afford it.

Isaac hired the P.R. company who charged silly Los Angeles rates and they set up a huge party at the Mayan Theatre. They organised free drinks all night, food, dancers and invited every A, B, C and D list celebrity in L.A. My budget was blown skywards. The launch party cost considerably more than I had allowed for in my cash flow forecast and was out of my control. I was not happy.

As the date for the shop opening drew closer, my initial reservations about Lee's commitment to the project were confirmed, she seemed to have lost all interest in the shop, the whole reason we were out there for, and only seemed interested in the launch party.

Meanwhile I was driving around L.A. like a lunatic, organising the signage, the security grilles, alarm and telephone systems, carrier bags and stationery, a till, mannequins, rails, mirrors, dressing room etc. desperate to get everything finished in time.

One day I was in the shop, painting, when Ringo walked in, he asked for Lee and I said she wasn't there. He took me out for a coffee and he said that he knew that the shop was all down to me. It was an odd situation, sitting down having a coffee with a real-live Beatle.

The day of the launch party and the day before the shop would open I was with Clive who had flown out to DJ. Clive and I went down to the shop and he helped me to finish off putting up the dressing room. We then had to drive around L.A. picking up business cards, tee shirts, posters etc.

There was a lot of media attention, particularly in the UK, about Planet Alice opening in L.A., understandably focusing on the Beatle connection and Lee and I were interviewed and photographed for countless newspapers and magazines. *People* magazine, *Hello! The Sun, The Daily Mail, Hola!* and *OK!* magazine were just some of the publications that wrote about us.

The launch party was a bit over the top. With swooping spotlights and a red carpet it was more like a Hollywood awards ceremony than a party to promote the opening of a new retail outlet. The TV crews filmed the guests arriving, looking for anyone famous. Despite the huge mail-out of invites to the Hollywood A-listers there were only a few well-known people who showed up. Alice In Wonderland regulars, Lemmy and Dogs D'Amour happened to be in L.A. at the time so came along, Ringo, Zak and Jason came, of course but the majority were unknown people who were there for the free party, rent-a-crowd courtesy of the P.R. company. Clive played the records, a few hired girls in Planet Alice outfits danced in cages suspended from the ceiling and the night went okay.

The next day we opened the shop. It was nothing like when we opened in the Portobello Road. No staff dancing in the window and no hordes of club regulars coming along to be the first to buy an outfit. However, the shop looked great, I have to say, the walls were painted in brightly coloured psychedelic swirls representing a unique planet, psychedelic mannequins sat in the window next to the Hoover Davidson and the crystal light projector shone in the far corner. In the centre of the shop was our fantastic purple Perspex counter and rails of our unique clothes were positioned around the shop floor. Ringo had bought us a statue of an Egyptian animal and an antique bench as a shop-warming present.

But all was not well in the Planet Alice camp, Lee and her little gang of hangers-on weren't talking to me and I was seriously beginning to regret doing the whole thing. I hated L.A. and apart from the sunshine couldn't see the appeal at all.

A black stretch limo pulled up outside the shop and parked. Nobody got out, and as the windows were blacked out, we didn't know who was inside. After about five or ten minutes two huge black bodyguards emerged and walked slowly around the shop, they nodded at me before getting back into the car. Another five minutes passed and they got out of the car again, this time with the diminutive purple legend, Prince. I'm not sure what he was calling himself then, the Artist Formerly Known As Prince, Symbol, Squiggle or just plain old Prince.

Prince walked around the shop flanked by these two blokes each about ten times bigger than him and touched half a dozen items of clothing. The bodyguards walked back to the car with him and then returned, picking up the clothes selected by Prince and bringing them to the counter. I folded up the velvet outfits and put them in a Planet Alice carrier bag. One of the bodyguards handed me a credit card, I had only just got the card machine and hadn't installed it yet so I couldn't accept the card. I explained this to Prince's minder who sighed and pulled out a massive roll of bank notes and peeled off the few hundred dollars to pay for the goods.

The first few weeks of the shop being open were painful. I never wanted to live in Los Angeles, my home was in London, Alice In Wonderland was in London, my family and friends were all in the UK and I just wanted to get back and organise the next batch of clothes and concentrate on the more lucrative side of the business, wholesale orders. I was keen to get a brochure together and contact all of my existing outlets as well as find new contacts to drum up orders for our new collections.

One day at Planet Alice, mega rock star legend and serious hero of mine, Alice Cooper, walked into Planet Alice. It was my day off and I missed him. What a shame, I could have apologised in person for the chewing gum incident at his back stage party all those years ago.

Alice Cooper was, in part, an influence on how I began Planet Alice in the first place and let's not forget: the Alice script was lifted from his *Killer* album. We even had a poster of the snake-adorned Alice on the door to the office. He knew Ringo and came to check out the shop, he chatted to Lee and left without buying anything. He was, however, very impressed with the Hoover Davidson.

Stop press... I have just heard, and this has not been confirmed, that the legendary vacuum cleaner is now in the possession of our favourite shock rock star. Now, if this is true, I am delighted. What more deserving person should have this iconic object cluttering up his house than Alice Cooper?

My Mum's health was deteriorating rapidly and so I flew back to the UK to see her. I was missing my family and friends, and with all that was going on in L.A. I couldn't wait to get out of there. Back in London I contacted Lee to find out what we should do next, as far as I was concerned I wanted to get cracking on the brochure and kick start the wholesale business, but Lee was beginning to believe that with me out of America she could run Planet Alice herself, without my help.

Meanwhile I put together a package with photos of our designs, photos of the shop and some press cuttings. I sent them to my contacts at the Seibu department store in Tokyo who replied straight away saying that they were very interested in doing another Planet Alice concession and wanted to see some samples of our new collections.

I also spoke to another contact of mine, a buyer at Harrods (and coincidently my future wife), who agreed to put our clothes into the most famous department store in London. Trash And Vaudeville in New York, shops in Munich, Milan and of course our friends in Iceland were all seriously keen. The product, the brand and the whole idea was obviously marketable and yet I was in limbo, not knowing what was going to happen and unable to do anything about it.

The eight-hour time difference between London and L.A. made communication very difficult, but it was now quite obvious that mine and Lee's relationship had broken down irretrievably so we had to decide what we would do next. Whilst I was loathe to give up on Planet Alice something had to be sorted out, after all, I had invested a lot of money in this project and I knew I could make it work, no doubt about it.

Lee was adamant that she could run the show on her own and according to her solicitor, the only way out was that she could return my original investment and I would have to walk away, Planet Alice Inc, the company we set up, would belong to Lee.

The money never came and it was almost impossible to contact Lee. If I phoned the house I always got the grandmother who didn't know what day it was, and if I phoned the shop no one would be there to answer it. It was reported in the UK press that Planet Alice was hardly ever open, Lee hardly ever went to the shop, and the shop assistant she hired thought he could follow in her example and not bother opening up either. In no time at all the shop folded and I could do nothing about it, and with it went my investment. Oh great.

It was tragic and totally unnecessary how it all fell apart, I was pissed off with Lee because I didn't feel she had the necessary commitment needed if the business was going to be a success and Lee was pissed off with me because she stumped up the cash for the launch party. The latter was actually irrelevant as I subsequently matched Lee's additional investment by settling the outstanding manufacturer's bills and the designers' wages for the next consignment of stock.

I was talking to Lemmy at Alice In Wonderland a couple of months later and he said that he had spoken to Lee in L.A. and that she was hurt by what went on at Planet Alice. "That makes two of us." I replied. It wasn't just money I had invested in the project but also an awful lot of my time, my contacts, my ideas and my brand. I had every right to be pissed off.

A few years after the L.A. shop closed down, Lee suffered from an unfortunate and serious brain illness and was rushed into a special clinic. The story was front-page headlines in the English tabloid newspapers. I was, by then, living in a remote village in the middle of nowhere and the day after the story of Lee's illness was reported I went down to the village store where I saw two journalists talking to the shopkeeper. I knew they were paparazzi, in a village where the locals held their trousers up with baler twine a girl in high heels and a smart suit stood out like a sore thumb. The camera with a lens half a metre long carried by her companion kind of gave the game away as well.

I don't know how on earth they tracked me down to this village some 300 miles from London or why they had travelled all that way to find me. They started to ask me questions about Lee, which I refused to answer, and asked me to comment on various personal issues that had apparently been reported to them by a 'close friend'. Again, I refused to tell them anything and drove off with the paparazzi following me, I soon lost them round the back lanes and went back to my farm where I hid my pickup truck in a barn and went inside the house and closed all the curtains. I stayed inside for the next few hours, a virtual hostage in my own home but never saw them again and the story died down. Lee recovered from her illness and to my knowledge is now absolutely fine.

The whole L.A. thing was an absolute nightmare and in some ways I blame myself. I blame myself for not appreciating that not everyone had the same hunger for success that I had. I didn't take on board Lee's young age and inexperience in business and although a contract was drawn up when we set up the company, in retrospect I should have had the whole thing tied up neater, so that we both knew what was expected of each other. However, it happened and neither Lee nor I can change that, these days I'm over it, I've moved on and now put the whole episode down to just one of life's experiences. Not everything will always go according to plan.

Whilst I was in Los Angeles, Clive and Joe were looking

after Alice In Wonderland for me. In my absence the club had quietened down considerably. I don't believe it was the fault of Clive and Joe at all, but without me to monitor the situation and do something about it Alice's, after eight years was reaching the autumn of her life. Whereas in the early eighties I profited from the second-generation baby boom, my target audience in the early nineties were babies of the seventies. With the advent of the pill and increased awareness of 'Burn the Bra' woman's libbers, considerably fewer children were born in the early 1970's than there had been a decade previously. These kids, now grown up were the kids that would now go out clubbing; only there was half as many. Still, it wasn't totally desperate, we had our busy nights and the fat lady, exercising her tonsils, would just have to wait a bit longer.

A year or two after Planet Alice closed down, I noticed that the future 'Rear Of The Year' winner, Tracey Shaw who played Maxine, the wife of local butcher Ashley Peacock on ITV's *Coronation Street* was wearing a Planet Alice top with a red fake fur heart stitched on the front. I thought it was hilarious, Maxine Peacock from *Coronation Street* wearing Planet Alice gear, long before she got whacked over the head by Richard Hillman.

I couldn't work out how she had come across our stuff, she was in Manchester, and we were in London or L.A. I didn't know whether she chose her own outfits or the costume department at ITV had come up with it, either way, she looked fabulous; exactly what Planet Alice was all about.

Alice In Wonderland's ability to showcase bands that subsequently went on to have hit singles continued with the arrival of Daisy Chainsaw. Led by their outrageous lead singer Katie Jane Garside they played at Alice's on the 14th October 1991. Dressed in rags and with netting and rag dolls strewn about the stage they made an immediate impact and were a great hit with the punters. The band came to the club regularly before getting a lot of press attention, a few TV appearances and then a top thirty hit single with 'Love Your Money.'

My mum had been fighting cancer for a few years now and eventually it got the better of her and in November 1991 she died. I went out and got totally pissed, going back to my flat in St. John's Wood I slung off my leather jacket and crashed out on the sofa. I had had the jacket, with a silver Mona Lisa painted on the back, for donkey's years, it was like a second skin to me, however, it was now so crusty that it could stand up on its own. Literally.

I woke up a few hours later and saw my jacket on the rug in front of me shaped exactly like me, my shoulders, my arms, it was me. I thought I had had another out-of-body experience at first until I realised that I was just pissed and my jacket was just crusty.

My mum's funeral was on a Monday and I had decided that I wouldn't go to Alice's that night. After the funeral we went back to my dad's house and had a few drinks remembering my mother and her life, as you do. Joe then drove me back to London and I changed my mind about not going to Alice's and he diverted via Soho. I was still wearing my suit and I just stood at the bar and drank. Strange thing was I remained completely sober, no matter how hard I tried the alcohol had no effect on me whatsoever.

An Alice regular called Jason came up to me and said "Hey Christian you look like you're going to a funeral." I replied: "I've already been to one, my mums'." "Oh Christian, you crack me up" said Jason wandering off laughing. A few moments later Jason came back up to me, white as a sheet, he wasn't laughing now.

"Someone's just told me it's true about your mum, I'm so sorry."

1991 was an odd year for me, starting off with great hopes for Planet Alice in America, dealing with the frustration and disappointment that it didn't work out as I hoped, coming back to the UK to pick up the pieces and then dealing and coping with my mum's demise. With no Planet Alice and very little activity with Doctor And The Medics all I had left was Alice In Wonderland.

As well as other bands already mentioned, Sidewinders, Electrocuted Elvis and well-known goth outfit The Sex Gang Children played that year.

I was sitting with my brother Julian in London's' Little Venice when a girl sailed past on a narrow boat. "I'm going to marry her one day." I said, and I was right. Carol was the tall blonde soul mate I had been searching for all my life and at the end of 1991 we started going out together. Carol had never been to Alice In Wonderland, being a good few years younger than me, she wasn't old enough to go there in the early days, and besides, she wasn't in London then but in Jersey working with horses. From then on my life was set to change once again and new adventures were on their way.

Planet Alice in Los Angeles

A mannequin at Planet Alice

Inside Planet Alice, 7223 Melrose Avenue, Hollywood

Lee Starkey at Planet Alice, Los Angeles

The Legend that was, the Hoover Davidson

CHAPTER TWENTY TWO

HORSES

In which I move to Wales, try out the Alice In Wonderland formula on the unsuspecting locals, start breeding horses and find the Pig In A Skirt most disturbing.

In early 1992 Clive had decided that he wanted to sever the contract with The Medics management team. Andrew King, Jenny Cotton and I had been looking after the band for about eight years and now it was the end of the era.

The split was perfectly amicable and we completely understood why he wanted to do it. The Medics had no record deal and apart from a few gigs here and there, there was little else we could do for the band.

On the odd occasion that we did get them a gig we would cream off the top twenty percent as per our agreement, the agency would then take another fifteen percent leaving the remainder for the band to pay all other costs and try and get something for themselves. The figures didn't stack up. Clive continued to DJ at Alice's and even though I had just lost one of my sources of income, there were no hard feelings.

It had been quite a laugh working with The Medics over the years and reaching number one was quite an achievement, I always thought they should have followed up 'Spirit' with 'Love Peace And Bananas' but was outvoted. However, one thing that never happened was a Christmas record, I don't know why we never thought of that idea, it could have been Clive's pension for the future. I am glad, though, that they never entered the *Eurovision Song Contest* at any stage in their careers and, contrary to what Richard Searle said, they never did record 'Agadoo'.

In the summer of 1992, I was reading *Horse And Hound* magazine when I saw an advert for a farm to let in west Wales. We happened to be going to Brecon to see Clive that weekend so rang up the estate agent and made an appointment to go and see it. Although I was originally a townie and then a city boy, I had always wanted to move to the country.

Carol had worked with horses for most of her life, either breaking in racehorses, competing in eventing or riding as a point-to-point rider. We had this idea that we could breed horses in Wales, where land and property is cheap, and sell the horses in England where they could fetch better prices. We kept the flat in St. John's Wood and the boat in Little Venice and signed the rental agreement for the farm. So Carol gave up her promising career at Harrods and a month later we were on our way to the middle of nowhere.

The day before we moved to Wales we had to go to a funeral, so after loading up the hired lorry with furniture and stuff, we got changed into our funeral suits. Outside the flat, for some reason, the boxer Frank Bruno was sitting in his BMW, he saw me in my suit with the lorry keys and wound down the window. "You're not driving that are you?" he asked, checking out my suit, "No I'm not," I replied, and pointing to Carol, said: "She is." Carol, wearing a black pencil skirt and high heels then stepped elegantly into the truck and started up the engine and we drove off, leaving Frank Bruno laughing his socks off.

The village we first moved to at the foot of the Cambrian Mountains was the strangest place I had ever lived in and full of the weirdest people I had ever met. Llanddewi Brefi was infamous in the early seventies as being at the centre of the notorious LSD drug factory bust, called 'Operation Julie.' How the hippies thought they could set up in the middle of nowhere and manufacture drugs in a place where nothing happened and everyone knew what everyone else was doing was beyond me.

When I lived in St. John's Wood in London the only person I knew in the entire mansion block was the little old lady next door and that was only because I did her shopping for her during the heavy snow. In Llanddewi Brefi, everyone knew everything about everybody, I was in the local pub and someone asked me if my mother in law had enjoyed her holiday. "How do you know my mother in law had been on holiday?" I asked. "The postman told me," came the reply, "He said she had sent your wife a postcard."

Llanddewi Brefi, long after we had left, became well known through the comedy show *Little Britain* as the home of Daffyd, 'The Only Gay In the Village.' Apparently the real village became a magnet for *Little Britain* fans who descended on the place in their hundreds, taking all the signs as souvenirs and photographing each other at the two pubs in the village. I can only imagine what the locals thought of it all, this was a place where the farmers would drink in the pub with their stained trousers held up with baler twine and sheep shit splattered on their faces.

Three quarters of the village were Welsh with the rest of the people English. The two groups rarely mixed although because we had animals and Carol knew a lot about horses, we were accepted by both lots. So, having swapped my leather jacket for a Barbour and a pair of Hunter wellies, I sold my classic sports car and bought a pick-up truck instead. We then started buying horses; the first was a two-year-old thoroughbred mare that was in foal and the rest followed soon after. Mucking out stables, exercising horses, learning to ride, fixing fences, chopping up firewood, I absolutely loved it, it was so completely different from my life in London.

I kept Alice In Wonderland going even though I now lived hundreds of miles away in Llanddewi Brefi and Clive and I took it in turns to run the night. Travelling down by either car or train every other week was a bit of a chore, but the club was mostly still just about busy enough to make it worthwhile financially, even after travelling costs were taken into account.

However, I was beginning to love my new life-style in Wales, but earning a living was a hell of a lot more challenging than it ever was in London. It got me thinking, if Alice's worked in London why not in Wales? Who the fuck was I trying to kid? London was the capital of England; Wales was the back end of beyond. However...

If I were asked to compile a list of things I would send to Room 101, top of that list would be: animals made to look sexy. The bunny rabbit in the Cadbury's Caramel advert, sheep with long eyelashes and Jessica Rabbit should not be allowed.

The only nightclub in the largest town in west Wales, Aberystwyth, at the time was called Porky's and their logo was absolutely awful. Not only did it feature a pig made to look sexy, but this pig was imitating the famous Marilyn Monroe scene in *Seven Year Itch* where she stands over the vent shaft and her skirt blows up. Can you imagine it? A pig? In a skirt? Yuk.

With Clive and I now both living in Wales, (albeit fifty miles apart,) we decided to see if Alice In Wonderland would work locally. So we approached Porky's in Aberystwyth and a nightclub in Swansea both of whom were keen to give it a go.

Porky's wanted us to use their 'sexy pig' logo on our leaflets and posters but I refused outright. The advertising did, however, have to be bi-lingual, which was a new one on me, writing psychedelic Welsh.

When Clive and I arrived at Porky's to set up, there was a flashing neon sign with the pig in a skirt logo. As I had only previously seen the club in the daytime, I hadn't noticed it before. Clive and I stared at the sign in utter disbelief, the bloody pig's skirt was flashing up and down. Skirt up, skirt down. Who the hell designed that?

It got worse. As if the logo and the flashing sign weren't bad enough, porcine depravity hit even baser depths. Inside the club was a specially commissioned painting of the same pig in the Marilyn Monroe skirt; only this time there was a boar in a suit smoking a cigar sitting behind her leering at the view that only he saw. Come on, it's just not right.

Getting publicity for the opening night was seriously easy, whereas in London a new club opens every night, in Aberystwyth it was almost front-page headlines of *The Cambrian News,* Clive and I were interviewed on *Radio Ceredigion* and when the doors opened a couple of hundred punters streamed in. Whereas the London Alice folk were cool trendy funky clubbers, in Aberystwyth they were a bit odd. The hippies came down from the mountains, the students from Aber University turned up, even the Young Farmers and a few other random nutters came to see what all the fuss was about.

One girl who came along for the first few nights was a girl from my village called Marianne. She later became the subject of the best gossip they had heard in Llanddewi Brefi for ages when her boyfriend, an ex-policeman called Andy commissioned a local artist, Jeff Wynne (who also lived in Llanddewi,) to paint her portrait. By an amazing coincidence Jeff used to live with the mother of Gaz Mayall who ran the Thursday night at Gossips, 'Gaz's Rockin' Blues' and helped bring Gaz up.

Jeff was an exceptionally talented artist whose portraits were so realistic you thought that the subjects were physically in the room. He could paint silver that you felt could be melted down and sold and if he painted water you almost thought you could dive in.

Jeff had a reputation for sleeping with most of his subjects so Andy insisted that he attended any photo sessions or sittings with Marianne. However, Jeff was a bit of a rascal and Marianne was a bit of a strumpet, secret photo sessions and private sittings were set up between them and it wasn't long before Marianne became the latest notch on Jeff's bedpost. Andy found out about it and after ditching Marianne and throwing a tantrum in the pub, told Jeff he could forget about the painting.

Jeff wasn't going to forget about the painting and a couple of weeks later he arrived at the pub where it was hung on the wall and covered in a sheet for the public unveiling later. That evening a packed pub waited in great expectation of the much-talked-about-painting, as the sheet was removed the whole pub fell into a hushed silence.

The painting Andy had commissioned was to be a tasteful portrait of Marianne sitting in a meadow in a long white dress, picking flowers. The painting that Jeff unveiled was of a stark naked Marianne wearing just black boots and stockings. To make matters worse, as a prop in the corner of the painting was a discarded Andy Pandy puppet. But it wasn't Andy Pandy's face grinning under the blue and white striped bonnet, but Marianne's ex-boyfriend Andy.

There were some seriously odd people living in west Wales but they didn't come odder than the Baby Eaters. They were a group of hippies who lived up in the mountains and ventured into town once every couple of months to cash their dole cheques, or in this instance check out what was happening at Porky's. I'm sure they didn't refer to themselves as the Baby Eaters but locally that was what everyone else called them.

Apparently whenever one of them had a baby, the birth had to be natural, in a bath, or standing up in a tepee with their whole community in attendance. They would then take it in turns to eat the newborn baby's placenta; apparently it was good for the soul.

They were the source of much gossip in the village, as were all the freaks that lived in the mountains, but no one was able to answer my question that was puzzling me no end. When the Baby Eaters ate the placenta, did they use a knife and fork?

A very strange bloke who turned up on the opening night was pointed out to me as the person who ran the infamous orgasmic clinic. Remember, everyone knew everyone. Apparently he took on some premises in nearby Lampeter and opened a clinic where he, apparently, would teach his female patients how to have the perfect orgasm. What? This bloke had no qualifications but set up his 'clinic' and distributed leaflets among the hippies in the mountains, the farmer's wives and anything looking vaguely female, in and around the town and the neighbouring villages.

Seeing as how half the population couldn't read or write and the majority of the rest only understood Welsh he actually stood a chance of getting some customers, by accident at least. According to someone who worked in a shop opposite, the only people who ever visited his 'clinic' were the ugliest, fattest, moustached women imaginable and the odd single farmer who peered through the net curtains in the hope of seeing the women in action. You couldn't make it up.

There's more to come... Another weird group of people who lived up in the mountains and made a special vigil to Alice's at Porky's were the Red People. I don't know why they were called that or what they were about but they would gather on certain days, the solstice or whatever, on a ley line in the hills and sit around a stone circle, light a fire in the middle and chant.

Some members of the local Welsh Young Farmers Club found out about this strange cult and one day went to the stone circle before the Red People had arrived. They hid a dozen or so fireworks among the ash of the unlit fire and covered them over with twigs; they then hid behind a bush and waited to see what would happen.

The Red People arrived and sat around the stone circle, as the sun went down they lit the fire and started chanting. Then all hell was let loose as the fireworks ignited and starting shooting off in random directions, the Red People ran for their lives, some thinking the world was coming to an end, others thought it was a sign from Lucifer himself.

Young Farmers are notoriously mental, add Welsh into the equation and you don't stand a chance. I was at a party once in Llanddewi Brefi when a Welsh Nationalist (the Nash) pulled off a stunt that made Alice In Wonderland's Health and Safety Nightmares look tame by comparison.

This bloke ran into the party, totally naked, with a lit Roman candle firework stuck up his backside. He burst through the front door of the fairly modest cottage and ran through the party with brightly coloured jets of fire and smoke screaming out of his bum. He disappeared out of the back door leaving the room full of acrid smoke. What a nutter.

Doctor And The Medics played on the second night at Alice In Wonderland at Porky's under the name of The Axemen. The band consisted of Clive, Steve and Wendi together with some backing tapes, and they went down well, although the locals were not quite sure about the Alice thing at all. After another week or so I was packing up to go home and I caught a glimpse of the leering boar and the pig in a skirt.

As I loaded my records and oil wheel projectors into the back of my pick-up truck I saw the flashing neon sign of the Marilyn pig with the skirt flashing up and down. What the fuck am I doing? I asked myself. This isn't what Alice's is supposed to be about. I pulled out the small bundle of fivers, the night's takings, from my pocket and decided that I was going to knock this Porky's thing on the head.

Although it was possible to pull a decent crowd to the place, they didn't want to pay a decent price to get in. We were earning a pittance for a lot of hard work and I had just about had enough. I took a long hard look at the flashing Marilyn pig sign and shook my head. Clive agreed with me so we closed it down. The same thing happened at Swansea.

Still, if nothing else it provided a few amusing stories, looking back on it now, it was fun for a week or too. Still, Alice In Wonderland in London was what we were really about and we would carry on with that show for a while longer at least.

Horses became my new obsession. We added to our collection by buying a dark bay section D cob mare that was already in foal. A few months after the colt was born we took her to be covered by a seventeen-hand Cleveland Bay stallion and ten months later out popped our next foal. With five hungry horses to keep and my savings long since dried up, it was difficult for a while. The horses, dog and goat came first and sometimes money was tight, what was left after paying the bills went on a bottle of wine and basic provisions. It was a far cry from my affluent days in the mid-eighties but I loved those horses and in time I would be back on my feet, bigger and better than ever. I was sure of it.

Carol and a new-born foal

Me in Wales

The Medics play at Alice's for the final time

Clive and I consider the future of Alice In Wonderland

CHAPTER TWENTY THREE

THE FAT LADY SINGS

After ten years and some remarkable experiences Alice In Wonderland finally closes down.

Despite all the strange people previously mentioned, most of whom were actually English, we loved living in west Wales, the scenery, the walks in the mountains, trips to the deserted secret beach, that was what we had left London for. We decided that we could stay there, for a while at least, and bought a small farm of our own, a run down small holding miles away from the weirdness of Llanddewi Brefi but still in Ceredigion.

After having our cottage completely re-built and Carol's dream stable complex constructed, circumstances changed, and after six or seven years in Wales, we decided to move on and go back to England. We loved the countryside, no doubt about it, and couldn't imagine moving back to a city, but where we were in Wales was a bit too rural, too far from an airport, too far from motorways and the time-warp that everyone was living in became a bit too stifling.

Whilst still in Wales I went to the local pub where I was introduced to a neighbour who had just moved into the area. His name was Andy Blade and he used to play in a minor punk band called Eater, I had never met him before, although I had seen Eater play at The Roxy Club a couple of times in the seventies. I had lived a very similar life to Andy Blade, both of us were one of six children brought up northwest of London, both listened to the same music, both played in a punk band, both lived in Los Angeles for a while before both ending up in the same village in Wales.

Carol and I became quite good friends with Andy and his then wife, Emma, until they split up and then we sort of lost touch. The coincidence continues, I have just found out that Andy Blade has also written a book, *The Secret Life Of A Teenage Punk Rocker* so I ordered a copy from Amazon. I had heard most of the stories from the horse's mouth but as I read the bit about him splitting up with Emma after Andy found out she had been having an affair with his best mate and former band member, I thought, surely he's not going to tell the Father Christmas 'Yo Ho Ho' story? But he didn't.

It was inevitable that as the years ticked by some of the Alice In Wonderland regulars started working on the next generation and a new baby boom occurred. It was only a matter of time before one of those kids would be named 'Alice' and eventually that happened on 27th November 1994. Alice Jewel Wilkins was born on what would have been Jimi Hendrix's 52nd birthday.

Her parents, Gordon and Nicki, chose a Medics gig at Alice In Wonderland as their first date. Gordon was an Alice In Wonderland regular from virtually day one and despite living miles away, came down to the club as often as he could right 'til the end. He was part of The Medics loyal Essex contingent and went on all of the Mystery Trips and special events as well as turning up to see The Medics at their other major shows.

When interviewed by an American TV crew who were filming the Lowestoft Mystery Trip, he was asked where they were going to which he replied: "I haven't got a clue, but I know we're going North." They weren't, they were going east, but then he, like most of the Mystery Trippers hardly knew what day it was let alone in which direction they were travelling.

Gordon made the fatal mistake once of deciding to go and see The Medics in Madrid to celebrate his birthday. After the gig and the usual party in someone's hotel room he got totally slaughtered and crashed out on the floor. Oh dear, not a wise move.

Various members of the band then stripped him naked as he lay comatose and with a felt tip pen wrote on his back: 'THE DRUGS ARE UP HERE MATE.' They then drew *Dads Army* style arrows pointing up his backside. The idea being that if, by chance, he was stopped at the Airport the following day, he would then be subjected to a humiliating and personal search. Luckily for Gordon, that didn't happen.

It took Gordon a month to scrub the graffiti from his skin and even longer to forgive the band members for their cruel but hilarious jape.

In recent years, the girl called Alice, now a teenager, appeared on stage with the punk band, Crass at the 'Feeding of the 5000' gig, doing the intro narrative for 'Big A Little A'. That's what I love about rock'n'roll; everything goes full circle. Crass supported The Bears (the punk band I played with in 1977), their lead singer, Steve Ignorant hung out at Alice's for a while, and then, totally unconnected, the daughter of an Alice regular joins the link. And Gordon? I still see him from time to time and whereas the inky arrows have long since faded, the 'DRUGS ARE UP HERE MATE' story hasn't. Certainly not now that's for sure.

Two important things happened for me in 1993, it was the year that Carol and I got married and also the year that I finally, after nine and a half years, closed down Alice In

Wonderland. The commuting to London every other week was getting a bit monotonous and my heart really wasn't in it any more. I wasn't going to do any more special events and I was no longer working with The Medics. The club had now just become routine, and I was just going through the motions on a Monday night. I was still earning money from it, but not enough to make too much difference. I talked to Clive about it and he agreed, after almost a decade and some fantastic times, it was time to lay Alice to rest.

Dreamgrinder, The Peace Frogs, Earthmothers and Pipedream were among the last of the bands to play at the club.

On Monday 19th April 1993 the last Alice In Wonderland (well sort of) took place. As could only be fitting for such an occasion, Doctor And The Medics played live, the club was packed and we all got pissed, just as we had done on numerous Alice nights previously. There had been some 450 Alice nights as well as the special events, shows abroad and guest DJ appearances. About 250 different bands had played and I estimate about 200,000 people had been through the doors. I was sad to see it stop, but all things come to an end and I felt that Alice's number was finally up.

I don't think we turned down any star bands of the future. I have boxes full of demo tapes of bands hopeful for a gig and I went through them recently to see if Oasis, Pulp or whoever had slipped through the net. I don't think so although I could be proved wrong. I'm fairly sure Jarvis Cocker came to Alice's once or twice as a punter though.

A few weeks after Alice's closed, Clive wanted to run a psychedelic night on the vacant Monday spot, he asked me if he could still use the Alice name and I told him that I'd rather he didn't.

Even though Alice In Wonderland wouldn't have been the great success that it was without Clive, I couldn't imagine it going on without me. Clive called his club Plastic Fantastic which trickled along for a few months until that too closed down.

In October 1998, what would have been the fifteenth anniversary of Alice's, Clive talked me into doing a one-off reunion party. We went back to Gossips for the show with the new-look Medics playing live. Clive and I travelled over from Wales and took it in turns to DJ; we even managed to track down Chris Duffell who flew over from Madrid where he was running an Elvis theme bar.

We charged just £2 entrance fee, the same price as the opening night fifteen years earlier and the club was packed, just like in the old days. Vom travelled over from Germany for the show and played on a few songs with the band and some old familiar faces showed up. As well as old regulars and bands that had played, The Damned, Lemmy, The Surfin' Lungs to name just a few, my dad came and recorded the show on video for the archives.

I decided to drag out my trusty crusty leather jacket (with the silver Mona Lisa on the back) for the reunion party. That jacket was, for more than a decade, my second skin, but had been left festering in a barn for the past five years.

So now, as well as blood, sweat, tears, alcohol stains and cigarette smoke it could add the new fragrances of mould, damp and rats piss. I gave it a sniff and it didn't seem too bad so wear it I would.

It was a great night and as the club filled up the temperature rose and my crusty leather jacket started loosening up. Heated from the outside by the ambient temperature and from the inside by my own body temperature my jacket started smelling a bit lively.

Numbed by alcohol (there's a surprise) I didn't notice but afterwards I did spare a thought for the dozens of old friends I hugged who must have thought that their old mate Christian had really let himself go.

I was totally oblivious to it all and it wasn't until Carol and I got back to our hotel room after the show and she was kept awake by the aroma that I actually realised, my trusty crusty leather jacket smelled like hell. I had to hang it out of the window so we could get some sleep. Still, what a night.

After the gig I decided, enough was enough and I shoved the jacket in the washing machine. Bad move. It shrunk. Another decade later and I gave it to my rock chick niece, Maddie, making her the custodian of the now not-so-smelly iconic piece of clothing. "Why did you wash it?" she asked. "Because it stank." I replied. "What did it smell of?" she asked, curious. I thought for a minute and not wanting to go into too much detail I replied: "Rock'n'roll, Maddie, rock'n'roll."

The premises at 69 Dean Street had been used for many things during its long life. Built on the site of Nell Gwynn's house in 1732, it was rumoured to have been haunted by Charles II most favourite mistress. Apparently it was used as an opium den for a while in Victorian times and in the twenties during the infamous Gargoyle Club days, was frequented by the likes of Noël Coward, Tallulah Bankhead, Francis Bacon, Lucian Freud and Fred Astaire. It went on to be a massage parlour, strip club and finally a nightclub. Gossips (formerly Billy's) in the basement was of course home to Alice In Wonderland for those crazy ten years.

One secret I kept quiet was that the basement had once been a chess club and one of the provisions of Gossip's lease agreement was that it had to remain available for anyone wishing to play a game of chess. For that purpose there was always a chess set under the counter. (Although half the pieces were missing.) Anyone could have turned up, demanded a game of chess and walked in without paying, no matter who was playing that night. Like I said, we kept it quiet.

In 2007 the lease was up at 69 Dean Street, Gossips closed down and it was sold to a hotel group and is now a five star boutique hotel. I often wonder if the premises are now not just haunted by Nell Gwynn but also by the ghost of Alice In Wonderland. Imagine if a well-heeled guest was awoken in the middle of the night by the cackling of the Doctor's psycho-babble echoing through the corridors or the pungent smell of the Smeg Monster seeping through the walls? I'm due to stay there next month when I next visit London so I'll let you know.

After closing down Alice's and for the good of my health and my sanity I had nothing more to do with the music business. Carol and I moved to North Somerset where we still live happily now. We did very well in the property market, buying, selling and renting out property both in the UK and abroad and have several properties with more planned for the future. We still live in the country with our horses and our dogs and spend the rest of our spare time travelling the world, exploring new places and having fun.

After years of growing old disgracefully I've finally quietened down, leaving my wild and reckless lifestyle where it belongs... in the past. (Until I decided to drag it all up again by writing this book of course.) The long hair and the leather jacket have gone and these days I'm more Versace and Paul Smith than Planet Alice. I still do my artwork and have become inspired recently to revive my psychedelic graphics for all to see. How this will work nearly thirty years on, time will tell. Still I've enjoyed doing it and so far it's attracted a lot of interest.

Watch this space.

Clive and I are still friends; he still lives in Wales with Wendi and the kids and still performs with Doctor And The Medics. Although Clive is the only original member of the band they still appear from time to time on TV, *One Hit Wonders, 2003 Top Of The Pops Special* that sort of thing. When Steve McGuire left and The Medics were officially all but finished, albeit for about five minutes, Clive decided to re-kindle the flame and see what would happen. Steve McGuire gave the new project his blessing with the classic statement: "If you can squeeze a little bit of life out of the rotten carcass that is Doctor And The Medics then good luck."

There was a TV series a couple of years ago hosted by Vernon Kaye called *Hit Me Baby One More Time* and Doctor And The Medics were asked to be on the show.

Various performers who had a hit or hits in the eighties were up against each other for another crack at the whip. Clive was on the same show as Shakin' Stevens, ironic seeing as how he was the butt of many an Alice In Wonderland joke years previously. Clive got the live audience vote but Shaky got the most viewers votes and then went on to win the whole competition. I watched it and voted dozens of times for The Medics, I needn't have bothered as Clive told me later that the whole thing was fixed.

When The Medics first arrived at the studio, Shakin' Stevens was rehearsing the final of the winning show, the programme makers had wanted Shaky to win and the votes were rigged so The Medics didn't stand a chance.

Clive also appeared on *Never Mind The Buzzcocks* in the identity parade, even though he looked exactly the same as he did in the mid eighties apparently no one recognised him. Even Phil Jupitas reckoned he hadn't got a clue who was the real Doctor even though they both went to the same school. Wendi summed it up by saying: "Not only was Clive on the sad bastards has-beens parade, nobody bloody recognised him."

Doctor And The Medics original guitarist, Steve McGuire, also appeared on *Buzzcocks* and you know what? Nobody bloody recognised him either.

We had the club, the band, the film, the film festivals, the mystery trips, the records, and the shops. The only thing missing was the book.

I had been thinking about writing a book about Alice In Wonderland, and all that went with it, for about five years, some days I would think it a good idea and other days I would ask myself: But why? There are hundreds of thousands of people more talented, more successful, more famous and more interesting than me who haven't written about their story, so why should I?

I was lying on the balcony of our apartment in Nice in the south of France when I decided that I would start writing. I had just finished reading Chris Moyles autobiography and I have to say, I wasn't that impressed. I can write a much more exciting story than that, I thought to myself, forgetting for a moment that Chris Moyles was a Radio One DJ with eight million listeners and his book was a best seller. I had to have a reason for committing myself to a lot of hard work and a lot of my time. It wasn't about ego and it wasn't about money. I just felt I had to do it while I still could.

I am under no illusion that the Alice thing is that relevant in the scheme of things, it didn't exactly change the world, I would leave that to others. But to some people it was relevant and it changed their world and that is why I decided to write my story, I believe it's a story that needs to be told and deserves to be told.

Looking back on the ten-year life of Alice In Wonderland and its associated spin-offs, I have very fond memories, I know it was special and I'm glad I was given the chance to do it. Along with the good times came the bad times and as well as the fabulous experiences came the unpleasant and scary moments. When I first started the whole thing with my initial investment of just £4 I had no idea whatsoever how it would change my whole life and what it would mean to me, and thousands of others. Yes, I have some regrets and yes there are some things that if I could go back and change I would. But that's not how it works and what happened happened.

It amuses me to think that sometime, many light-years away in the future, an alien girl covered in green jelly-like goo and wearing her time travelling costume made out of what looks like cling film, may stroll into a second hand cyber bookshop and pick up a copy of this book. She'd look at the brightly coloured cover, flip it over and read the spiel on the back, skip to the photos of the various freaks of nature among the pages and think to herself:

WHAT THE FUCK WAS THAT ALL ABOUT?

Lightning Source UK Ltd.
Milton Keynes UK
UKOW041358190412

191087UK00014B/55/P